THE CONNOISSEUR'S
GUIDE TO IRELAND

THE CONNOISSEUR'S
GUIDE TO IRELAND

A SELECT COMPENDIUM FOR THE DISCRIMINATING TRAVELER

DON FULLINGTON

An Owl Book
HENRY HOLT AND COMPANY
NEW YORK

Published by Henry Holt and Company, Inc.,
115 West 18th Street, New York, New York 10011.
Published in Canada by Fitzhenry & Whiteside Limited,
195 Allstate Parkway, Markham, Ontario L3R 4T8.

Library of Congress Cataloging-in-Publication Data
Fullington, Don.
The connoisseur's guide to Ireland : a select compendium
for the discriminating traveler / Don Fullington.
        p.   cm.
"An Owl book."
Includes index.
ISBN 0-8050-0632-X (pbk.)
1. Ireland—Description and travel—1981-   —Guidebooks.
I. Title.
DA980.F84   1989
914.15'04824—dc19   88-10298
                                                          CIP

Henry Holt books are available at special discounts
for bulk purchases for sales promotions, premiums,
fund-raising, or educational use. Special editions
or book excerpts can also be created to specification.

For details, contact:

Special Sales Director
Henry Holt and Company, Inc.
115 West 18th Street
New York, New York 10011

First Edition

Designer: Ann Gold
Printed in the United States of America
1   3   5   7   9   10   8   6   4   2

To happy Nora

CONTENTS

County Cork; Blairs Cove, Durras, County Cork; The
Blue Haven, Kinsale, County Cork; Aherne's Seafood
Bar, Youghal, County Cork; Chez Hans, Cashel,
County Tipperary; Galley Cruising Restaurants, New
Ross, County Wexford; Doyle's Schoolhouse
Restaurant, Castledermot, County Kildare; Le Coq
Hardi, Dublin City; The Lord Edward, Dublin City;
Bewley's, Dublin City; The Kish, Dublin City; King
Sitric, Howth, County Dublin; Restaurant Mirabeau,
Sandycove, County Dublin

ACKNOWLEDGMENTS

Many thanks to the Irish Tourist Board, especially Paddy Derivan, Simon O'Hanlon, Mark Rowlette, Margaret Cahill, Pat Delaney, Catherine Cullen, and Mary McGreal. At Aer Lingus, Pat Hanrahan. Literary agent Patrick Delahunt at John Schaffner Associates. And editor Peter Bejger at Henry Holt. Along the way: Jane, Patricia Tunison Preston, Francis, Tom Kennedy, Michael, Mary, Hope Delon, Marie Duffy, and radio personality Pegeen Fitzgerald.

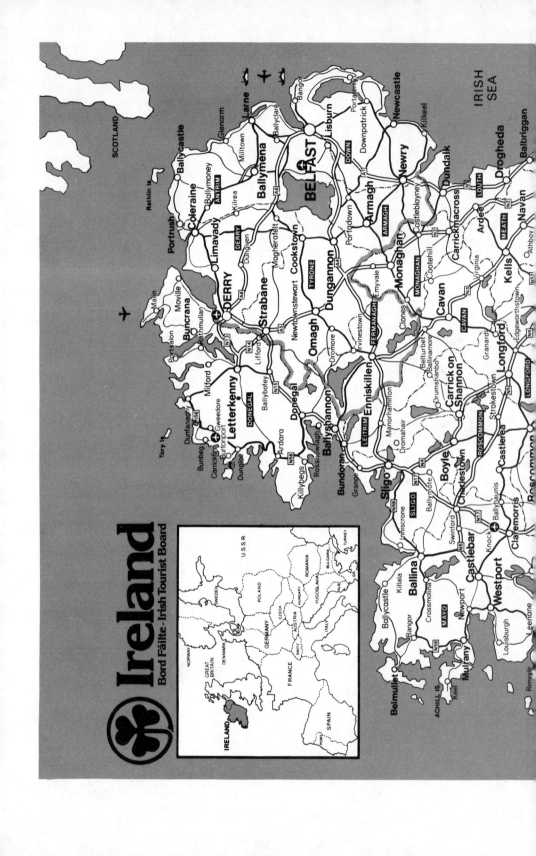

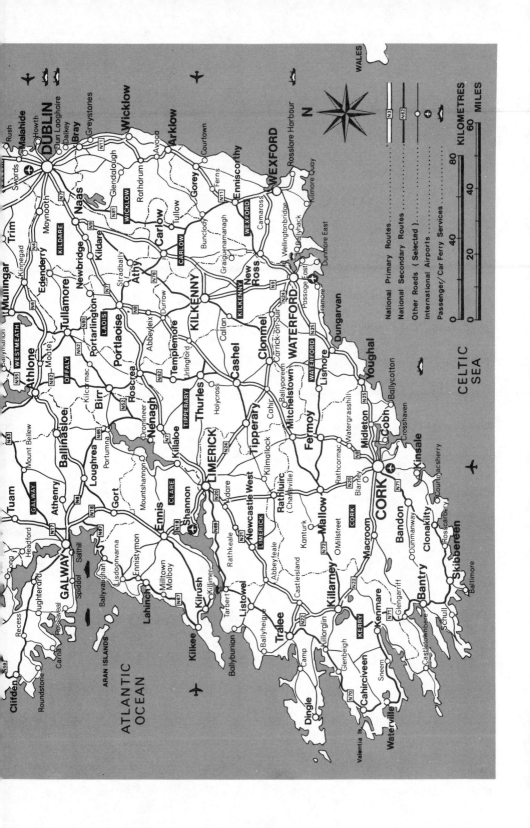

INTRODUCTION

"Romantic Ireland's dead and gone," wrote famed Irish poet William Butler Yeats in his poem "September 1913." How his words, taken at face value today, would have turned against him. Of course, Yeats meant them in a completely political sense and therefore is spared any embarrassment, but contemporary Ireland is a romantic's dream come true—with magnificent country inns and Georgian estates operated as lodgings, with intimate new restaurants and special treasures of shops, with quiet pubs and fine cultural events. All this, combined with the haunting beauty of its landscapes and seascapes, makes Ireland one of the most enchanting countries in the world.

There has never before been a comprehensive guide to Ireland for the connoisseur, and it is most needed. This book is planned for those who wish to appreciate the rich quality and values of the country's past, to take the time to discover and absorb its beauty.

This, then, is not a book for those wanting to take The Grand Tour of Ireland, for people who frantically pack and unpack their suitcases on a daily basis. Rather, it is for those who want a slower-paced, higher-quality vacation—which in so many ways is far more rewarding.

In this book you'll find the best Ireland has to offer—beginning with a county-by-county rundown of the country's lodgings. Included are detailed, slow-paced itineraries of the most elegant places and fascinating things to do—from picnics to little boat trips to dining in candlelit restaurants to shopping in tiny, out-of-the-way craft shops to viewing spectacularly beautiful landscapes. There are even chapters that suggest some unusual holidays.

Here, then, is the connoisseur's guide to Ireland.

Discovering the Special Places

There are 2 kinds of lodgings discussed in this book. Those in the first 12 chapters are featured in the greatest detail. They are the most dramatic examples—on all counts—of the true romantic elegance of Ireland. They range from the regal to the grandiose to the rustic, and they have one thing in common—all are captivating.

There are many reasons why some of the lodgings appear in chapter 13, Other Lodging Possibilities; poor quality is not one of them. Some may have added too many modern wings onto old abodes; others may be newer lodgings that don't strive for a sense of Old World atmosphere yet have a certain intimate charm; some may not have dining rooms (a major drawback when couples want a romantic evening with wines but don't want the danger of a drive afterward); some may be the only existing premises in a key scenic area but may not be terribly charming. So carefully read the descriptions of these before you decide. As you do, bear in mind that this is not a ratings book. It's a guide designed to help you find what's best for you—and your personality.

A Further Word About Places

The lodgings, restaurants, and pubs you will find in this book are all referred to favorably. Any that were below standard were eliminated to avoid wasting space and time. This does *not* mean, however, that every place not featured here is undesirable. No guidebook could cover every establishment in Ireland, and new ones are opening constantly. If you discover a place that interests you, which is not discussed here, check with the nearest Irish Tourist Board (Bord Failte) office to obtain an accurate rundown before committing yourself.

A Word About Price Categories

For lodging costs, the following guidelines have been used:
- *Inexpensive* starts at under $15 per person sharing per night and goes up to as much as $30.
- *Moderate* ranges from $30 to $55 per person.
- *Expensive* is anything from $55 upward.

For dining rooms and restaurants, the following guidelines have been used:

- *Inexpensive* is anything up to $15 per person.
- *Inexpensive to moderate* includes those places offering meals in both ranges.
- *Moderate* is in the $15 to $25 range.
- *Moderate to Expensive* means $15 to $30.
- *Expensive* means $30 and up.

A Very Important Note

The U.S. dollar value of the Irish pound fluctuates daily, and what a few years ago seemed expensive or moderate now seems inexpensive. But this can all change overnight. It's impossible for a travel guide to keep pace with currency fluctuations. The financial sections of daily newspapers are the most reliable sources for up-to-date information. In making reservations for both lodgings and restaurants, ask for current prices so you can translate them into the current dollar value. Even then, the pound's value could change before you get there.

Also note that Ireland is now a member of the European Monetary System, so English currency is no longer acceptable in the Irish Republic—nor is Irish currency accepted in Great Britain.

The Irish pound is divided into 100 new pence. Notes are issued in paper Irish pounds in denominations from 1 to 5, 10, 20, 50, and 100. Coins range from ½ pence to 1p, 2p, 5p, 10p, 20p, and 50p.

On Changes of Prices, Dates, and Hours

Nearly all the lodgings in this book post their prices with the Irish Tourist Board each year and therefore are bound by those prices (they can lower them but they can't go above them) for that year. Many of the restaurants, including all those incorporated in the lodgings, do the same and, therefore, are also bound to hold to these for the given year. But here there's more leeway, since the prices given to the Board are usually for the standard full dinner. If you select from the à la carte menu, sometimes the prices can vary dramatically. A good rule of thumb is to check with the establishment or the Board in advance. As for lodgings' opening and closing dates, it's almost always the case that hoteliers will increase rather than decrease the span of their season. Ireland is rapidly growing into a year-round holiday destination. Of course, restaurants in lodgings would follow suit. However, free-standing restaurants are more fickle. One year they might be closed on Mondays, the next open Mondays but closed Sundays. Usually they do remain true to their colors for a year at a time. The same could be said for the hours, although most restaurateurs who are changing are expanding rather than cutting their hours. The majority of the restaurants included here are of top quality. However, coffee shops and cafes, which do come and go, have been included for your convenience. It's always wise to check and reserve in advance.

On Credit Card Changes

Lodgings, but especially restaurants and stores, occasionally add or subtract the credit cards they accept. If you have any concern, phone the establishment first—and they'll be most delighted to tell you.

Hotel Booking Agents in the United States

There are a number of American agents with whom you may make your own confirmed reservations. (If a lodging is represented by one of these, that information appears in the lodging's review.)

- **American Wolfe International**, 6 East 39th Street, Suite 803, New York, NY 10016; 212-725-5880 or 800-223-5695.
- **Ashford Castle Inc.**, 30 Rockefeller Plaza, Suite 3318, New York, NY 10112; 212-315-3588 or 800-346-7007.
- **Best Western Hotels**, Best Western Way, P.O. Box 10203, Phoenix, AZ 85064; 602-957-4200 or 800-528-1234.
- **BTH Holidays**, 185 Madison Avenue, New York, NY 10016; 212-684-1820 or 800-223-1074.
- **David Mitchell & Co.**, 200 Madison Avenue, New York, NY 10016; 212-696-1323 or 800-372-1323.
- **Doyle Hotel Group**, 757 Third Avenue, New York, NY 10017; 212-593-4220.
- **E and M Associates**, 45 West 45th Street, New York, NY 10036; 212-719-4898 or 800-223-9832.
- **Great Southern Hotels**, 122 East 42nd Street, New York, NY 10168; 800-522-5258 (NY), 800-223-8944 (other states). Also: 19634 Ventura Boulevard, Suite 305, Tarzana, CA 91356; 800-331-3824 (CA), 800-423-8866 (other states).
- **Leading Hotels of the World**, 747 Third Avenue, New York, NY 10017; 212-838-3110 or 800-223-6800.
- **Loews Representation Int'l.**, 666 Fifth Avenue, New York, NY 10103; 212-841-1111 or 800-223-0888.
- **Reservations Systems, Inc.**, 6 East 46th Street, New York, NY

10017; 212-661-4540 or 800-223-1588 (US) or 800-531-6767 (Canada).

- **Robert Reid Associates**, 845 Third Avenue, New York, NY 10022; 212-832-2277 or 800-223-6510 or 800-223-5077 (New England states) or 800-223-5352 (Mid-Atlantic states).
- **Salt and Pepper Tours**, 7 West 36th Street, Suite 1500, New York, NY 10018-7911; 800-522-6558 (NY) or 800-223-7733 (other states).
- **Selective Hotel Reservations**, 19 West 34th Street, Suite 700, New York, NY 10001; 800-522-5568 (NY) or 800-223-6764 (other states).
- **Trusthouse Forte (Ireland)**, 12 East 41st Street, New York, NY 10019; 212-541-4400 or 800-442-5886 (NY) or 800-223-5672 (other states).
- **Utell International**, 10605 Burt Circle, Omaha, NE 68114; 402-493-4747 or 800-448-8355.

NOTE: Further vital statistics on Ireland, including airline and car rental information, appear in chapter 21.

1

THE COUNTRY ELEGANCE OF COUNTY DONEGAL LODGING ESTATES

The Sand House

Ireland is a land of the mystic. It is an enigma. This is probably most evident in County Donegal. Go out on the lovely strand that fronts Mary Britton's Sand House, look out over the endless seascape and imagine what the famous Irish writer James Stephens was thinking of when he wrote his classic *The Crock of Gold*, which, even to James Joyce, was the soul and essence of romantic Ireland.

The evening was full of peace and quietude, the mellow, dusky sunlight made a path for her feet. . . . She saw a figure rise from the fold of a little doon. The sunlight was gleaming from his arms and shoulders. . . . She had never seen so strange a face before. Her eyes almost died on him as she gazed and he returned her look for a long minute with an intent, expressionless regard. His hair was a cluster of brown curls, his nose little and straight, and his wide mouth drooped sadly at the corners. His eyes were wide and most mournful, and his forehead was very broad and white. His sad eyes and mouth almost made her weep. . . . When he turned away he smiled at her, and it was as though the sun had shone suddenly in a dark place, banishing all sadness and gloom.

> —James Stephens
> *The Crock of Gold*

The Sand House couldn't be any closer to the rolling Atlantic without being in it. Indeed, its name comes from the wonderful 2-mile-long sandy carpet just outside its doors, while its façade resembles that of a

giant sand castle. If you happen to walk into one of the sea-front
bedrooms when the tide is full, you most likely will feel you are in the
middle of the sea. This view and the thundering sound that accompanies
it is the most spectacular feature of the hotel. You could easily spend
hours sitting in the window. Even at night, if there's moonlight, it's
positively breathtaking.

Besides the view, this relatively modern hotel has a rustic elegance
comparable to that of Ireland's other historic country estates. This lovely
hotel is quite cozy.

Many fine features distinguish the Sand House, which is expertly
managed by owners Mary Britton and her son Conor. There's enough
reason to come here for its restful lounges, where turf and log fires burn
continually. There are 2 pubs with totally different personalities—and
both are fascinating. One is sophisticated and decorated with muted
stained glass, dark woods, and hammered copper. It's pleasant and
comfortable; so you might like to spend some time here, chatting and
relaxing. The other pub, decorated with fishnets, is a sort of surfer/
swimmer/beachcomber lounge, where you can stroll in barefoot from
the beach if you wish. Probably no other pub in Ireland is comparable
to this California-style enclave. On weekends, there are ballad sings
here.

The Sand House has immaculate and beautiful bedrooms abundantly
furnished with antiques. Every year Mary Britton wisely tracks down
additional pieces because she loves to surround herself and her appre-
ciative guests with them. Although all the rooms are very carefully
appointed, ask for one overlooking that dramatic seascape. A Sand
House sunset will long linger in your memory.

DINING AT THE SAND HOUSE: Mary Britton must have Ireland's cleanest,
most efficient kitchen—one where a crumb wouldn't dare be found.
But even more important are the fine foods that come through its doors
into the totally disarming and relaxing dining room. If you enjoy seafood
at all, be sure to try one of the amazingly fresh, heaven-sent fish dishes.
Especially fine are the poached fresh salmon served with an equally
fresh and deftly prepared hollandaise, or the grilled fresh sea trout, a
specialty of the house. Another unusually fine entree is the simply grilled
trout topped with butter-fried slices of almonds and slivers of lemon.

A meat aficionado will be equally pleased with the Sand House,
where entrees include superbly prepared barbecued spring lamb, hon-
eyed loin of pork, thinly sliced delicate veal with fresh mushrooms, and

succulent roast prime ribs. These meats tend to be much more flavorful than those from other countries (including the United States), because the Irish pay particular attention to the care of livestock and the grazing conditions.

Special mention should be made of the vegetables, which are so carefully prepared that a vegetarian would feel gratified. The kitchen uses only the finest local produce, delivered daily. Some of the entrees also are particularly good—fresh salmon mousse; terrine of duckling; an apple, fresh shrimp and celery salad, fresh crab and cucumber mousse, and fresh Donegal Bay oysters. Special desserts include homemade blackcurrant and apple pie, as well as gooseberry pie. The wines are fine and moderately priced, as is the food. Lunch is from 1 to 2:30 and dinner from 7 to 11.

PARTICULARS: The Sand House (072-51777) is open from April to October and has a full license. It is moderately priced, with breakfast included, and accepts AmEx, Diners, and Master. There are 45 bedrooms, all with bath. (U.S. agents: Robert Reid; Salt and Pepper Tours; Selective Hotel Reservations.) Sports amenities include tennis, pony trekking, miniature golf, surfing, sailboarding, and canoeing (equipment available at the hotel). The surrounding area is relatively flat and excellent for running or walking. There are two 18-hole championship golf courses 5 miles away. *Finding the Sand House:* It's 11 miles south of Donegal Town and 32 miles north of Sligo Town, off the N15. Watch for the signs for Rossnowlagh.

Rathmullan House   RATHMULLAN

Northern Donegal was one of the prime locales of Lughnasa festivals, pre-Christian harvest festivals named after the god Lugh. Carried over into Christian times, they often were spiced with romantic and sexual endeavors. Across Lough Swilly from Rathmullan House is the Inishowen Peninsula. At its center is the 2,019-foot mountain Slieve Snaght. On its summit in late July, people from the surrounding areas would gather for merrymaking. They drank from a well whose waters were said to have strong curative and preventive powers—as well as aphrodisiacal qualities. There was dancing, singing, drinking, game

Rathmullan House, County Donegal

playing, and much flirtation. Couples would often dart off with the pretense of berry picking, when in fact there was much lovemaking taking place—resulting, inevitably, in a flurry of weddings a few months later. Another similar event was held on Loughsalt Mountain, some miles west of Rathmullan. Young men and women waited all year for this event, hoping for the beginning of a passionate courtship.

To say that Rathmullan House is a rambling anachronism, as some have described it, is not to give it its due. This wonderful estate exquisitely set out above the shores of Lough Swilly—amid ancient oak trees, weeping elms, and stately gardens—is not only of the past but it remains in the past. Built in 1780 and extended in 1890, the gleaming white bay-front house, with its dining pavilion, once was the country estate of the Batt family, Belfast linen merchants.

The current owners, Bob and Robin Wheeler, undertook a grand refurbishment to restore the house and grounds to their former glory. And what a success it is. Once inside the antique-filled house, you forget the present and lose yourself in time. Here you'll find a grand library, a drawing room, even a coffee room with intricate pargeted (ornamental plasterwork) ceilings, crystal chandeliers, rich oil portraits, cozy settees and divans, and white marble log-burning fireplaces. Many of the bedrooms are richly furnished with comfortable antiques and are extremely attractive, especially those overlooking the lough. There's also a fascinating dungeonlike cellar bar where Francie Cooney holds forth, serving drinks and telling comic stories that will keep you amused for hours. Someday this man may become immortalized for his tales. (He also knows his history.)

DINING AT RATHMULLAN: The lovely Pavilion Room, overlooking the long stretches of manicured lawns and the handsome gardens, is the setting for enjoying Rathmullan's fine cuisine. Seafood is a specialty here, and among the excellent choices for entrees are lemon sole on the bone, poached local salmon with brown butter sauce, sea trout, and Lough Swilly lobster. The lamb, beef, and poultry dishes are good as well. Starters include homemade spicy tomato soup, onion soup, baked grapefruit with sherry, smoked mackerel, and egg mayonnaise with fresh prawns. Vegetables and fresh fruit desserts are deftly prepared. Wines are good and most are moderately priced, as is the dinner, which is served from 7 to 9. Afterward, take a stroll along the shore and look across Lough Swilly at the flickering lights of Buncrana and the Inishowen Peninsula. Lunch is served from 1 to 1:45. Before that, or perhaps even before breakfast, you might enjoy an invigorating swim in the lough, with views of the green rolling hills of Inishowen.

PARTICULARS: Rathmullan House (074-58188) is open from April 5 through October 5 and has a full license. It is moderately priced, with breakfast included, and accepts AmEx, Visa, Master, and Diners. There are 21 bedrooms (16 with bath), plus some self-contained, lough-side chalets. (U.S. agents: Robert Reid; David Mitchell.) In addition to the swimming, amenities include fishing in Lough Swilly. The hotel also has its own boat on Glen Lough for sea trout fishing. Tennis, croquet, and pony trekking are nearby, and there are 4 golf courses in the region. *Finding Rathmullan House:* It's just outside Rathmullan village, on the L77 Portsalon road.

NOTE: Some maps and reference materials refer to Rathmullan as Rathmullen, so don't be confused. They are one and the same.

Suggestions for Your Visit   COUNTY DONEGAL

¶ Although County Donegal is part of the province of Ulster, which includes Northern Ireland, it is in the Irish Republic. Near its southern tip, only a narrow 5-mile strip of the county separates the sea from Northern Ireland, thus giving Donegal an almost insular feeling. As such, it seems to become a country of its own, tucked away from the rest of the world. And since so much of the county is undeveloped, it's like a frontierland.

While Donegal is not the largest county in Ireland (County Cork is), it seems far larger because of its road configurations. This ruggedly beautiful county has narrow, winding, switchback roads that lead around and up craggy mountains, through hidden valleys, and along jagged coastlines. The miles—while weaving through constantly enthralling scenery—take longer to drive here than they do in any other part of the country, so don't attempt to see all of Donegal in a few days. You'll only disappoint yourself. Take the time to enjoy sections of it, as suggested below.

¶ Both of the County Donegal lodgings described—Sand House and Rathmullan House—need time for enjoyment. Both have attractive, long stretches of beachfront property and fascinating interiors—all of which invites lingering for hours, if not days.

¶ If you are staying at the Sand House in Rossnowlagh, nearby are the ruins of the 13th- or 14th-century **Kilbarron Castle**, resting on a rocky promontory, and near it are the remains of the 14th-century **Kilbarron Church**. Also in Rossnowlagh is the Franciscan Friary, which houses the **Donegal Historical Society Museum**, with much of interest on Donegal archaeology and folklore. It's open daily, all year, from 10 A.M. to 8 P.M. Nearby is the **Coolmore Art Gallery**, which is open daily and offers landscape paintings by local artists.

¶ You will want to use the Sand House as a base for exploring southern Donegal. The first suggested journey is a relatively long one, approximately 113 miles. This covers Donegal's splendid southernmost promontory, which includes Donegal Town, Killybegs, wondrous Slieve League, Glencolumbkille, the Glengesh Pass, Ardara, Portnoo and Narin Strand, Maas, and Glenties. After a swift beginning, the roads become narrow and twisty, requiring slower driving. If you feel a journey of this length is more than you wish to undertake, you can—and should—shorten it. It's a good idea to start early on this journey if you plan to do it all.

¶ From Rossnowlagh, take the L24 over to the N15 and head north to **Donegal Town** (11 miles). Quite likely, you will want to park your car and stroll about this interesting old town with 16th-century castle ruins, 17th-century church, and a ship's anchor shorn from one of Napoleon's frigates when his fleet unsuccessfully tried to thwart the British in an Irish uprising in 1798.

The center of town is diamond shaped, with streets spoking off in all directions. Here you'll find a variety of fascinating shops, including **Magee of Donegal** (a big shop with a variety of tweeds handwoven by the employees, tweed items, and other clothing crafts, with a tearoom adjoining); **The Gift Shop** (watercolors and oils of the area, tweed-woven pictures, Belleek, porcelain, Irish books, other crafts, souvenirs); **The Antique Shop** (glass, paintings, china, jewelry, brass, silver, oil lamps)—all on The Diamond. **Kelly's The Tweed Shop** (Donegal tweeds and Donegal handknit sweaters) and **Wool 'n Things** (Aran knitwear, Irish crocheted and linen items, Donegal tweeds) are both on Main Street. Then there's **David Hanna & Sons Ltd.** (tweed hats) on Tyrconnell Street.

If you're hungry at this point, the **Hyland Central Hotel** on The Diamond offers good basic Irish meat and fish dishes in its homey dining room, which is open all year for lunch from 12:30 to 2:30 and for dinner from 7 to 9:30. Prices are moderate; AmEx, Master, and Visa are accepted. **The National Hotel** on Main Street, a fascinating place loaded with antiques, has a very pleasant dining room serving traditional dishes all year, with lunch from 12:30 to 2:30 and dinner from 7 to 11. It's inexpensive, but no credit cards. Both of these places have most interesting bars.

Before leaving the Donegal Town area, you may wish to visit the **Donegal Craft Village**, which is located just outside the town on the N15 Ballyshannon road. It's a small complex of shops and workrooms where Donegal artists and craftsmen produce their wares. Included are hand-crafted tweed apparel items, hand-designed batik wall hangings, hand-weaving, pottery, porcelain ceramics, jewelry, metalworking, and furniture. It's open year-round from Monday through Saturday from 10 to 5.

From Donegal, head west on the N56 through the somber hilly village of **Mountcharles** (with **Gillespie Bros. Tweed Shop** and **Jack Furey's** hand embroidery), then past **Jean's** (fascinating old barn craft shop with authentic Irish hearthcrafts, pottery, jewelry, fashions, and toys plus coffee and delicious homemade desserts—open 7 days a week) and continuing westward through Inver and Dunkineely and on into Killybegs, 17 miles from Donegal Town.

Although granted a charter by King James in the early 17th century, **Killybegs** resembles a 19th-century village built around a fine harbor. It is one of Ireland's major fishing ports. Besides Irish fishing vessels, trawlers from many foreign ports tie up here. The arrival of a fishing fleet heralded by hundreds of seagulls is an impressive sight. If you'd like to eat here, **The Sail Inn** restaurant and fishermen's pub has good bar food as well as à la carte seafood and meat dishes. The pub is open from 9 A.M. to midnight, with bar lunch from 12:30 to 2:30. The à la carte upstairs restaurant is open all year for dinner from 6:30 to 10:30, except Monday. It's inexpensive to moderate and has music nightly during the high season. There's also the small **Cod End Restaurant**, which specializes in inexpensive seafood dishes and has a wine license. It's open all year for lunch from 12:30 to 2:30 and for dinner from 7 to 10. Then there's the **Harbour Bar**, offering pub grub, but during the summer there are seafood dishes and nightly entertainment.

Also in Killybegs is the **Donegal Carpets** factory, where handwoven and knotted carpets, rugs, and wall hangings have been made since the end of the 19th century. Their carpets adorn famous buildings around the world, including the White House. You can watch them being woven and then visit the on-site craft shop to make purchases. It's open all year from Monday through Friday from 9 to 12:30 and from 1:30 to 5:30, except the first 2 weeks in August. For more crafts, there's the **Niall Mor** shop in the village.

From Killybegs, continue traveling westward. After 8 miles, you'll come to the charming little village of **Kilcar**, where the waters of Ballyduff and Glenaddragh stream down from the mountains. This village is one of the centers of the handwoven tweed industry. Here you may visit **Connemara Fabrics Ltd., Studio Donegal**, and **Gaelrarra Eireann**, open all year Monday through Friday from 8:30 to 5. The latter two shops are open Saturday and Sunday during the summer and offer weaving demonstrations.

Traveling 3 miles farther westward, you'll come to the sleepy little village of Carrick, set out on the Glen River above beautiful Teelin Bay. From here, detour for 2 miles to Teelin village, but just before you get to the village (and this is very important), *do not* take the road signposted for Slieve League. While this leads to some scenic wonders of the formation, it is nothing remotely like what you will see if you continue on into Teelin and take the right-hand turn to Bunglass (cliffs). Here is one of the heartbeat points of this tour—and one you will never forget. It's 2 miles from Teelin village. The road can be cliffside scary and above all should not be attempted on a misty day. As you head skyward, you may feel like a jet on takeoff. If you squint below, you'll see Carrigan Head, with a lone signal tower. Don't panic; you will soon come to a car park. It's past secluded Lough Mulligan, atop the cliffs that rise over 1,000 feet from the sea. Slieve League itself is 1,972 feet. Walk a few feet from the park and suddenly the cliffs and the sea are spread out before you in wondrous splendor. These breathtaking cliffs extend for 3 miles and vary in color due to the mineral content and rockside vegetation. This undoubtedly is one of Ireland's and the world's scenic wonders. You may want to have a picnic or stroll about these cliffs. There are good, well-worn tracks, as these walks are popular with the tourists, but be careful to stay away from the sheer drops, especially on a windy day. Below, the furious waves lash themselves over jagged rock formations known as the Giant's Desk and Chair, spraying off into rainbow plumes over the sea.

¶ You may find that you have stayed at Slieve League longer than you expected and prefer to return the 39 miles to the Sand House over the same route. Or you may wish to continue on from Carrick to Glencolumbkille (10 miles). As you do, you'll enter the Owenwee Valley, where you climb 600 feet before descending into the glen. **Glencolumbkille** (or *Gleann Cholaim Cille*, the Glen of [Saint] Columcille) is one of the most remote and beautiful areas (again especially for seascapes) in the country. This lonely valley, which runs back between the hills from Glen Bay, is where the saint decided to build a monastic retreat during the 6th century. Of all the Irish saints, Columcille is believed to have been the one most enamored of solitude. He certainly found it here.

While at Glencolumbkille, be sure to visit the **Folk Museum**, which consists of cottages reproduced to represent different periods of Irish history, including period furniture and utensils. Here, as well, are a good tearoom and craft shop. The complex is open daily from Easter through October, Monday through Saturday from 10 to 6 and Sunday from 1 to 6.

Also in Glencolumbkille is the **Straid Gallery**, with impressive paintings of the Donegal area. It's open daily during the summer months.

If you wish to eat while you're here, the **Glencolmcille Hotel**, near the Folk Museum, is open daily from March through October for lunch from 12:30 to 2:30 and for dinner from 6:30 to 10, offering moderately priced Irish fare, especially fresh seafood. No credit cards are accepted.

While in this area, you might like to walk to **Glen Head**, another sheer cliff that rises some 700 feet from the sea and is slightly north of Glen Bay. A drive 9 miles to the south leads to **Malinmore**, which offers both dramatic cliff scenery and a fine beach.

From Glencolumbkille, you may wish to head back to Rossnowlagh over the same route you've traveled or you may wish to continue the tour, journeying northeast toward **Ardara**, 16 miles away. The road has no classified route number, but as you travel, you'll climb through the spectacular **Glengesh Pass**, almost 900 feet before you drop down (usually along with the winds) into the windswept but lovely little village of **Ardara**, where the Owentocher River flows into nearby Loughros More Bay. This town has a feeling of antiquity about it, a sense that time stopped here long ago. While taking in the town, renowned for its tweedmaking, look at some of the shops, such as **Campbell's Tweed Shop** (tweed apparel and Irish crafts); **Kennedy of Ardara** (Aran knits, handloomed knitwear with demonstrations, Irish linens, Tyrone crystal, Irish pottery, and rugs; the shop insures and handles mail orders); **J.F. Hernon** (fine handknit sweaters, Irish caps and scarves); **John Molloy** (tweeds); **W. McNelis & Son** (handwoven tweed fashions, knitwear, china, and crystal)—all on Main Street. And **McGill's** (handknit fisherman's sweaters, socks, other Irish crafts)—on the West End; **C. Bonner & Son** (handknit sweaters, tweed fashions, crystal, china, pottery, rugs, souvenirs)—on the Glenties Road.

If you are interested in eating here, there's the rambling old and interesting **Nesbitt Arms Hotel**, which serves basic Irish fare, with lunch from 1 to 2:30 and dinner from 6 to 9. It's open all year, is inexpensive, and accepts MasterCard. The moderately priced **Woodhill House Restaurant** with magnificent mountainside views, is open June through August for dinner from 6 to 10. It has a full license and serves very good meat and fish dishes, but accepts no credit cards. **Nancy's**, located in a Victorian house full of antiques, is an interesting pub.

Leaving Ardara, you have another decision to make. If you're anxious to head back at this point, take the Glenties Road (T72) for about 5 miles east, then turn right on a road (L74) leading south for Donegal Town (17 miles away), passing through Kilrean and Frosses. After Frosses, you'll come to the main N56, where you turn left and go through Mountcharles, back into Donegal Town, and then 11 miles south to Rossnowlagh and the Sand House. From Ardara, this is 33 miles.

If you're not ready to return to Rossnowlagh as you leave Ardara, there's another 18-mile loop you may wish to add to your journey. If so, head northwest 10 miles on the L81 to the lovely twin fishing villages of **Portnoo** and **Narin**, also seemingly untouched by the world. Resting at the foot of gently sloping hills, they are located on the shores of beautiful **Gweebarra Bay**. Here you'll find secluded strands and coves that you're likely to share only with a couple of seabirds. At Narin is a magnificent 2-mile-long strand that faces Iniskeel Island, with ruins of a 6th-century church. You can walk to the island at low tide, but be sure the tide is *very* low when you start out; it comes in with a vengeance.

From here, take the road east (L81) for 4 miles to Maas village, where you pick up the N56 (or T72) southwest into **Glenties**, one of Ireland's tidiest towns. Here are **Campbell's of Glenties** (craft and knitwear shop) and **Melly's Art Gallery** (Donegal landscape paintings). Just outside of Glenties, heading west again toward Ardara, you'll come to a left-hand turn onto the L74 headed for Donegal Town—17 miles away. Take it and pass through Kilrean and Frosses. After Frosses, pick up the main N56 again. Turn left here and pass through Mountcharles and then Donegal Town, where you'll take the road south 11 miles back to Rossnowlagh.

¶ A much shorter journey from the Sand House is to Donegal Town, where you can pick up the N15 (or T18) headed north toward **Bally-bofey**. In about 5 miles, you'll come to **Lough Eske**, with beautiful tree-lined shores. Ringed by the **Blue Stack Mountains**, it's a lovely place for walks and a picnic. If you wish, leave the main route and drive around the lake (15 miles), passing forested estates, including the baronial 17th-century Tudor **Lough Eske Castle**. The 2-story castle has a 4-story tower and a dramatic porch. Fire gutted it some years ago, but one wing is still used.

Back on the N15, 2 miles north of Lough Eske, you'll come to the lonely yet fascinating **Barnesmore Gap**, formed by 2 enormous granite hills—Croaghconnellagh (1,724 feet) and Barnesmore (1,491 feet). From earliest times, this glacier-carved trough has been a key route between southern and northern Donegal. As such, it was once a favored haunt of highwaymen, and this spot saw many a robbery. It's worth a hike with a picnic basket to the top of these hills. From the first peak, you'll have excellent views of Lough Eske, Donegal Town, Donegal Bay, and the Blue Stack Mountains. From the second peak, you can see all the way to Lough Derg and into Northern Ireland. If you're not in a climbing mood, you may just want to stop at the rustic **Biddy O'Barnes** kitchen-cottage pub, where brown bread is thrown in for free—if you ask.

From here, you may wish to return to your lodging over the same route—or, if you're hungry, you can travel 8 miles farther north on the N15 to Ballybofey, where **Jackson's Hotel** is just off the main road. The dining room is one of the best in County Donegal, with excellent food and meticulous service. The salmon is superb, but so are the other selections (both meat and fish). Even the pub foods in Jackson's Bar are good. Jackson's is open all year for lunch from 1 to 2:30 and for dinner from 5:30 to 9. It's inexpensive to moderate and accepts no credit cards. From here, continue on the same route back to your lodgings.

¶ The Sand House is also an excellent base for exploring the **Sligo** area by driving out to the N15 and taking it south 10 miles to Bundoran, and then an additional 22 miles into Sligo Town. (For touring ideas in Sligo, see Suggestions in chapter 2.)

¶ Another area easy to explore from Rossnowlagh, by heading south to **Ballyshannon** on the N15 (5 miles), is the **Lough Erne** part of **Northern Ireland**. Here you may first wish to travel about a mile south of the village on the same N15 to visit the new **Donegal Irish Parian China Company** factory and shop for moderately priced, eggshell-colored translucent china vases and ornaments with color relief work (Irish rose, shamrock, hawthorne, etc.). Open Monday through Friday from 9 to 5. Then head back to Ballyshannon village, where you'll travel east on the L24 for 4 miles to Belleek, which is in County Fermanagh, Northern Ireland. Here the famous Belleek porcelain is made. But before you cross the border, take a few minutes to stop by the **Celtic Weave China Company**; it's on the right, just as you pass the Irish Republic Customs. This tiny place is operated by three young china enthusiasts. Basketweave artists Tommy Daly and Seamus Mullin and hand painter Patricia Daly were formerly employed by the Belleek factory but became disenchanted with working conditions there and simply moved the few feet across the border into the Republic and opened their own factory. It's open yearly Monday through Saturday from 9 to 6. Anytime you go in, the threesome will delight in showing you the exacting and delicate process involved in making woven china baskets and floral ware, including the hand kneading of the Parian bone mix, the weaving of the open trelliswork, the shaping of the basket and the tiny flowers and, of course, the intricate hand painting. You may purchase items here and by mail order. AmEx, Master, and Visa are accepted for these truly lovely items. They are expensive, but considering the handwork and the fact that it takes each item 6 to 8 weeks to reach completion, they're more than worth it.

From here, cross the border into Belleek and visit the world-famous **Belleek Porcelain Factory**, which began operation in 1857. The beautiful cream ornaments made here require delicate handwork to create, and you can watch the artisans doing it. There are 20-minute guided tours all year Monday through Friday from 10:15 to noon and from 2:15 to 4. The Belleek shop is open Monday through Saturday from 9 to 5 (closed the first 2 weeks in August) and does accept credit cards. Remember that if you're paying with cash here, you must have British pounds; Irish ones are no longer accepted, except at a great premium and loss to you.

¶ If you are staying at Rathmullan House, it is a fine headquarters for seeing some of the magnificent beauty of northern County Donegal. The town of **Rathmullan** is a fascinating place to explore on foot. Its old buildings hark back to the days when it was a famous naval and mercantile port. You might like to visit the quaint **Pier Hotel Bar** or have a meal at the moderately priced **Water's Edge Restaurant**, excellent for such dishes as boned duckling, steak, pork, and seafood. The latter is open from 7:30 to 10 Monday through Saturday and noon to 2:30 on Sunday, with a wine license; Master, Visa, and Diners are accepted.

Rathmullan was the site of an incident that occurred in 1587 and nearly altered the course of Irish history. Fifteen-year-old Red Hugh O'Donnell, who was later to become a famous Irish freedom fighter, was in Rathmullan visiting relatives when British soldiers sailed into port and lured a group of young men whom they considered anti-royalist onto their boat with the promise of a drink. Among them was Red Hugh, who until this point had been, along with his family, pro-British. The boat set sail, and the men eventually were taken to Dublin Castle, imprisoned, and tortured. So embittered was Red Hugh that, upon his escape, he joined forces with Hugh O'Neill and the duo led the Nine Years' War against British domination. Finally, in 1607, they were forced to flee the country, leaving their vast estates in Ulster to fall to the British and thus initiating the Ulster Plantation in the country's northeast—the Northern Ireland of today.

¶ A beautiful drive from Rathmullan is around the **Fanad Peninsula**, about 42 miles round trip. Head north on the Knockalla Coast road to Portsalon, passing the 1,203-foot Knockalla Mountain (ideal for climbing), the cliffs overlooking Ballymastocker Bay, and the panoramic views across Lough Swilly to the **Inishowen Peninsula. Rita's Bar**, an old traditional Irish pub, stands by the splendid beach here. A couple of miles farther on are the fascinating rock-formed tunnels called the

Seven Arches, eroded from the cliffs. A little farther along is the **Great Arch of Doaghbeg**, which is so enormous it could house a large boat. Continue on from here to **Fanad Head**, with dramatic seascapes. Drive southward from here along the shores of Mulroy Bay (affording great views of the Donegal highlands), through Tamney, Rossnakill, Kerrykeel, and on to Milford—all charming villages. The **Robert Mc-Causland Craft Shop** is in **Milford**. Also on Main Street here is the 19th-century **Moore's Inn**, with good, inexpensive pub food.

From Milford, head south on the T72 to **Ramelton** (or Rathmelton, as it is often called). This is an absolutely fascinating town, a painter's dream. With a river coursing through it and a tree-lined main street, it is somewhat reminiscent of another of Ireland's special towns—Westport, County Mayo. There are some delightful early-17th-century houses and a church here. If you're interested in dining, there's the good **Mirabeau Steak House**, located in an old Georgian house. It's open all year for dinner from 6 to 11, has a wine license, is moderately priced, and accepts AmEx, Diners, and Master. Near the river is an interesting old pub.

From Ramelton, it's about 7 miles north on the L77 back to Rathmullan. En route, you'll pass **Rathmullan Wood**, which offers lovely forest walks, another fine view of Lough Swilly, and excellent picnic areas.

¶ A more extended journey (32 added miles) than that above, and one with spectacular views, takes in the **Rosgill Peninsula**, with its dramatic, end-of-the-world Atlantic Drive. The decision point for this side trip is Milford village. Instead of heading south on the T72 to Ramelton and then back to Rathmullan, head north 10 miles on the T72 to the charming little resort town of **Carrigart**, on the beautiful shores (excellent for swimming) of Mulroy Bay. A good resort lodging and restaurant here is the **Carrigart Hotel** (reviewed in chapter 13, Other Lodging Possibilities). If you're interested in shopping, there's **Nothing But McNutt** (handwoven tweeds and other Irish crafts with good little restaurant attached; open April through September only) and **The Pharmacy** (good selection of Irish crystal in this drugstore)— both on Main Street.

From here, drive on up through **Rosapenna**, where in the late 18th century violent, desertlike sandstorms buried farms and mansions alike, rendering them uninhabitable, and **Downings**, a pleasant resort village. The **Beach Hotel** in Downings is open June through September and offers local seafood, a buffet, and bar food. And if you're interested in tweeds, there's **McNutts of Downings Ltd.**

After Downings comes the **Atlantic Drive**. The road meanders up and down this lonely peninsula that separates Sheephaven Bay from Mulroy Bay and offers sensational views of Tranarossan Bay and the hills of Donegal. You can look across Sheephaven Bay to the west and see Horn Head, an equally dramatic promontory. Or you can look to the east for a fine view of Melmore Head; to the southwest is Muckish Mountain. But always you're surrounded by the glittering splendor of the open Atlantic. Do, of course, aim to take this tour on a fine day. The Atlantic Drive circle from Carrigart and back is 12 miles.

¶ Another rewarding drive leads over to **Dunfanaghy** and **Horn Head**, with its stunning views of the Atlantic. Head south from Rathmullan 6 miles on the L77 to Ramelton. Continuing on the L77 but heading west, you will reach Kilmacrennan in about 7 miles. From here, head north on the main road (L76) up through the lonely Barnes Gap, 9 miles to Creeslough. A couple of miles off the Creeslough/ Carrigart road is 16th-century **Doe Castle**, which was originally a fortress of the MacSweeney family. Surrounded by the sea on 3 sides and a moat on the 4th, this castle once had a drawbridge and was the scene of many battles between the MacSweeneys and rival northern clans. It also had connections with the Spanish Armada. The castle is in good condition and may be viewed at any time.

Back on the main road headed for **Dunfanaghy**, you'll pass **Ards Forest Park**, which has lovely scenery and is a good place for a picnic under ancient trees or a swim from the silky white strand at the forest's edge. A fine 18th-century homestead called Ards House also used to stand here. Once run as a feudal estate by the extravagant Wray family, it changed hands many times over the years, until the Franciscan order bought it. Sadly, in 1965, for no known reason, they had the building demolished. From here, you'll pass through **Port-na-Blagh** (or **Portnablagh**), where the **Port-na-Blagh Hotel**, overlooking the sea, has a good restaurant. It's open until 9 P.M. each day from April through September and is moderately priced but accepts no credit cards.

The next town you'll come to is Dunfanaghy, 7 miles from Creeslough. Follow the sign in the village that turns right toward **Horn Head**. This is a high, very narrow road—one to be avoided in bad weather—with sheer drops to the sea. When you reach the top of the spectacular cliffs and begin to curve around them, you see no more ground ahead of you—just the vast Atlantic. Suddenly you feel as though you could forget where you are. And that's the danger: some people are so taken by the feeling and the overwhelming beauty that they literally forget for an instant. But an instant can be fatal here, so be prepared and remain calm. When you have found a place to park, you can walk back and linger over the dazzling view. The route will circle about and bring you back to Dunfanaghy.

Before you leave Dunfanaghy to head back to Rathmullan (on either the same route or cutting off at Creeslough for Carrigart then going down to Milford and around to Rathmullan), you may wish to visit a couple of craft shops. In Dunfanaghy proper, there's the **Tweed and Fashion Shop**, with lovely though expensive Irish apparel (open April to September only). A short distance outside the village, on the road to **Falcarragh,** is The Gallery, one of Ireland's best antique/craft/painting shops. Located in a Georgian country home, it reveals superb taste and is worth seeking out.

¶ Some of you may be interested in visiting **Glenveagh National Park**, one of Ireland's newest national parks. Set amid mountains on 24,000 acres, it is in one of the loneliest, most remote interiors of the county. Formerly the Glenveagh Estate, it has a lakeside castle, complete with waterfall, where Lady Sarah Churchill, Yehudi Menuhin, Cecil Beaton, and John Betjeman often visited. A ravishingly young Greta Garbo was said to have ensconced herself here with a lover. On a dingy day, this mountainous, boggy area can be dramatically bleak; on a clear day, it can explode with beauty.

The baronial Victorian castle—lurking in mountain mists like something out of *Dracula*—was built in 1870 on the shores of Lough Beagh by the Adair family. John George Adair, described as an up-and-coming educated country squire, proceeded to acquire rights to adjoining lands, running them as a feudal estate but promising the tenants generous rights and favors. But something went wrong. Either Adair was a trickster or his tenants reacted to his kindness with greed. Suddenly there were bitter disputes, many of Adair's sheep were stolen, and his Scottish steward was murdered. Adair became so enraged that, despite vigorous protests, he evicted nearly 50 families from his lands and ordered their houses demolished.

Adair became the hated outsider, as the local people banded together in their mutual anger (as indeed they would in Ireland today, especially in Donegal). It was said that even the constables wept as they unwillingly enforced the evictions. An unhappy Adair later married an American woman whose father had been a general in the Union Army during the Civil War. Strangely enough, Adair died in a St. Louis hotel room in 1885, leaving his Irish dream in ruins. The estate then became the property of his wife, whom the locals looked upon with a great deal more fondness. While she lived there, Glenveagh flourished, and happier days returned. In the late 1930s, the estate was purchased by Henry McIlhenny, a former curator and vice president of the Museum of Decorative Arts in Philadelphia. His ancestors were among those evicted by Adair. During the next 30 years, Gatsbyesque parties were frequent here, and many noted homosexuals were said to have dropped by—causing much tongue-wagging among the locals. It was McIlhenny who developed the magnificent gardens and forests that today boast plant specimens from all over the world.

In the 1970s, McIlhenny bequeathed the estate to the Irish nation, and it was developed as a national park open from July 1 through September 30. Visitors are taken by bus from the park's visitor center and parking lot to the castle and gardens, where there is also a pleasant, inexpensive tearoom. Hours are 10:30 to 6:30 daily, and there is a moderate fee.

It might be a good idea to carry some insect repellent on this excursion, since at certain times of the year (depending on the weather) there are horseflies and at other times midges (smaller versions of the American mosquito).

To reach Glenveagh from Rathmullan, take the L77 south to Ramelton (7 miles). Then head west for 8 miles on the same L77 to Kilmacrennan. Turn right onto the main road (N56) and head north for about 2 miles. On the left, you'll see a signpost for Gweedore. It's a narrow road (again the L77). When you come to a signpost for Church Hill, do not take it. Continue on the Gweedore/Bunbeg road until you come to the national park. This is about 7 miles from Kilmacrennan, making the total journey from Rathmullan about 22 miles. Do not expect to find a gas station on these last miles on the Gweedore road; fill up in advance.

On your return to Rathmullan, you may follow the same route or you might like to take the turn for Church Hill. At **Church Hill**, there's the **Glebe Gallery**, housing the art collection of well-known Irish painter Derek Hill. Included are works by Picasso, Renoir, Corot, Degas, Braque, and Jack B. Yeats (brother of poet William Butler Yeats). From Church Hill, proceed on the L82 to New Mills, where you pick up the L74 into **Letterkenny**. Here you'll find **Gallagher's Hotel** on Upper Main Street, a good place for a hearty Irish meal. It's open every day all year, with lunch from 12:45 to 2:30 and dinner from 5:30 to 8:45. Meals are inexpensive to moderate, and Visa and Master are accepted. From Letterkenny, pick up the T72 north to Ramelton (8 miles) and then the L77 north for 7 miles to Rathmullan. On this route the distance from Glenveagh to Rathmullan is about 30 miles, or 8 miles longer than the previous route.

¶ There are many other fine journeys in northern County Donegal, but most of them are too distant for using Rathmullan House as a base—that is, if you want to keep your holiday more romantic than frantic. For instance, there's the coastal **Gweedore** section, with its dramatic Bloody Foreland. In **The Rosses** section are the quaint seaside town of Dungloe (rambling old **Sweeney's Hotel** has surprisingly delicious food), the neighboring fishing village of Burtonport, rugged offshore Arranmore Island (reached quickly by ferry) and hilly Annagry village. (**Teach Killendarragh** is an excellent off-the-beaten-path gourmet restaurant serving fine fish and meat dishes. It's charming and unusual for this part of the country and even rents tasteful B&B rooms. Moderately

Errigal, County Donegal

priced; Visa accepted. Phone 074-3108). These places are approximately 45 to 50 miles away from Rathmullan. The islands are farther.
Often the roads are not the best—and then you still have to return.
If you think this rugged coastal area of Donegal is of interest, there is
a splendid rent-an-Irish-cottage complex (one of the country's finest)
on **Cruit Island** (see chapter 15, Special Holidays), but remember that
you have to fend for yourself at such a facility.

NOTE: A word is relevant here about the **Inishowen Peninsula**, which
neighbors Rathmullan's **Fanad Peninsula**. Here again, the distances are
vast (getting there is a major effort), but it is a scenic wonder, especially
the **Malin Head** area—Ireland's northernmost point. It is best not to
attempt it unless you are spending a good deal of time here and, above
all, feel enormously rested.

Finally, almost anything you do in County Donegal will be memorable, but doing too much can be a mistake. The problem is to know
when you've had enough here—because almost every area casts a spell
over the traveler (unless the weather is horrendous, which usually isn't
the case). Remember that Donegal is a world of its own—almost as
ethereal as Brigadoon. It's not only a separate state; it's a unique locale.

2

THE UNUSUAL ESTATES
OF COUNTY SLIGO/LEITRIM

Drumlease Glebe House

And I shall have some peace there, for peace comes dropping slow,
Dropping from the veils of the morning to where the cricket sings;
There midnight's all a glimmer, and noon a purple glow,
And evening full of the linnet's wings.

—W. B. Yeats
"The Lake Isle of Innisfree"

He stood among a crowd at Dromahair;
His heart hung all upon a silken dress,
And he had known at last some tenderness,
Before earth took him to her stony care.

—W. B. Yeats
"The Man Who Dreamed of Faeryland"

Just down the road from Dromahair, County Leitrim, is Cairns Hill Forest Park. There are 2 hills here—Belvoir, meaning "fine view" (of Lough Gill), and Cairns, referring to burial chambers. On each hill is such a chamber, dating from prehistoric times. Legend has it that these were the tombs of 2 Celtic warriors—Romra and Omra. Romra had a stunning daughter called Gille (which is Gaelic for "beauty"). One day while Gille was bathing nude with water from the nearby Tobernalt well, Omra came upon her and was enraptured by her beauty. Since the waters from this well (which still exists today—see Suggestions at the end of this chapter) purportedly have aphrodisiacal powers, Gille was filled with overwhelming desire for this strong and handsome young man. Unable to resist, the two embarked on a passionate but furtive affair. But after weeks of ecstasy in the surrounding woodlands, Gille's father came upon them by accident. Since he and Omra were mortal enemies, they soon engaged in battle. The father, being older and less strong, was fatally wounded. Omra, thinking him dead, turned away. At that moment, Romra mustered enough strength to stand and slay his daughter's lover, and then he succumbed. Grief-stricken, Gille drowned herself in the nearby lake, which from then on was named after her—Lough Gill.

If you are an admirer of W. B. Yeats and would love to sequester yourself amid the truly beautiful and unchanged wood and lakeland beauty of which he wrote, you could find no better place than Drumlease Glebe House. But even if you're not a Yeats fan, don't miss this wonderful 1830 Georgian estate.

Tucked away on its own, it might seem a bit too lonely, perhaps even austere, from the outside. Yet this may be all to the good, because it belies the thrill of discovery when you enter.

Beyond the wonderfully rustic feel that so many such houses in Ireland now have, there is a quiet elegance, a sophistication here that sets this estate apart. This is not to say, however, that it's stuffy and uncomfortable. To the contrary, this place beguiles even the tensest person to relax and savor its charm. It is absolutely hypnotic.

Besides the immaculate, unusually cozy period furniture and the beautiful oil paintings, the color schemes are cheery and warm. There's also a fine collection of Irish books. To say that you will feel sad to depart is to make an understatement. But then, you have to see it for yourself.

As for the bedrooms—with matching wallpaper and homespun spreads and drapes—they are the stuff of dreams. There's a dramatic use of white with the doors, casements, and multipaned windows. And the antiques are treasures. The house is surrounded by woodlands with the quiet little River Bonet coursing through the estate. Would that we all could awaken every morning to this.

With only 7 bedrooms in this former Protestant bishop's homestead, guests are assured of privacy and good service—and the pleasant new owners, the Greensteins, have ample time to spend on each of their guests.

DINING AT DRUMLEASE GLEBE HOUSE: As with the rest of the house, the dining room also weaves a spell. Candlelight is essential to the intimate mood of the room, with its lovely antiques—especially the sideboard from which the fine cuisine is served. Beautiful silver candlesticks and old Irish crystal add to the romantic aura. There's one set meal each night, and it varies daily. It might be a beautifully prepared tender roast leg of lamb served with an excellent plum sauce. It's placed before you in fine china, as are the tasty vegetables. Dinner may begin with fresh vegetable soup with herbs from the garden and end with a delicious chocolate dessert with fresh peaches and cream. There are excellent wines at reasonable prices. The dinners, which are at 7:30, are moderate to expensive and well worth it. Nonresidents must reserve in advance.

PARTICULARS: Drumlease Glebe House (071-64141) is open from March to October, has a wine license, is moderately priced (breakfast included), and accepts Visa. There are 7 bedrooms, 4 with bath (newly installed but designed to look old-fashioned in keeping with the rest of the house). All rooms have hot and cold running water, but those without baths have them adjacent. (U.S. agent: Robert Reid.) There is an outdoor swimming pool on the estate. Other sporting activities include excellent fishing on the private waters of Lough Melvin (said to be one of the purest lakes in western Europe and containing a unique species of trout—the sonaghan), fishing for salmon in Lough Gill (5 minutes away), coarse fishing for pike in Corrigeencor Lake (4 minutes away). Boats, engines, tackle, and ghillies (guides) are available for hire through the owners. Deep-sea fishing is also available, and rental of boats and equipment can be arranged. Golfing is available at the 18-hole Sligo Golf Course at Rosses Point (17 miles) or Strandhill (18-hole) Golf Club (17 miles). Horseback riding is available at the Sligo Riding Centre at Carrowmore (15 miles). This is the perfect location for discovering the beauty of Yeats country. *Finding Drumlease Glebe House*: It is in County Leitrim 12 miles from Sligo Town on the L16 Dromahair Road, which hugs the upper shore of Lough Gill.

Temple House

Come away, O human child!
To the waters and the wild
With a faery, hand in hand,
For the world's more full of weeping than you can understand.
        —W. B. Yeats
          "The Stolen Child"

Although this haunting poem was written about an area about 19 miles north of Ballymote at Glencar, it expresses the mood of this part of the country—and especially of the Temple House demesne.

"The past is like a foreign country. They do things differently there," wrote L. P. Hartley in his Edwardian-era English novel *The Go-Between*. There may be no better quotation to describe this 1,050-acre estate with its own private lake and its owners Deb and Sandie Perceval. This is one of Ireland's most eccentric places, and one that will fascinate from the moment you drive up the long, iron-gated roadway and then walk through the pillared entryway and into yesterday.

These people even talk in a language that seems foreign, but you will be perfectly charmed by them. They and their relatives (whom you probably will meet) make up one of the most refreshing families around. They don't talk history here—they live it. An evening with them makes yesterday seem like today. Of English extraction, the Percevals are more Irish than the Irish. Their distant forebears helped the Irish in this area of Sligo during the most tumultuous of times when the British ruled. It is unquestionably true that you lose touch with reality after one night here. Heaven knows what several weeks would do.

You most likely will want to spend the daytime wandering around this approximately 100-room (they've lost count) abode, being totally engrossed by its Georgian and pre-Georgian antiquity. And then there are the sprawling grounds, which include the remains of an ancient castle built in 1200 A.D. by the Knights of St. John, or the Knights Templar, a private lake, and terraced gardens. If you want to escape everything about today's mad world, this is the place to go.

It's very difficult in such a short space to list all the assets of this estate. It's a place where gleeful children once used tricycles to transverse the palatial interiors, where there are such features as a "half-acre bedroom" (and it must be), a "twins room" in which every magnificent antique is duplicated, a secret room with Oriental antiques, and a dining room so special that it is even equipped with Victorian high chairs for elegantly attired babies. In this household people talk of half-testers and canopied beds as if they were modern furniture—would that they still were.

Despite all this, the Percevals will not force you into their pattern of life. After dinner, you may even opt for your own rustic Georgian sitting room, complete with fireplace and separated from the other guests. How romantic can you get!

As enormous as this estate is, there are just 5 bedrooms—and only one with a full private bath. The Percevals decided not to divide the dramatic second floor into smaller, modern quarters. You will see that this is to your advantage, and there's never a problem finding an un-occupied and fascinating old-fashioned bath down the hall.

Temple House should be declared a national monument, forever protected by the Irish State. It's worth any amount of trouble to spend a night here—one you'll never forget.

DINING AT TEMPLE HOUSE: The dining room is splendid, with an enor-mous antique oval table where all the guests sit and share the dinner—a rural Irish dinner. There are no choices—only one set meal each night—but it's a good one composed entirely of local ingredients. On one night, the appetizer was fresh tomato soup with lovely herbs and bits of tomato enhancing the taste. The lamb entree was truly succulent and tender, as were the sweet peas and cauliflower with Irish cheese sauce. Fresh fruits were a delicious dessert, as was the homemade choc-olate ice cream. Wines were inexpensive and fine. There's true value here. Food was moderately priced.

PARTICULARS: Temple House (071-83329) is open year-round and has a wine license. It is inexpensively priced, with breakfast included, but accepts no credit cards. There are 5 bedrooms, all with hot and cold running water, 1 with bath. (Bathrooms are down the hall.) There are terraced gardens and 1,000 acres of woodland walks. Among the sport-ing possibilities are: boat hire on Temple House Lake (well known for its pike fishing—some 30-pounders have been caught here—as well as perch, bream, tench, rudd, and eels; fishing equipment also for hire); shooting on the estate—for woodcock, snipe, and duck—may be ar-ranged; birdwatching, with more than 50 varieties. Golfing is available at the Sligo (18-hole) Golf Club at Rosses Point (17 miles) or Strandhill (18-hole) Golf Club (17 miles). Horseback riding is available at the Sligo Riding Centre at Carrowmore (15 miles). *Finding Temple House*: It is about 12 miles south of Sligo Town. Take the N4 south to Collooney and then pick up the N17 Tubbercurry Road, south past Ballinacarrow. Soon you will come to a road that dips down to the left. It will bring you shortly to the estate.

Coopershill House   RIVERSTOWN

When you are old and gray and full of sleep,
And nodding by the fire, take down this book,
And slowly read, and dream of the soft look
Your eyes had once, and of their shadows deep;

How many loved your moments of glad grace,
And loved your beauty with love false or true,
But one man loved the pilgrim soul in you,
And loved the sorrows of your changing face;

And bending down beside the glowing bars
Murmur, a little sadly, how Love fled
And paced upon the mountains overhead
And hid his face amid a crowd of stars.

—W. B. Yeats
"When You Are Old"

Approaching the Coopershill demesne, you may develop a sudden sense of foreboding. Surrounded by stately trees, this is a dark-looking mansion, even darker-looking on a cloudy day. But once you pass through its doors, the warmth of the Georgian homestead surrounds you.

This 3-story structure, owned by the O'Hara family since it was built in 1774, sits amid 500 acres of forest and farmland. Hidden from the world and sporting lovely antiques and silver, it is the perfect place to escape. Enjoy a sherry or a coffee by the fire in the drawing room, with extremely comfortable overstuffed furniture, antique piano, brass candleholders, and old books. Then, as you retreat to your bedroom, pass through the hallway lined with deer heads (a hark back to centuries past when deer roamed this forest) and spears from ancient India. Most of the bedrooms have four-poster or canopied beds. There are antique dressing tables, wardrobes, chaise lounges, and books. The carpets are Oriental, and there usually are fresh flowers everywhere.

A special note should be made of the delightful family that holds all of this together and makes it so pleasant for the guests. Joan O'Hara, now in her seventies, and her children, Jane and Tim O'Hara, are the charming hosts who ensure your relaxation.

DINING AT COOPERSHILL: The dining room is large though quiet and intimate, with enormous multipaned windows overlooking the forest, oil portraits of the O'Hara ancestors, and separate antique tables. You are served a set 5-course meal, which changes each night, from a magnificent antique sideboard with Georgian silver. The food, all from the O'Hara farm, is excellently prepared. Roast lamb and beef entrees get raves from many guests. Country-fresh soups and vegetables are perfectly prepared, and desserts are equally delicious. The price is moderate, as it is for the good wines. Dinner is at 7:30 and nonresidents usually are not accepted.

PARTICULARS: Coopershill House (071-65108) is open from Easter through September and has a wine license. It is moderately priced, with breakfast included, but accepts no credit cards. The 5 bedrooms all have private baths. (U.S. agent: Robert Reid.) There are many delightful woodland walks here, but no shooting is allowed. Sporting facilities include a small river flowing through the estate where pike and perch may be caught. Golfing is available at the Sligo (18-hole) Golf Club at Rosses Point, where ocean swimming also is possible (17 miles) or the Strandhill (18-hole) Golf Club (17 miles). Horseback riding is available at the Sligo Riding Centre at Carrowmore (15 miles). *Finding Coopershill House*: It is about 12 miles south of Sligo Town on the N4. Watch for the signposted road for Riverstown and turn left onto it. Coopershill House is signposted.

Suggestions for Your Visit   COUNTY SLIGO/LEITRIM

¶ You may become so intrigued by these places and their grounds that you won't want to leave them. So plan to spend time at them.

¶ While these lodgings are in different areas, each is approximately

12 miles from **Sligo Town**, which dates back to 807 A.D. and is fascinating to visit. From Drumlease Glebe House, take the L16 west along the upper shores of Lough Gill; from Temple House head north on the L11 until you come to the N17, where you turn right or north and just outside of Collooney, pick up the N4 north to Sligo Town; from Coopershill drive out to the N4 and take it north, right into Sligo Town.

It must be said right away that Sligo is scarcely a town anymore. It now verges on being a city by Irish standards. Its bustling streets are among the busiest in the Northwest, and many of them are now one-way. *Tip*: Find yourself a car park (there are quite a few), ditch the car, and walk around. (You'll be unusually fortunate if you do find a place to park on the streets, so don't waste your time.) There is a signposted walking tour of Sligo and a guidebook to indicate places of interest along the 1½-hour route. The trail, which traces the history of Sligo from the earliest times to the present day, begins at the Tourist Board office on Temple Street, where the booklet is also available. Conducted walking tours begin at this point as well. They depart at 11 A.M. during the summer season and are of similar duration. Escorted evening tours highlighting the legends and romance of Sligo are available through *Unique Travel*, Drumcashel School, Clogherevagh, Sligo Town (071-5848).

If you're hungry here, there are plenty of places to eat. Of interest among them is **Beezie's Dining Saloon** on O'Connell Street. It started life in the early 1900s with a classic mahogany bar, marble counters, and stained-glass partitions. Fortunately, these features of the old pub have been retained and are echoed in the later restaurant extension. The food is hearty—boiled ham, shepherd's pie, mixed grills, chicken—and plentiful, at inexpensive to moderate prices. This is a colorful place that blends the best of old and new. (*Men only*: Note the old-time marble urinal; they don't make them like that anymore!) Open noon to 11, every day. Also good are **The Bonne Chere Restaurant** on High Street (poultry and beef dishes), which is open all day, every day, with full license and moderate prices (AmEx, Visa, Master) and **Kate's Kitchen** on Market Street, with inexpensive snacks, good fresh salads, and a wine license. The latter is open all day but closed Sunday and bank holidays.

If a pub is of interest, try **Tommie Regan's Pub** on High Street, visually one of Ireland's finest. Old framed mirrors, antique lamps, mahogany snugs, and upholstered stools complement the antique bar fixtures.

And if a little shopping is in order, you might try some of these: **C & M Enterprises**, Old Market Street (antique items, furniture, prints, vases); **Sligo Crafts**, Market Yard off High Street (Irish earthenware crafts made on the premises, including pitchers, wine jugs, plates and other dishware, lamps); **Wehrly Bros.**, O'Connell Street (Irish jewelry and glass); **Mullaney Bros.**, O'Connell Street (beautiful Irish apparel for both men and women, including tweeds and cashmeres); **P.F. Dooney & Son**, O'Connell Street (knitwear for men in strikingly handsome colors); **Castle Crafts**, in a lane off Castle Street (owner creates his own wares, including pottery, paintings, and framed prints); **Keohane's**, Castle Street (books of Irish interest); **Joy's Craft Centre**, Castle Street (Irish handwoven baskets, pottery, glass, patchwork pictures, sheepskin rugs).

Here is a listing of Sligo's finest in entertainment and annual events:

- **The Hawk's Well Theatre**, Temple Street (071-61526/61518), under the Tourist Board offices, is a venue for traditional music and Yeats memorabilia, with plays and films by other Irish artists.
- **The Yeats Summer School**, operating for 2 weeks in mid-August, draws admirers of the poet from around the world to its seminars led by prominent lecturers. The schedule includes excursions through the scenic Yeats country as well as to such famous Yeatsian haunts as Lissadell House and Thoor Ballylee. This is one of the world's most popular summer literary courses. Request applications and sign up well in advance through Kathleen Moran, The Yeats Society, Douglas Hyde Bridge, Sligo (phone 071-2693). Lodging reservations must be made far ahead.

¶ Just outside of Sligo Town, east on the L16, is **Lough Gill**. With its 22 islands, it is surrounded by woodlands and mountains and is connected to Sligo Town by the Garavogue River. One of this lake's islands, **Innisfree**, was immortalized by William Butler Yeats in "The Lake Isle of Innisfree." You may, if you wish, circle the lake by car, until you reach the turnoff for Hazelwood. Take this half-mile road for a fine view of the lake and also to see **Hazelwood House**, a grand example of an 18th-century Palladian country home. This is also a lovely spot for a picnic.

Returning to the main road, continue on through Dromahair. (This is in County Leitrim, 12 miles from Sligo Town.) Next, you will pass by a road leading to the remains of 16th-century **Creevylea Abbey**. A little farther along, another road is signposted for Innisfree. This road gives you a fine close-up view of the island, as well as access to a tea/

craft shop open during the summer months. Still farther on the main road, you'll pass the entrances to Slish Wood forest walk with a peaceful stream and Dooney Rock forest walk with a steep, stepped climb that affords fine views of the lake. These are also great places for picnics. Back on the main road, you'll pass a signposted turn for **Tobernalt**. In pre-Christian times this was an assembly site for *Lughnasa,* one of the 4 great harvest festivals, where the god Lugh was honored. His name became the Gaelic word for the month of August. Water from the well here is thought to have curative as well as aphrodisiacal powers. The next turn off the main road is for **Cairns Hill Forest Park**, from which there are splendid views of the lake. Continue from here until you come to the N4, where you turn right if you want to head back to Sligo Town (the total circle from Sligo and back is about 25 miles) or left if you are staying at Ballymote or Riverstown and wish to return there.

Perhaps the best way to see Lough Gill is aboard the water bus **Inisfree Express**. The boat seats 70, has a full liquor license, and departs from Sligo Town's Riverside area at the entrance to Doorly Park and near the **Blue Lagoon Sing-Song Lounge Bar and Restaurant**. Each afternoon in the summer season (through September), the boat cruises down the Garavogue River and into Lough Gill, stopping at Innisfree Island. It takes 1½ hours and is very inexpensive. There's even a commentary on the history and folklore of the lake and its surroundings, and Yeats poetry is recited as it pertains.

¶ For William Butler Yeats fans who love his haunting poem "The Stolen Child" (a section of which appeared earlier in the discussion of Temple House), and for those who just like beautiful scenery, 7 miles northeast of Sligo Town on the N16 is **Glencar Lake and Waterfalls**— the setting of the poem. The 2-mile lake stretches through a verdant valley. At the valley's eastern end are the 2 waterfalls; one of them has a spectacular unbroken fall of 50 feet.

¶ Five miles northwest of Sligo Town is **Rosses Point**, another Yeatsian landscape. There's a 3-mile sandy beach below the high banks and some fine views of the sea. Approximately a half mile out is **Coney Island**. (New York's Coney Island is said to have been named after it.) It is accessible on foot from the Strand hill (village with beach, 4 miles west of Sligo on the L132) side when the tide is out. Across Drumcliffe Bay is Lissadell House (see below). At Rosses Point, there's an 18-hole golf course, plus a yacht club and a sail-training center.

Exciting news is that Damien Brennan, brother of one of Ireland's finest hoteliers (Francis Brennan, The Park Hotel, Kenmare, County

Kerry), has opened a splendid new restaurant here called **Reveries**, which is touted by many as one of Ireland's finest. (For review, see chapter 14, Special Restaurants.) If you're looking for a relatively good hotel nearby to stay at so you can eat here, **Ballincar House** is just about 2 miles down the road, and it serves good food. (See the review in chapter 13.) **Lissadell House** is another place to stay, if you wish to visit Reveries, but don't want a long drive home. It's a little farther away, about 5 miles, on the main Sligo to Donegal road. It's a very basic-but-spotless bed-and-breakfast place that's inexpensive and has 5 rooms with bath. It's open all year, but doesn't accept credit cards.

¶ Five miles due north on the N15, under the shadow of Benbulben Mountain, is **Drumcliffe**, location of the churchyard where Yeats is buried. On the marker is the epitaph he wrote:

> *Cast a cold eye*
> *On life, on death.*
> *Horseman, pass by!*

After Drumcliffe, a road to the left follows along the shore of Drumcliffe Bay through the village of Carney to **Lissadell House** (about 4 miles). This was the homestead of Eva Gore-Booth and her more famous sister, Constance, who later became the Countess Markiewicz and played a leading role in the 1916 Easter Rising (rebellion). After her release from prison, she was the first woman to be elected by the Dublin constituency of Sinn Fein, the Irish Republican Army's political wing, to the House of Commons in Westminster. She immediately refused it and instead chose to sit on the separatist Dáil Éireann, as minister for labor. The Dáil to this day forms the Irish Republic government. Yeats immortalized Lissadell and these women when he wrote in his poem "In Memory of Eva Gore-Booth and Con Markiewicz":

> *The light of evening, Lissadell,*
> *Great windows open to the south,*
> *Two girls in silk kimonos, both*
> *Beautiful, one a gazelle.*

The house, still the home of the Gore-Booth family, was built between 1830 and 1835. The austere Greek Revival architecture makes it appear haunted amid the stately forests. Yeats visited here often. The house, along with its gardens, is open to the public from May 1 through

Lissadell House, County Sligo

Benbulben Mountain, County Sligo

September 30, every afternoon except Sunday, from 2 to 5:15. The last tour stressing the antiques and oil paintings begins at 4:30. There is a tearoom serving homemade baked goods and preserves, and hand-knits and souvenirs are available for purchase. Nearby in the pine forest is a picnic site.

Just a short distance from here is **Ellen's Pub** at **Maugherow**. Built in 1610, this is the oldest and the last of Ireland's thatched pubs. During the summer months, there are traditional music sessions each night. The pub is adjacent to one of northern Sligo County's fine beaches. Farther along this road, off Streedagh, 3 large ships of the Spanish Armada broke up, and more than a thousand bodies washed onto the strand.

¶ Continuing on for a few miles, you'll eventually meet up again with the N15 Sligo road. At this point, you will be 10 miles north of Sligo Town at **Grange Village**, site of the **Sligo Crystal Glass Ltd.** factory. It is open all year, Monday through Friday, from 8:30 to 5:30. The shop is also open on weekdays during the summer months. Also in Grange is **The Spinning Wheel Sweater Shop**, open June through September, Monday through Friday, from 9:30 to 5:30.

For the adventurous, Grange is the village beneath the vast, flat-topped **Benbulben Mountain**. If you ascend to 1,800 feet, you'll see spectacular seascapes and panoramas (north into Donegal and south to Glencar Lake, Drumcliffe, and Rosses Point) on a clear day. The 6½-mile round trip takes about 4 hours on foot.

¶ Due west of Sligo Town, on the L32, is the **Strandhill Peninsula**. **Strandhill** (a seaside resort) is at the westernmost point, 5 miles from Sligo. Two miles out, a left turn leads to the low hill of **Carrowmore**, where megalithic remains from the Bronze Age include a 2-mile line of burial chambers—dolmens, cairns, and stone circles. This is thought to be one of the largest such concentrations in northern Europe. Two miles farther west is **Knocknarea Mountain**. Knocknarea (or *Cnoc na Ri*, "the Hill of Kings") is 1,080 feet high and the legendary grave (a 50-foot stony cairn) of the prehistoric Queen Maeve, once the leader of the Connaught province. You may, if you wish, climb to the top of this lovely mountain and enjoy—on a clear day—the spectacular views. These include the Blue Stack Mountains and the Slieve League cliffs of Donegal to the north; the hills of Slieve Daeane brushing the southern shore of Lough Gill; and magnificent seascapes to the west. It is best (and relatively easy) to ascend the 900 feet to the top on the southeast side of the mountain near Grange House. It takes about 1½ hours to complete the 2-mile trip. This climb is quite popular. On the southwest side of the mountain is the **Glen of Knocknarea**, a deep, mile-long chasm, 30 feet wide. Although it is overgrown with plant life protruding from the crevices in the limestone, a nature footpath runs through it.

Near here, at **Culleenamore**, is an excellent award-winning restaurant called **Knockmuldowney** (071-68122) located in a Georgian country home. Serving superb fish dishes as well as excellent meats (including game and poultry), it's open Tuesday through Saturday evenings from 7:30 to 10, has a wine license, is moderately priced, and takes AmEx, Master, Visa, and Diners. (See the review of the lodging in chapter 13.)

¶ If you are staying at Coopershill in Riverstown, 3 miles due south is **Heapstown Cairn**, a Neolithic passage tomb. Nearby is the area known as Moytirra, where it is thought 2 legendary battles were fought in pre-Christian times. You may continue south from here, skirting Lough Arrow (many beautiful islands), or you may cut over to the N4 and in a short distance come to the **Carrowkeel Passage Tombs**, on 5 ridges called **Bricklieve Mountains**. It's about 1½ miles to the top, and you can spend hours here exploring the tombs, which date from about 2000 B.C. The views are spectacular, especially at sunset.

¶ If you are staying at Temple House near Ballymote, consider a visit to **Ballymote Castle**, around which the town developed. Built at the beginning of the 14th century by Richard de Burgo, the Red Earl of Ulster, it has 6 towers and enormous towered entrance gates. Although now in ruins, at one time it was said to be the strongest castle in the province of Connaught. *The Book of Ballymote* was compiled here in the 15th century, when the castle was in the hands of the MacDonaghs. This book provided the key to the linear system of writing called Ogham. Based on the Latin alphabet, it appears on many standing stones in Ireland that date from the 4th and 5th centuries. (The *Book of Ballymote* is displayed at the Royal Irish Academy on Dawson Street in Dublin.)

Also at Ballymote are the ruins of a 15th-century **Franciscan abbey.** In the surrounding countryside are many examples of pre-Christian ringed forts, circular dwelling houses of Celtic farmers, and underground rooms and passages.

Four miles south of Ballymote on the L11 is **Keshcorran Hill**, where there are 17 caves on the west face that held the remains of such animals as cave bear, reindeer, and Irish elk—long since extinct in Ireland. Legend has it that in one of these caves a she-wolf dwelled and nurtured

the child who was to become the wisest of all the ancient Irish kings—
Cormac Mac Airt. The ancient *Lughnasa* harvest celebration in honor
of the Celtic god Lugh was held in front of these caves. On the last
Sunday in July, called Garland Sunday, the locals would all meet here
for great merriment, apparently sparking a great number of courtships
and love affairs. The tradition has survived to modern times, although
Lugh is no longer honored. The summit of the hill offers spectacular
views of the area.

A SPECIAL NOTE ABOUT COUNTY DONEGAL: If you are staying at any
of the County Sligo/Leitrim lodgings described here (or, for that matter,
any that aren't mentioned here) and are considering using them as
headquarters for touring County Donegal, perish the thought. Donegal
does not become interesting until you reach the area around Donegal
Town, which is 41 miles from Sligo Town. Bundoran, the first major
destination in County Donegal, is a brash, noisy holiday town. Granted,
the roadway from Sligo has been greatly improved, so you can speed
right along, *but* above Donegal Town, where so much of interest lies,
the roads become twisty and narrow and travel takes much longer. If
you want to see County Donegal, do yourself a favor and either go to
the Sand House in Rossnowlagh, an excellent springboard for all of
southern Donegal, *or* go all the way north to Rathmullan and Rathmullan House, an ideal base for seeing northern Donegal. (Both are
covered in the Donegal chapter of this book.) To explore Donegal from
a base in Sligo/Leitrim not only will exhaust you but also could ruin
your holiday.

3
OUTSTANDING
COUNTY MAYO LODGINGS

Newport House

During medieval times in Ireland, unlike in many areas of Europe, many marriages seem to have been as flimsy as they are in America today. One such was performed only a few miles from Newport House—at Carraigahooly, or Rockfleet Castle, which is still in excellent condition if you wish to visit it (see Suggestions at the end of this chapter). Grace O'Malley, the famous Pirate Queen of Connaught, came here to live with Richard Burke (or Richard-an-Iarainn—"of iron") after their marriage, sometime around 1566. The terms of the marriage were such that after a period of a year, either party could cancel the contract and dismiss the other. At that time, Grace and her O'Malley clan controlled most of the coastal territories in this part of Ireland, except for the northeastern reaches of Clew Bay, including Carraigahooly. These were controlled by Richard. The story goes that Grace romanced him—to the point of becoming pregnant. They married, went to live in Carraigahooly, and continued to have such a fevered relationship that Richard was blissfully unaware of imminent treachery. All the while, Grace was garrisoning Richard's castle with her own clansmen. Three months after their son was born, the first anniversary of their marriage occurred, and Grace blithely called out to Richard, "I dismiss you." And that was that.

If you were to happen upon Newport House and wander about its stately halls and rooms, unaware that it was a lodging, you would think you

Newport House, County Mayo

were in a museum full of beautiful art and furnishings. There is a special delight upon entering such a place, because you're not just seeing a collection of antiques; rather, you're being absorbed by a segment of the past.

If you can imagine a 200-year-old home (mansionesque, mind you) on 30 acres rich with extravagant sitting rooms (which would be roped off in a museum but which you can actually use here) you'll have some idea of what ivy-covered Newport House is like. Built on earlier foundations in 2 varying stages of Georgian architecture, it was the original home of a branch of the O'Donnell family, descended from the fighting Earls of Tyrconnell and the cousins of the famous "Red Hugh" O'Donnell, who controlled northern Mayo. (They were transplanted to Mayo from the province of Ulster by Oliver Cromwell.)

During the first half of the 19th century, the *Cathach* (Battler), *Battle Book of the O'Donnells*, was discovered at Newport House. Its vellum pages contain the Psalms written in Latin. Historians believe the book, which is now in the Royal Irish Academy in Dublin, dates from about 650 A.D. and is the handiwork of St. Columcille. Its name derives from the legend that it would ensure victory when the book was carried in the hands of an innocent priest about the O'Donnell army camp before the men went into combat.

This alluring homestead contains a spectacular center staircase that sweeps gracefully up to branch off in 2 directions for the second floor, then comes together again to rise to the top floor. A magnificent glass-domed ceiling edged with elegant Georgian plasterwork designs holds court over the grand hallway that shimmers in sunlight on a clear day. Then there are small pargeted alcoves, priceless tables, three-cornered settees, a library with antique books, Regency mirrors, silver serving pieces, and a magnificent collection of artwork, including grand oil paintings.

With all this, it's difficult to think of Newport House as a hotel that caters to fishermen. Not only is it that, but it's considered one of Ireland's best, with fishing right on the grounds and a fishing guide who will provide you with maps of the best fishing spots.

DINING AT NEWPORT HOUSE: The quiet dining room exudes the aura of the past as well. It serves fish from the estate's own waters and vegetables and fruits from the grounds. The menu is quite simple—and good. Appetizers may include sea trout mousse, pâté, and a light, delicately cooked spinach and tomato salad. The fresh turbot and salmon baked in a shell with a rich cream sauce are truly superb. Other entrees include very tender roast beef and lamb, well-prepared salmon, sea trout, and turbot. The wine list is long and the menu is moderately priced. Non-residents must reserve. Lunch is served from 12:45 to 2:15 and dinner from 7:30 to 9:30.

PARTICULARS: Newport House (098-41222) is open from April 1 through September 30 and has a full license and a laundry. It is moderately expensive, with breakfast included, and accepts AmEx, Diners, Master, and Visa. There are 20 bedrooms (15 in the main house, the rest in 2 smaller houses near the courtyard). (U.S. agent: Robert Reid.) Sporting facilities include full match-size billiards and snooker table; table-tennis room; shooting on 25 thousand nearby acres; croquet; walking; running; riding; and pony trekking, under qualified instruction, and hiking on key hills and wooded paths; fishing on private waters of the Newport River and the Lough Beltra West—as well as on the Beltra East and other lakes and rivers by arrangement; arrangements for cruising down the Tidal River to the islands or sea fishing on the waters of Clew Bay; golfing nearby—a championship 18-hole course near Westport (8 miles) and Newport House's own 9-hole course near Mulrany (11 miles); swimming at nearby beaches. *Finding Newport House:* It's on the N59 (or T71), on the southern outskirts of Newport village.

Ashford Castle   CONG

On the banks of the Cong River, near Ashford Castle, is a cave called Pigeon Hole, once the haunt of wild birds. Inside is a wide, deep stream running through an unknown course, and the only sound is that of rushing underground waters. As the story goes, an Irish maiden once fell deeply in love with a wiry young *Fir Blog* (allegedly the country's first settlers, from the Mediterranean). But she had another admirer who seethed at their affair. In a fit of passion, the rejected suitor killed the Fir Blog and rowed the body out onto Lough Corrib, where he threw it overboard. When the body drifted ashore and the maid discovered the tragedy, she vanished. But soon afterward, in the cave where the lovers had held their passionate rendezvous, a beautiful white trout began to appear frequently. Rumor had it that this was the bereaved girl's spirit, which eventually disappeared for good. To this day, in the deeper confines of the cave, an eerie white light creeps out over the waters. It is thought to emanate from the maiden's spirit, lighting the way through eternity for her lover's return.

There are so many special features to the lodgings of Ireland, and each location has a unique atmosphere that varies markedly from the others. But the place that seems the most lavish, the most splendid—the place where you could imagine pampering yourself in the grandest manner— is County Mayo's Ashford Castle.

When you pass the gatehouse and through the massive iron gates that enclose Ashford's thousands of acres, you'll most likely feel you've stepped into the pages of Evelyn Waugh's *Brideshead Revisited*. A leisurely curving road finally brings you within sight of the castle, vast and imposing. A composite structure endowed with every flourish known to castellated architecture, Ashford is straight out of a fairy tale.

The original structure (still part of Ashford) was built in the early 13th century by the de Burgo family, who took part in the Norman invasion. For years, the de Burgos feuded with the O'Connors for su-

Ashford Castle, County Mayo

premacy in this area of Ireland, only to be superseded by the Oranmore and Browne families. During the 18th century, Sir Geoffrey Browne constructed a French-style chateau designed to connect and integrate with the older castle. In the mid-19th century, the estate was sold to Sir Benjamin Guinness, who expanded it to its present 26,000 acres, built the road, reclaimed the land and installed a drainage system, and planted thousands of trees. It was he who added 2 major extensions to the Browne section of the castle.

His son, Lord Ardilaun, later designed the gardens and laid out more than 20 miles of attractive walkways. Still dissatisfied, he decided that the castle needed a more baronial air, even at the estimated cost of £2 million. So in 1884, with a crew to rival that of a Cecil B. deMille production, he undertook to have the stonework cut just as the ancient Egyptians did it. (Is there any other way?) Some 31 years later, with the western portion of the refurbishing complete, Lord Ardilaun died. Many feel his work at Ashford was inspired; it certainly is dramatic.

The estate was controlled by the Iveagh Trust for the Guinness family until it was sold to Noel Huggard, who started transforming it into a grand hotel at the beginning of World War II. Recently, an American,

John Mulcahy, assumed ownership and picked up where Lord Ardilaun left off, completing the restoration at a cost of millions of pounds. Presently, Ashford is under the ownership of a consortium.

The structure looms over Ireland's second-largest lake, Lough Corrib, and is approached via a formidable stone bridge. Entering the castle, you'll be struck by the lavish elegance of its appointments. From the massive carved oak doorway onward, the sense of grandeur is enhanced by suits of armor, hundreds of oil paintings, plush carpeting, enormous fireplaces, a sweeping staircase, carved wainscoting and ceilings, and priceless antique furniture.

The castle is so vast that you literally get lost in it. Numerous lounges overlooking the grounds are furnished with wonderfully elegant (but comfortable) old armchairs, divans, and settees. Solicitous attendants ply you with tea or sherry.

DINING AT ASHFORD: Perhaps influenced by the glitter of the old Waterford chandeliers overhanging the massive dining room's Doric columns, some claim that Ashford offers the finest and most regal dining experience in all of Ireland. Well, the food is very good, but so many truly superb restaurants have opened recently in Ireland that they all vie with one another and have converted the country to a gourmet's paradise. At Ashford, the crabmeat appetizers are highly recommended, as is the smoked trout with raifort (horseradish/cream/mustard) sauce. The pâté is good, and so is the courgette (zucchini) quiche. The chilled avocado soup is wonderful, but the fresh carrot soup is just a little too sweet and creamy. Among the entrees: beautiful roast beef—tender and rare; succulent roast rack of lamb. Poached fillet of sea trout in a delicate sorrel sauce, fresh poached salmon, and escalope of veal in lemon butter are all praiseworthy. One hearty and very tasty dish is the boned chicken breast stuffed with duck liver pâté and covered with fennel sauce. The vegetables are excellent—especially spinach puree, broccoli hollandaise, potatoes dauphinoise (sliced and baked with Swiss cheese), as well as the unusual Chinese leaves and deep-fried salsify (oyster plant). There is also a fine dessert cart (fresh strawberry mousse is recommended), in addition to a good cheese tray. The wines can be extremely expensive or reasonable, depending on your choice, but the lower-priced wines are good. Dining at Ashford is expensive, and if you're not a resident, you should reserve in advance. Lunch is from 1 to 2:15, dinner from 7:30 to 9.

As well as this dining room, Ashford has an elegant new French restaurant called **The Connaught Room**. Under the glitter of more vast chandeliers and overlooking Lough Corrib, this smaller, more intimate room serves superb haute cuisine and wine on the finest china and crystal that was designed especially for Ashford. The carefully prepared meat and fish offerings boast sauces that are made by the order rather than in advance. Everything is à la carte and expensive, but well worth it. Because this room is small, reservations are required, even if you're staying at the Castle. Dinner is from 7 to 10.

PARTICULARS: Ashford Castle (094-71444) is open all year and has a full license. It is very expensive and breakfast is not included. AmEx, Master, Visa, Diners are accepted. There are 78 elegant bedrooms, including 6 executive suites that include bedroom, large sitting room, bath, and cocktail bar. All bedrooms have bath and phone, as well as a view of either the lake or the Cong River. Make reservations well in advance, especially in high season. (U.S. agent: Ashford Castle Inc.) Sporting facilities at Ashford include golfing over a 9-hole course on the grounds; tennis; running; walking; hunting—pheasant, snipe, duck, and woodcock in season; fishing; boating. Also, a new health and leisure complex has been added, which includes an exercise equipment room, whirlpool, steam room, and Turkish bath. In addition, there is a lovely craftshop. *Finding Ashford*: It's near the village of Cong on the L101.

Suggestions for Your Visit   COUNTY MAYO

¶ Without question, you will want to save plenty of time to enjoy both museumlike Newport House and Ashford Castle, which can only be described as regally lavish. It wouldn't be difficult to spend weeks at Ashford amid the splendor of its many lounges and sitting rooms— to say nothing of its grounds. So, above all else, *do* take the time.

¶ At Ashford, you may want to go boating on **Lough Corrib**. You can arrange for your own private rowboat, you can hire a boat and boatman who will offer you fishing gear and advice (if you wish), or you can cruise on the *Corrib Queen*—a craft that carries 50 passengers. All are quite reasonable. The *Queen* goes around the lake's islands, including Inchagoill Island, where the boat often stops. Before your departure, you can arrange to have a luncheon cold plate and a bottle of good wine served to you on the island for a modest price. (Inchagoill, one of Lough Corrib's largest islands, houses the ruins of 2 ornate stonework churches, one of which is attributed to St. Patrick around the year 500. Nearby, a stone obelisk with one of the oldest Christian inscriptions in Europe is said to mark the burial spot of his nephew, St. Brendan the Navigator.) There are several cruises a day of a few hours' duration. But you can also make arrangements for longer trips on the *Corrib Queen* to the village of **Oughterard**, or even all the way to **Galway City**. You can enter the **Maam River** and travel up through the breathtakingly beautiful Maam Valley to Maam Bridge and back.

¶ Whether or not you're a religious person, there's a very pleasant journey from Cong to **Ballintubber Abbey** in **Ballintubber**, 17 miles to the north and just off the main Castlebar road to the right (3½ miles from Partry village). This is the only known church in the English-speaking world where Mass has been celebrated daily for almost 770 years, despite Henry VIII's attempts to suppress the abbey and an attack by Cromwell that left it roofless for a time. Ballintubber was founded in 1216 by Cathal O'Connor, the King of Connaught, on the site of a 5th-century church established by St. Patrick. It is perhaps one of the most beautiful and peaceful of all rural churches, and it exudes a special aura of romance. Walking through its early-Gothic main entrance, you're struck by the sight of gleaming whitewashed walls, rustic beamed ceilings, flagstone floors, and simple wooden benches. The nave is lighted by 8-pointed windows. Over the altar are 3 stained-glass Norman windows, crowned by a 4th, all framed with double dogtooth molding. The ancient monks' quarters extend to the right of the church. While here, sit for a moment in the church and absorb the sense of calmness and lightness.

From here, if you wish to continue touring, it's a good idea to cut over from Ballintubber village to the L101 and head north about 11 miles to the charming and captivating coastal village of **Westport**— situated on a hill and in a hollow surrounded by trees and mountains and resting on an arm of beautiful Clew Bay. The main street, or Mall, drifts along both banks of the **River Carrowbeg**, connected by quaint stone bridges and lined with lime trees. Here you may well want to stroll about and do some shopping. On High Street are **Old Market Crafts** (Irish jewelry, clothing, knits); **Western Hand Knits**; and **M. Molloy Iron Monger & Grocer** (Waterford glass, china, prints, fishing flies). On Bridge Street are **Hugh Coen** (old books, antique dishes, copper items, vases); **Carraig Donn Boutique** (Irish glass, sweaters, sheepskin rugs, other crafts); **The Aran Shop** (Irish sweaters); **The West Crafts & Gift Shop** (Irish crystal, adjoining tearoom); and **Shan-**

ley's (men's clothing, sweaters, tweeds). **The Mall Gift Shop** (Irish sweaters, books, crystal) is on the South Mall and **McAleer & Sons Ltd.** (locally made lambskin rugs and slippers) is slightly outside of town at The Quay.

If you're hungry, Westport offers **The Parlour Inn** (open every day; moderate and inexpensive meat and fish dishes such as baked ham, fresh trout, savory pancakes, hamburgers) and **The Boxty Restaurant** (open every day; inexpensive snacks and meals)—both on Bridge Street. Slightly outside of town, at The Quay, are several restaurants. **The Asgard Tavern and Restaurant**, a small, old pub with a nautical theme, has won food awards and serves very tasty homemade soups, farmhouse pâtés, lamb stews, and beef curries. It's inexpensive (larger moderate meals also) and accepts AmEx, Visa, Master, and Diners. It's closed Monday. **Ardmore House Restaurant**, an intimate dining room and bar overlooking Clew Bay, specializes in homemade brown bread, pâtés, and soups as starters and fresh seafood (especially lobster, salmon, sole, mussels) as entrees. Steaks and curries are also available; moderate; AmEx, Master, Visa; closed Sunday. **The Chalet Swiss Restaurant** has a warm, intimate atmosphere and specializes in fresh seafood, veal, steak dishes, and continental cuisine. Prices are moderate; AmEx, Master, and Visa are accepted; closed Tuesday.

One-and-a-half miles west of the village, on the T39 near The Quay, is **Westport House**, a magnificent Georgian mansion owned by the Marquess of Sligo (a direct descendant of Grace O'Malley, the Pirate Queen of Connaught). Occupying the site of the old O'Malley castle, it was built in 1731 and furnished with the best that Georgian artists and craftsmen could provide, especially Irish silver, paintings, crystal, and furniture. Visit the downstairs drawing rooms, with grand fire-places and chandeliers, then ascend the sweeping marble staircase to the bedrooms. Shops here offer Irish crafts, antiques, and old books. There's a tearoom, which was the main kitchen in the old days, featuring delicious homemade Irish barm brack cake. The house is open daily from 10:30 to 6, June through August. In April, September, and the first 5 days in October, it is open afternoons from 2 to 6. Additional reasons for visiting Westport include a children's zoo and Grace O'Malley's former dungeons, which have been turned into a mock-scary setting for children. On the grounds are horse and pony riding, horse-drawn caravans, boats, bikes, and holiday homes for rent.

There's a pleasant return route to **Cong** if you backtrack on the L101 through Mace and Killavally. Then, after about 3 or 4 miles, branch off to the right (before coming to Partry) and head south, hugging the beautiful shores of Lough Mask with the Partry Mountains on your right. You'll pass through Tourmakeady, Trean, Maumtrasna, Conbur, and over to Cong. The distance from Westport on this route is about 30 miles.

An alternate route (about 20 miles) from Westport back to Cong follows the N59 and passes through the striking Erriff Valley, between the Partry Mountains and the Sheefry Hills, through such towns as Knappagh, Liscarney, Carrowkennedy, Erriff Bridge, and down to Leenane (in County Galway). **Leenane** is on Killary Harbor, the only Scandinavian-type fjord in all of Ireland. It's a spectacular setting. Here you'll have access to the **Killary Shop**, a very attractive and well-stocked Irish crafts store with a rustic restaurant extension serving everything from good snacks to 4-course meals. Try the homemade pâté. Open all

Westport House, County Mayo

day; wine license; AmEx, Diners, Visa, Master; inexpensive. Also in Leenane is **Mweelrea Craft Shop**, which features Irish pottery and sweaters and has an inexpensive tearoom of its own. From Leenane, pick up the L101, cutting down through the lovely **Joyce Country**, with its cool lakes, verdant glens, and grand mountains. It's named after the Joyce family, stalwart men and women who moved here from Wales in the 13th century and whose descendants still live here. Although James Joyce was a self-proclaimed descendant of this clan, he never wrote about this area. This road will bring you to Maam Bridge, then Cornamona on the shores of Lough Corrib, then up to Clonbur, and back over to Cong—about 24 miles from Leenane. The total distance on this route from Westport to Cong is about 44 miles.

¶ For those staying at Ashford Castle, the Connemara region of County Galway is within easy reach. Its heart, the village of **Clifden**, is only 45 picturesque miles away (through Leenane), and the area is well worth exploring. See Suggestions at the end of chapter 4.

¶ A tour of historic **Galway City** (28 miles away) is an excellent idea. See chapter 4 for all the possibilities.

¶ If you are staying at Newport House, the village of **Newport** has **Dorac Crafts, Curragh Crafts**, and the **Newport Foundation Craft Shop**—each with a variety of Irish crafts. Also, an interesting pub here, called **Chambers**, is decorated with old Irish farming equipment.

¶ Quite likely you will want to travel the 8 miles south on the N59 from Newport to Westport village, described earlier in this section.

¶ You may wish to travel the N59 coastal road north of Newport to **Achill Island**—a distance of 23 miles to the beginning of the island, accessible by bridge. On the way, you'll pass the 15th-century ruins of **Burrishoole Abbey**, with its central tower still intact. Near that is **Carraigahooly**, or **Rockfleet Castle**, where the Pirate Queen dismissed her husband (see the romantic legend at the beginning of this chapter). Just outside the little resort village of Mulrany is **Rossturk Castle**.

Achill is Ireland's largest coastal island—15 miles long and 12 miles wide. Crossing the bridge from the mainland you enter **Achill Sound**, the island's main town for shopping. Attractions here include bathing, surfing, fishing, boating, and boating excursions. This town is a good point from which to explore the less-traveled and nearer southern tip of the island. Farther afield, to the north, is the resort village of **Keel**, which has an incredible 3-mile beach. The island has its own great mountains, heather-covered hills, spectacular cliffs, and underwater caves for exploring. It's also an ideal place for running, hiking, and picnicking. Achill has for some time been very popular with tourists, especially Irish tourists, so it won't be quite as removed from the world as you might expect. It's quite a lively place. At **Keel**, there are 2 seemingly trendy restaurants: **The Amethyst Restaurant**, which accepts Visa, has a seating capacity for 50, is open daily April to September, has a wine license, and specializes in tandoori and vegetarian dishes (inexpensive to moderately priced), and nearby, the **Chalet Seafood Restaurant**, which has patio dining and a view of Keel Bay and the Minaun cliffs. It seats 70, has a wine license, and is open from noon onward from June to September 20. It's moderately priced but accepts no credit cards. From here, you will have to backtrack to Newport on the same road.

¶ Also north of Newport, but still in County Mayo and on the same N59 (which later changes to the T58—you just continue north from **Mulrany** instead of heading west for Achill), is the **Mullet Peninsula**. The most familiar town here (and that isn't saying much) is **Belmullet**, about 43 miles from Newport. It's one of the most remote, windswept villages in Ireland, with fine nearby beaches and seascapes. Because of its distance from popular tourist sites, you will not find a variety of dining places, but there is a very basic hotel (10 rooms without baths, very inexpensive) called **Western Strands**, plus a few B&Bs—one with licensed premises (**M. Maguire Murphy** at Drom Caoin, Ballinavode). The **Western Strands** is a grade-C hotel—by Irish Tourist Board standards—but at least it's there, and it offers inexpensive food, all day, all year. You might prefer to take along a picnic lunch instead.

NOTE: It is not wise to combine this excursion with a tour of Achill Island, as each offers many sights and the combined mileages are too great.

¶ Southwest of Newport is **Croagh Patrick**, Ireland's 2,500-foot holy mountain, where legend has it that in the year 441 St. Patrick spent 40 days of Lent fasting and praying for the Irish people. Each year, on the last Sunday in July, there is a pilgrimage to its summit, where mass is celebrated in a modern oratory. From Newport, take the N59 for 8 miles to Westport and then take the T39 Westport to Louisburg road for 5 miles to Murrisk where you begin the climb, which usually takes about an hour and affords spectacular views of Clew Bay, Achill Island, and the Nephin Beg range of mountains to the north; the Partry Mountains to the south; and Clare Island and the sweep of Atlantic to the west.

4 CONNEMARA'S ENCHANTED ESTATES, COUNTY GALWAY

Abbeyglen Castle

Rain on Rahoon falls softly, softly falling,
Where my dark lover lies.
Sad is his voice that calls me, sadly calling,
At grey moonrise.

Love, hear thou
How soft, how sad his voice is ever calling,
Ever unanswered and the dark rain falling,
Then as now.

Dark too our hearts, O love, shall lie and cold
As his sad heart has lain
Under the moongrey nettles, the black mould
And muttering rain.

> —James Joyce
> "She Weeps over Rahoon"

James Joyce's lover/common-law wife/mother of his 2 children (eventually they did marry) Nora Barnacle was from Galway City. She was born at No. 8 Bowling Green, a tiny house that is still standing. Joyce wrote the poem above about Nora's former lover—a gentle boy in failing health. On the rainy night before she was to leave for a Dublin convent, he left his sickbed and came to her window at No. 5 Nun's Island to sing of his love (he had wanted to become a singer). And from that, as the Irish say, "he got his death in the rain" from exposure. This story is also told in prose in "The Dead," the last of the moving short stories in Joyce's *Dubliners*.

In the past, going to the Abbeyglen Hotel was a rather disappointing experience. While it had excellent food and a terrific view of the picturesque village of Clifden and the mountains, the interior was too modern and uninteresting. Now that has changed dramatically. Owner Paul Hughes has taken his lodging and turned it into a castle. The entire façade has been reconstructed with twin towers and castellated windows. In one of the towers is a spiral staircase that leads to a library/ cocktail bar and onto the battlements, where cocktails are also served in fair weather. There's now a grand foyer, and the sitting rooms are resplendent with antiques. The bedrooms have been lavishly furnished with canopied beds, period chairs, settees, and dressing tables, as well as with reproductions of antique ceiling moldings. To complete the estate, a gatehouse and drawbridge are being added to the grounds.

DINING AT ABBEYGLEN CASTLE: The lodging now boasts 2 fine restaurants and also serves food in the cocktail lounge. The downstairs restaurant is somewhat more intimate than the original upstairs room, which is larger. The food is excellent. For starters, there's often a wonderful salad called Melina—filled with fresh shrimp, walnuts, celery, apples, and melon and served on a bed of Bibb lettuce with a sprightly dressing. Delicious. Then there's an eloquent lobster-and-tomato quiche. The mushroom soup is beautifully done, with chunks of fresh mushrooms and cream. The scalding onion soup rivals that of New York's Brasserie in its heyday.

Entrees include a succulent roast lamb (served rare on request); an equally flavorful and tender steak béarnaise; poached salmon with a superb, freshly made hollandaise; simply prepared but delicious lobster and scallop dishes. For dessert, the fresh lemon mousse is a must. Even people who loathe dessert love this. Wines are excellent and moderately priced, as are the meals. Lunch is from 1 to 2:30, dinner from 7:30 to 9.

PARTICULARS: Abbeyglen Castle (095-21124) is open most of the year, but closed for parts of January. AmEx, Diners, Master, and Visa are accepted. (U.S. agent: Reservations Systems.) There are 36 rooms, all with bath, shower, bidet, and telephone. Prices are moderate, but breakfast is extra. The Abbeyglen has its own outdoor heated swimming pool and a tennis court. It's located near excellent lake and sea fishing and an 18-hole golf course is 15 minutes away. Pony trekking may be arranged. Nearby are many fine beaches. *Finding the Abbeyglen*: It's just outside Clifden on the Sky Road—which reveals one of Ireland's most dramatic seascapes.

Currarevagh House   OUGHTERARD

During the 15th century, when trade with Spain was at its peak, a tragic triangular love affair and its consequences rocked County Galway. James Lynch Fitzstephen, as mayor and chief magistrate, traveled to Spain to promote good trade relations. Here he befriended a wealthy merchant named Gomez and his son, who was a darkly handsome young man. When he returned to Ireland, Fitzstephen took the son back with him and introduced him to his own son, Walter, an attractive lad of similar age. The young men became close friends. Walter was having a fervid love affair with a beautiful girl named Agnes. Her father, a merchant, spoke fluent Spanish, so he began inviting young Gomez to his house for conversations in Spanish. Well, one thing led to another, and Gomez found himself paying daily visits to Agnes's house—even when her father wasn't there. One day, they embarked on an equally passionate affair. For a time, she was able to keep both affairs going without Walter's realizing he had been betrayed by his new friend. But when Agnes's infatuation for young Gomez grew far stronger, she tried to drop Walter. Brokenhearted, he asked if she loved someone else. She confessed that she had fallen deeply in love with young Gomez. Upon hearing this, Walter's rage was unbearable. He stalked young Gomez, stabbed him to death, then fled into the Galway countryside. Within a day, a group of citizens, led by Walter's father, found and jailed him. His father, as chief magistrate, sentenced him to death by hanging. Even though his wife and family begged him to commute the sentence, he adamantly refused. When no one would carry out the hanging, he contained his emotional grief. Father and son received the sacrament and James Lynch Fitzstephen executed his own son. He then went home, never to leave it again. On that day the word "lynch" became a verb for the first time.

- -

"Far away from the world" would be an apt description for most of the lodgings in this book, and of course that's a large part of their appeal. Currarevagh House probably can lay claim to being one of the most isolated spots in the country. Lost in its stately woods 4 miles from the nearest Connemara town (Oughterard) and gracing the gentle shores of Ireland's second-largest lake (Corrib), this rustic, old country estate provides the world's most precious commodity—peace. You could lose yourself on Currarevagh's 150 acres for weeks and never notice time passing. The wonderfully long walks weaving among stalwart trees, rhododendron, and rare shrubs can be thrillingly romantic on a sunny day as well as on a windswept, mist-lashed day.

And certainly that holds true for the lodging as well. It's a mid–19th-century country mansion that, thanks to the Hodgson family (owners for 5 generations), has kept its aura of olden times. June and Harry Hodgson are the current diligent and affable owners. Once you step into their home, you'll most likely feel—as with many places described in this book—that you are going back in time. Of particular interest is the enormous sitting room, with marble fireplace, overstuffed chairs, and window settees that overlook the manicured lawn and spectacular lake. Here you can sit and sip a sherry or partake of a splendid afternoon tea complete with homemade scones and an array of rich cakes.

A fine, old, balustered staircase rising past the quaint bar leads to the house's snug, antique-furnished bedrooms, where the accommodating staff will turn down your cozy quilts at night before you return to your room to retire.

DINING AT CURRAREVAGH HOUSE: The dining room offers truly wonderful foods in a rustic setting. The moderately priced dinner, which is served at 8, consists of 5 hearty courses. There is no selection. You must take the meal of the day, but what a meal! Among the marvelous entrees served on different nights are roast pork with forcemeat balls, an enormous mixed grill (including bacon, liver, kidney, lamb chop, Irish sausage, french fries), and a superlative thinly sliced roast lamb that has a haunting flavor and literally melts in your mouth. The locally grown vegetables are especially good and roast stuffed potatoes are excellent. Starting courses include deviled eggs in parsley sauce, sea trout, and smoked salmon. Then there are fine desserts (baked Alaska and *Bombe surprise*) plus good French and Irish cheeses. The fine wine list includes an inexpensive house Burgundy.

Currarevagh does serve lunch at 1:15—but doesn't stress it. Dinner is their pièce de résistance. Although they are extremely modest about the breakfast, this wonderful meal is one of the finest in all Ireland. The extremely hearty ingredients include bacon, egg, sausage, black-and-white pudding, fresh jams, breads, fruits, and fresh cream from local cattle. You can also serve yourself to beef tongue displayed nobly on a magnificent antique sideboard. And don't forget the splendid afternoon tea.

Another understatement about Currarevagh is that you'll never go hungry. The scurrying staff is always on hand to serve you second helpings. It should be noted that because the dining room only has enough space for overnight guests, the estate rarely accepts diners who aren't residents.

PARTICULARS: Currarevagh (091-82313) is open from Easter to early October and has a full license. There are 15 bedrooms, 11 with private bath. It is moderately priced, with breakfast included. No credit cards are accepted. (U.S. agent: Robert Reid.) Reserve well in advance; it is very popular. Among the facilities are excellent trout fishing, also fishing for pike, salmon, and perch. The Hodgsons own their own boats, which may be rented at a small charge. There is a tennis court, and golfing and riding facilities are nearby. The owners hold the sporting rights to 5,000 acres of moorlands, which are stocked with woodcock, snipe, grouse, and pigeon. *Finding Currarevagh*: Take the N59 from Galway City to Oughterard. Drive along the Main Street until you come to a left-hand turn for Glan. Follow the narrow road (taking special care to drive slowly and cautiously because it is 2-way) for 4 miles to Currarevagh's gate.

Cashel House   CASHEL

And we will talk, until
Talk is a trouble, too,
Out on the side of the hill;
And nothing is left to do,

But an eye to look into an eye;
And a hand in a hand to slip;
And a sigh to answer a sigh;
And a lip to find out a lip!
   —Old Galway verse
      translated by James Stephens

Promotional material for the Cashel House Hotel in Cashel states that it's a "hideaway in an idyllic setting." Well that it is, but "magnificent" should be included as well. This wonderful 19th-century country house (some say unequivocally that it is the best in Ireland) poised at the headland overlooking Cashel Bay, with the verdant slopes of Cashel Hill in the background, is ideal for a romantic holiday.

William Makepeace Thackeray once lingered here over his work. More recently, French statesman Charles de Gaulle and his wife were so taken with Cashel House that they spent a fortnight here. Despite the many years between these visits, there has been no change in Cashel's tranquility and seclusion. Its natural beauty offers both aes-

Cashel House, County Galway

thetic pleasure and activity. Sea sports and horseback riding adjacent to the 50 acres of floral gardens (including rhododendrons, azaleas, camellias, and rare magnolias) compete with the woodlands, planted with trees from around the world.

The interiors of this gleaming white structure can only be described as charming. Lovely period sitting rooms are resplendent with antiques, art, and cheery turf fires. There is a fine library as well as a very bright and pleasant bar. Beautiful flowers from the gardens bedeck all these rooms. The bedrooms and bedroom garden suites are elegantly appointed and very comfortable.

If you happen to be out enjoying the gardens and hear the faint sounds of young children's laughter, it's coming from a distant schoolyard. The voices are almost musical, and are a joy to hear.

DINING AT CASHEL HOUSE: The sprightly dining room is without question among the growing list of Ireland's finest. Dubliners drive all the way to Cashel (174 miles) just to have dinner and stay overnight here. While there are fine meat dishes here, especially Connemara roast lamb, it would be a shame not to experience the wonderful seafood dishes. Among the starters are delicious smoked salmon quiche, fresh seafood cocktail with an excellent blend of shellfish, and marinated mussels. Entrees might include baked trout béarnaise, poached salmon hollandaise, and superb lobster selected from Cashel's own lobster tank and prepared in whatever manner you wish. There's a fine selection of desserts, including a succulent rhubarb tart. The wine list is excellent and reasonable. Dinner, moderate to expensive, is served from 7 to 9. There's a fine bar lunch from 1:30 to 2:30, including many fish and shellfish selections.

PARTICULARS: Cashel House (095-21252) is open from March 1 through October 31 and has a full license. There are 32 rooms with bath. These include 13 elegant garden suites. Cashel House is moderate to expensive (breakfast included) and accepts AmEx, Master, Visa, and Diners. (U.S. agents: Selective Hotel Reservations; Robert Reid; David Mitchell.) Cashel House has its own tennis court and a small, private, sandy beach across the road. There's an 18-hole golf course at nearby Ballyconneely, fishing in nearby lakes and rivers, and deep-sea fishing at nearby Roundstone, Clifden, or Cleggan. Horseback riding may be arranged. Other possibilities are mountain climbing (Cashel Hill, which shelters the town), walking, and running. (If you do the latter along the main road, it is twisty and narrow, so be careful of traffic.) Cashel

House is in an excellent location for touring Connemara. *Finding Cashel House*: Follow the N59 from Galway City, through Oughterard, to Maam Cross and Recess. Two miles beyond Recess, turn left and continue for 4 miles before turning right into Cashel. The distance from Galway is about 40 miles.

Zetland Hotel   CASHEL

You have taken the east from me; you have taken the west from me,
You have taken the moon, you have taken the sun from me,
And my fear is great that you have taken God from me!
  —Translated from the Irish Gaelic by Lady Augusta Gregory
  Donal Oge: Grief of a Girl's Heart

The Zetland Hotel, Cashel, is located in an area that 19th-century writer William Makepeace Thackeray described as "one of the most wild and beautiful districts that is ever the fortune of the traveller to examine." Built as a private homestead in 1850, this mansion, which once entertained the royalty of England, has been converted into a grand hotel. While it attracts anglers from all over the world because of its special facilities (see Particulars, below), it is a thoroughly charming place to stay, regardless of your interests.

The hotel is owner-managed with great care and concern by John Prendergast, who trained at the Ritz in Paris. The lovely public rooms have grand turf fires and are tastefully furnished with period antiques and reproductions, as are the very comfortable bedrooms. (Try to obtain one facing Cashel Bay.) The lounge bar is very pleasant, and very good pub grub is served here at lunchtime. You may also want to try the more rustic Fisherman's Bar.

DINING AT THE ZETLAND: The intimate dining room overlooks the beauty of floral gardens, trees, shrubs, and lawns that sweep down to the sea. Excellent seafood is the specialty here, as befits the hotel's proximity to the water. Especially superb are the salmon, sea trout, and shellfish dishes. Scallops with champagne sauce and turbot hollandaise are particularly memorable. The vegetables and fruits are all fresh from the estate's own garden. There's a good cheese board, and wines are fine and moderately priced. Dinner, which is moderately expensive, is served from 7:30 to 9. Nonresidents must reserve.

PARTICULARS: The Zetland Hotel (095-31011) is open from April 1 to October 31 and has a full license. There are 15 expensive bedrooms, all with bath and breakfast included. AmEx, Visa, and Master are accepted. (U.S. agent: Robert Reid.) The Zetland's brochure states that it stands "in the heart of Connemara's wild beauty, with the sea at your feet and the magical mountains of the West all around." This is not an overstatement. The hotel owns rights to some of the finest sea trout and salmon fishing waters in the country. This includes some 3½ miles of river (the Gowla Fishery) and numerous lakes. Deep-sea fishing may also be arranged. Boats, boatmen, guides, licenses, permits, and fishing equipment are all available through the hotel. The area is excellent for mountain walks and climbs, ocean swimming, and running. There's an 18-hole golf course nearby; riding and pony trekking may be arranged through a local stable. Rough shooting for snipe and woodcock is available in season. For picnickers, the hotel prepares picnic lunches. *Finding the Zetland*: Follow the N59 from Galway City, through Oughterard, to Maam Cross and Recess. Two miles beyond Recess, turn left and continue for 4 miles before turning right into Cashel and the Zetland Hotel. The total distance from Galway is 40 miles.

Ballynahinch Castle BALLYNAHINCH

Slender graceful girl, be no longer inconstant to me; admit me, soft
slender one, to your bed, let us stretch our bodies side by side.
—Irish, author unknown
probably 15th or 16th century

And I thought, my sweetheart, that you were the moon and the sun,
and I thought after that that you were the snow on the mountain,
and I thought after that that you were lightning from God,
or that you were the Pole Star going before and behind me.
—Traditional Irish folk song

One of the most romantic settings for vacationing in Ireland is unquestionably that provided by Ballynahinch Castle in Ballynahinch. If you did no more than stroll the estate's endless nature paths, watching the hypnotic rush of the swirling river that makes the water reeds dance in the glitter of the afternoon sun, you would feel fulfilled. But there is so much more here than that.

The castle, at the base of Benlettry (one of the mountains known as the Twelve Bens), overlooks the lovely Owenmore River. It was built in the late 16th century by the Normans and later became an O'Flaherty fortress. In the 18th century, the Martin clan flattered English royalty so successfully that they were rewarded with lands all over Connemara, including Ballynahinch. The enraged O'Flahertys, now dispossessed, were accomplished duelists, but no more so than the Martins. Despite all the feuding that ensued, the property remained in Martin hands. This eccentric family continued courting the throne and soon were being treated like royalty. One of them, dubbed "Humanity Dick," had a rare impulse to do something constructive, and he established the Royal Society for the Prevention of Cruelty to Animals. Thackeray wrote about this enigmatic man, whom he found a fascinating character study.

The Martins prospered until the potato famine (1845–47), when they lost their home and many of their Connemara lands. The castle faded from prominence until the Roaring Twenties, when it was purchased by the Maharajah Jam Sahib of Nawanagar—reportedly a lover of famed dancer Isadora Duncan and better known as Ranji Singh, the famous cricketer—who lavished money on it and turned it into a *Great Gatsby* kind of place. It was converted into a hotel in 1945.

Today it is a disarmingly peaceful spot amid mountains, woods, and hills streaked with lonely rivulets and a fine anglers' river. Inside are grand sitting rooms, libraries, elegant period furniture, art, and log fires. The stately bedrooms, also enhanced by beautiful antiques and named after previous inhabitants—Humanity Dick and the Maharajah—are extremely comfortable. An unexpected feature here is the unusual bar. With an outside entrance, it is a very basic fisherman's pub planned so that when the fishermen come back with their catches they can feel comfortable going straight in for a drink in their boots and fishing gear.

DINING AT BALLYNAHINCH: The dining room is slightly disappointing in that it strives for a stateliness and intimacy that it doesn't quite achieve. One tends to wish it would strive a little harder, because it's well on its way—with art, period furnishings, and spectacular view of the waters below. The food is another surprise here. Although very good, it is traditional Irish fare, and, like the bar, it seems out of context with the castle itself. As with the rest of Ireland's finest lodgings and

Ballynahinch Castle, County Galway

restaurants, you would expect a slight French touch in some of the menu's offerings. The food *is* good, however, and the castle and its surroundings are a charm. Seafood (salmon is recommended) and meats are local. Fruit and vegetables are grown on the hotel's grounds. There is a relatively short selection of wines, but all are good and reasonable. Expensive dinners are served from 7 to 9. Lunch from 1 to 2:15, or pub lunch in the bar.

PARTICULARS: Ballynahinch (095-21269) is open from April 1 to October 31 and has a full license. It is expensive, with breakfast included, and accepts AmEx, Visa, Master, and Diners. (U.S. agent: Reservations Systems.) There are 20 rooms, all with baths. The Ballynahinch Fishery is famous and very popular with salmon anglers. Tennis, pitch and putt, and river swimming are available at the hotel. Nearby are riding facilities, ocean swimming, and fishing. This is a superb location for touring Connemara, for climbing, walking, running. It's 7 miles from Clifden (Connemara's main town) and 42 miles from Galway City. *Finding Ballynahinch:* It's on the Galway-to-Roundstone coastal road (L102), 10 miles north of Roundstone, and it's signposted.

Crocnaraw House   MOYARD

During the 16th century in County Galway, Spanish influence sparked many lively romances. For centuries, Galway traded exclusively with Spain, and many young Spaniards thus came to Ireland. Because promiscuity was quite commonplace, the British introduced an edict in 1585 pronouncing that "no young man, prentice or otherwise, shall wear gorgeous apparel of silks either within or without their garments." To further discourage romantic young males, the edict went on to blacklist "fine knit stockings either of silk or other costlie materials. Ruffles, thick and/or starched and embroidered pantofles [slippers] shall be worn." As for the girls, they were refused "hats and capes unless colored black, and any gorgeous clothes or costly hatbands of gold thread."

Perhaps one of the coziest and most interesting places in Ireland is the charming little Georgian country home known as Crocnaraw House.

Located in the wilds of Connemara at Moyard, it's far away from the hectic world. This is an ideal escape spot for those who long for quiet. Some 21 years ago, Mrs. Joanne Fretwell bought this estate. With the addition of impeccable period furnishings and a splendid gardener's hand, she turned it into a lodging that so impressed its clientele that many returned year after year.

The estate is now operated by Mrs. Fretwell's daughter, and many visitors are so pleased with it that they correspond regularly. Recently, a wealthy American purchased a valuable painting from an art gallery and had it shipped to Crocnaraw House because he was so thrilled with its "wonderful peace."

With gentle gardens that have won national gardening awards, a lovely turf-fired sitting room, and snugly delightful and bright bedrooms, Crocnaraw House provides country charm with elegance.

DINING AT CROCNARAW HOUSE: Basic and sizable (a little too much so) meals are served in a small and delightfully intimate dining room. The menu, while emphasizing seafood, also contains fine meat dishes. The incomparable roast chicken is probably the best in the country. A popular appetizer is the fresh carrot soup with a touch of orange mint. Vegetables and salads are simple and first class; most of the menu's ingredients come from the estate's own farm and gardens. Homemade chocolate ice cream is a favorite dessert. The wine list is short but pleasant. Meals are moderate to expensive. Dinner is served from 8 to 9:30, lunch from 1 to 2:30, afternoon tea from 4 to 6. It is open to nonresidents, but reservations are suggested.

PARTICULARS: Crocnaraw House (095-41068) is open from Easter to mid-October and has a full license. There are 10 (6 with bath) moderately priced rooms. Breakfast is included. (U.S. agent: Robert Reid.) AmEx is accepted. Crocnaraw House is located north of Clifden in one of the most beautiful areas of Connemara, amid the Twelve Bens mountain range and the rugged seacoast. Nearby are the famed Kylemore Abbey and Connemara National Park. This area is ideal for fishing, golfing, swimming, and cycling—to say nothing of long walks and panoramic drives. *Finding Crocnaraw House*: If you take the spectacular N59 from Clifden northward for about 6 miles, you'll see the sign.

Rosleague Manor   LETTERFRACK

She's my pulse, she's my secret, she's the scented flower of the
apple, she's summer in the cold time between Christmas and Easter.
                                        —Traditional Irish folk song
                                            before 1789

I do not know with whom Edan will sleep, but I do know that fair
Edan will not sleep alone.
                                        —Irish, author unknown,
                                            probably 9th century

One of the prettiest Georgian manors in Ireland sits out on a hill amid
elegant gardens and trees overlooking Ballinakill Bay and the haunting
mountains of Connemara. Rosleague Manor, near Letterfrack, is aglow
with dazzling turf fires, superb Irish oils and watercolors, and crystal
chandeliers. The antique furniture is among the finest in the country.
It's difficult to think of a lodging as stately while at the same time as
cozily entrancing as this lovely inn. Its lightness and cheeriness are
enhanced by many floral arrangements in period vases.

The Foyle family has graciously hosted guests here for years. The
current owners, Patrick and Anne Foyle (brother and sister), make a
point of chatting, introducing guests in the manor's snug bar and sitting
room, and ensuring that everyone has a pleasant stay.

The bedrooms at Rosleague are as bright and cozy as the rest of the
rooms in the manor; many have antique furnishings.

DINING AT ROSLEAGUE: The pleasant dining room, overlooking the estate
grounds, has much to offer. Starters include smoked Killary salmon,
rich homemade country pâté, fresh mixed seafood salad, and homemade
mulligatawny soup (beautiful if the day is a bit nippy). Entrees include
such excellent meat and fish dishes as an exceptional lamb liver with
orange flavoring, black sole on the bone (among the best anywhere),
poached salmon or sea trout, chicken Kiev, and roast pork or beef in
red wine sauce. A special word is deserved for the vegetables, which
are home grown and magnificently prepared—so much so that you could
easily make a meal of these alone. Order parsnips if they happen to be
available. The wine list is surprisingly long, modest in price, and very
good. Moderate to expensive dinners are served from 8 to 9:30. Reservations are required for nonresidents.

PARTICULARS: Rosleague (095-41101) is open from Easter to November and is fully licensed. There are 15 moderately priced rooms, all with bath and breakfast. (U.S. agent: Robert Reid.) Visa and Master are accepted. The manor has an immaculate sauna. Nearby are clean, sandy beaches, and skin diving may be arranged at the manor. There are several deep-sea angling centers. The area abounds with lakes and rivers, providing first-rate salmon, sea trout, and brown trout fishing. Boat trips are available to the local offshore islands, especially Inishbofin. There are lovely short drives in this area, and Connemara National Park is only a mile down the road. Pony trekking and mountain climbing are possibilities. There's a fine 18-hole championship golf course at nearby Ballyconneely. *Finding Rosleague*: It's 9 miles northeast of Clifden on the N59, just before the village of Letterfrack.

Renvyle House   RENVYLE

A house to dream of the past in, of rollicking Irish hunting parties, surprise visits and lavish hospitality and joviality, of rattling good stories told over the turf fire in the capacious dining room, of ghosts upstairs, of fascinating Irish Dianas with unfathomable grey eyes changeable in colour like the Connemara streams, of knightly squires and sprightly crimes.
             —Ode to Renvyle House from a 1920s Irish magazine

Renvyle House is said to be a fine example of an Irish haunted house. On their honeymoon, William Butler Yeats and his wife stayed here, and by candlelight she conjured apparitions of the house's previous inhabitants. To this day, seances are held here, and it is said that Yeats's ghost itself now walks the halls. Genial current owner Hugh Coyle can cite tales of haunted bedrooms but insists all the apparitions are of the peaceful, friendly sort.

Connemara's Renvyle House is perched on a promontory at what seems to be the end of the world. (Actually, it is one of the westernmost points in Ireland.) This fascinating place appeals to all sorts of people— spiritualists, the theatre and literary set, filmmakers, fishermen, lovers, married couples with children, old people, young people, those looking for quiet, and those wanting a riproaring good time. They all make their way to Renvyle—and somehow they all seem to find what they want in this menagerie. Many return again and again. This said, it must also be noted that Renvyle is not for everyone. It is not for romantics who want to see few people and no children. But this is not to detract from its charm.

Renvyle House is located on the frontierlike horizon just outside the tiny village of Renvyle. Writer, politician, and surgeon Oliver St. John Gogarty owned the house in the 1920s and wrote:

My house, too, stands on a lake, but it also stands on the sea.
Water lilies meet golden seaweed. It is as if, in the faery land of
Connemara at the extreme end of Europe, the incongruous flowed
together at last; and the sweet and bitter blended.

Built more than 150 years ago, this was first the residence of the Blake family. During the civil war of 1923, it was burned almost to the ground by the IRA. (Instead of supporting their free-all-Ireland campaign, Gogarty compromised in favor of the Northern Ireland partition.) He was so deeply attached to Renvyle, which he used as his vacation home, that he painstakingly reconstructed it and expanded it to take in lodgers, since he could no longer support its cost.

Writing further of Renvyle and the environs, Gogarty noted:

Behind me, islands and mountainous mainland share in a final rec-
onciliation at this, the world's end. I am sitting on a little terrace
overlooking the lake, watching the wider shimmer of the ocean beyond a thin line of green in the middle distance . . . behind me a
wing of the long sea-gray house stretches for forty years.

The house and its surroundings still seem very much the same— simultaneously stark and gentle, isolated from the world. But once inside, a warmth pervades its cozy lounges, turf fires, rustic Irish bar, solarium, the old library, snooker room, and antique-filled bedrooms. The latter are a special treat, with Victorian furniture and bath fixtures that sweep you into another world. Be sure to ask for an old room. Renvyle has added a very extensive new wing, which is acceptable, but certainly not as charming as the older sections. Since the Victorian rooms are in the minority, reserve well in advance. Also, you may want to request a room that's not over the bar/lounge, because there are Irish sing-songs (sing-alongs) each night in season, and people stay up late singing and talking.

The thrilling feature of being at Renvyle is that no matter what the weather—from misty white mornings to the dazzling sea-and-lake glitter of sunny afternoons to black, moonless nights—you will experience the landscape's mysterious, almost ethereal quality. Be sure to take ample time to stroll about and partake of the many moods. The lakeshore, the lawns, the strand, and the fantastic white seastone beach are all very special treats. Swimming in the wonderful clear waters at Renvyle is most invigorating, and boating on the shimmering lake is dreamlike. After dinner, if the night is clear and spiced with the buoyant North Atlantic wind, take a leisurely walk out across the seaside golf course. This is the perfect end to a Connemara day.

DINING AT RENVYLE: The food in the rustic dining room is good, hearty Irish fare, including such appetizers as grilled turbot, asparagus crepes, and smoked salmon, and such entrees as roast duckling, Irish beef Burgundy, fresh Killary salmon, poached lemon sole, steak béarnaise. Lunch is from 12:30 to 2:30, dinner from 7:30 to 8:45. Meals are moderate to expensive, with good and relatively inexpensive wines.

PARTICULARS: Renvyle House (095-43444) is open mid-March through January 1 and has a full license. It has 68 moderately priced bedrooms, all with bath and breakfast included. Reserve early for peak season. Visa and Master are accepted. Excellent game fishing, sea angling, riding (stables at the hotel), tennis (2 hard courts, one soft), croquet, boating (boats available at the hotel), golfing (a 9-hole course and a clock course at the hotel, 2 championship courses at nearby Ballyconneely), diving (Connemara Diving School and Station located behind hotel), swimming pool, lawn bowling, football pitch. Indoors are: snooker, table tennis, pool table, darts, chess, draughts (checkers), backgammon, sauna, solarium, library. *Finding Renvyle*: It's 62 miles from Galway City. Take the N59 through Oughterard and out to Clifden, then up the 9 miles to Letterfrack. From here, take the road marked for Tully Cross and follow on through the short distance to Renvyle.

Suggestions for Your Visit   COUNTY GALWAY

¶ As with all the locales in this book, start off by enjoying the special qualities of your lodging and its surroundings. If you don't start off doing this, save plenty of time to do so during your stay.

¶ Since all of the lodgings described in this chapter are in Galway's Connemara area—with its rugged purple mountain ranges, dazzling seascapes, and clear deep lakes—it is well worth spending a goodly amount of time touring the region. The distances are relatively short, so you can cover quite a bit of territory in a short time. But don't. Travel at a leisurely pace and enjoy it.

The rustic and very attractive coastal village of **Clifden** is in the heart of Connemara—about 24 miles from Cashel, 9 miles from Letterfrack, 13 miles from Renvyle, 7 miles from Ballynahinch, 7 miles from Moyard, 32 miles from Oughterard. Clifden is a pleasant town to stroll about and shop. Some of the most popular shops are **The Silver Shop** (Irish silver crafts and jewelry, tweeds), **The Celtic Crafts** (marble items, Belleek china, Irish books, tweeds, leathers, other crafts), **Millar's Connemara Tweed Shop** (tweeds, knitwear, Irish pottery, woodcrafts, glass, oil paintings), **Tara Jewellers** (Claddagh rings, Belleek), **The Weaver's Workshop** (handweaving), **Connemara Pottery** (potterymaking)—all on Main Street; and **Gerald Stanley & Sons** (crafts, knitwear, and tweeds), and **Atlantic Craft Shop** (small native craft items)—both on Market Street.

There are a number of restaurants in Clifden. Besides those at **Abbeyglen Castle**, there are **O'Grady's Restaurant** on Market Street (snug and candlelit, specializing in fresh fish; moderate to expensive; AmEx, Visa, Master; wine license; open noon to 10); **Marconi Tavern and Grill** on Main Street (seafood dishes such as baked mussels and grilled salmon steak; inexpensive to moderate; open daily till 10); **Connemara Delicatessen** on Main Street (all-day coffee shop specializing in fresh fish and smoked salmon dishes; inexpensive; upstairs is an exhibit of contemporary Irish paintings); **Billy's Vintage Car Bar** on Main Street (soups, salads, snacks; inexpensive all-day service); **Atlantic Coast Hotel** on Market Street (good Irish fare; inexpensive; AmEx, Master, Visa; open all day till 9 P.M. but closed October to April).

If you want a drink, try **Griffin's Bar and Lounge** on Main Street (drift into the back room here at night for good, down-to-earth traditional music); **The D'Arcy Inn** on Main Street (small, Tudor-style bar frequented by young people for talk and song; good pub food); **E. J. King's**, Castle House (another young people's place with traditional music at night and a small cafe); the **Atlantic Coast Hotel** on Market Street (rather dingy basement bar/lounge that at night offers wistful traditional Irish music); the **Celtic Hotel**, Market Hill (traditional music at night, but the place can get rather rowdy).

¶ From Clifden, take the **Sky Road** behind Abbeyglen Castle. This 9-mile stretch, which climbs around the northern promontory, is one of Connemara's highlights. The sweeping seascapes are so compelling that you must remember to be careful while driving on the rather treacherous roadway. About halfway up is a parking area where you can stop. (If you're an experienced runner or hiker, this is your road.) From Cleggan, a fishing village, you can take the mail boat to **Inishbofin Island** to see ruins of the 17th-century monastery founded by St. Colman and the remnants of a Cromwellian castle.

Next, drive on to **Moyard**, where there's a delightful little luncheon restaurant called **Doon**. (See the review in chapter 14, Special Restaurants.) Then travel on to **Letterfrack**. Just outside this sleepy fuchsia-filled village is one of Ireland's finest craft shops. Called **Connemara Handcrafts**, it has a wide array of most Irish crafts, along with a very good tearoom. The place is a must. AmEx, Diners, Master, and Visa are accepted. Also in Letterfrack are the **Connemara West Centre** and **Village Handcrafts**.

Near Letterfrack is the splendid new **Connemara National Park**, 3,750 acres of mountains, heaths, bogs, grasslands, dense woods, and lonely streams. In season, there are magnificent rhododendron, some of Ireland's most beautiful wildflowers (bluebells, primroses, sorrel, and wood anemone, to name just a few), and majestic woody specimens (the wonderful gorse, holly, heather, and rush are superlative examples).

The beauty of Connemara National Park will entrance you for hours (if you have the time). You can choose from the Ellis Wood nature trail (with peaceful, heavily wooded paths that lead you far from the world's hectic pace) or the more adventurous climb along the Scruffaunboy nature trail (with awesome views of the Connemara mountains and the offshore islands).

¶ From Letterfrack, there are 2 possibilities for little journeys. One is just a few miles down the road toward Leenane, through Kylemore Pass, which brings you to the majestic **Kylemore Abbey**. This is one of the last castellated mansions built in Ireland. Constructed by a wealthy English merchant around the time of America's Civil War, this vast estate, mirrored in one of Kylemore's 3 peaceful lakes, is now a girls' school run by the Benedictine order. The nuns operate a craft shop selling pottery and an inexpensive tearoom. From here, you could continue on (or return to Letterfrack) for another 10 or so miles, crossing along the top of the Maamturk Mountains (Lough Fee to the left) and descend to Killary Harbor, Ireland's only Scandinavian-type fjord. Then proceed to **Leenane**, where you'll have access to the **Killary Shop**, an attractive Irish craft store with a rustic restaurant extension serving everything from good snacks to 4-course meals. Try the homemade pâté. The restaurant is open all day, has a wine license, and accepts AmEx, Diners, Visa, and Master (prices are inexpensive to moderate). Also in Leenane is the **Mweelrea Craft Shop**, which features Irish pottery and sweaters and has an inexpensive tearoom of its own. From here, you may want to take the most expeditious route back to your lodging—or you may want to drift around, discovering still more unexpected pleasures of Connemara and the neighboring Joyce Country.

The other short journey from Letterfrack involves driving the few lonely miles out the isolated **Renvyle Peninsula** to Renvyle, which feels like the end of the world. Here there's a fascinating beach of white, satin-smooth stones and rocks.

¶ If you are passing through the Connemara gateway village of **Oughterard**, this is an excellent center for touring beautiful **Lough Corrib** (second-biggest lake in Ireland). You can either travel by road around it or go boating and/or fishing on it. Oughterard village has 2 fine hotels—**Sweeney's Oughterard House** and the **Connemara Gateway Hotel**—both featured in chapter 13 of this book. The village also boasts **Keogh's** (fine crystal and china) and **Egan's** (handknits for all age groups, Irish sheepskin rugs, stoles, scarves, hand-embroidered linens, and local marble products).

A few miles down the road from Oughterard toward Galway City is the village of **Moycullen**, where hand-carved marble products are available at the **Connemara Marble Shop**. There's also **Moycullen Crafts and Antiques**. A little off the main thoroughfare is a crystalmaker who hand-cuts crystal that some insist is cheaper and finer than Waterford. He calls his operation **Connemara Celtic Crystal**. Moycullen boasts a good seafood restaurant called **The Silver Teal**, with fine French cuisine. Especially good are the lobster, crab, and mussel dishes. Intimate atmosphere and moderate-to-expensive prices; full license; open 12:30 P.M. to 11:30 P.M. All major credit cards are accepted.

A few miles farther down the road toward Galway City is one of Ireland's most highly touted new restaurants—**Drimcong House**. (See the review in chapter 14 of this book.) Just before entering Galway City is another good, new establishment, **Casey's Westwood Restaurant**. Entrees include salmon with champagne sauce, roast pork with cider sauce, calf's kidneys in port wine sauce, and pastry-wrapped baked scallops in wine sauce. Intimate atmosphere and moderate-to-expensive prices; full license; open for lunch from 12:30 to 2:30, dinner from 7:30 to 10:30. Good pub lunches (fried plaice, pâté, lasagna, salads) are available.

¶ Most people staying in County Galway lodgings probably will want to spend at least a day or a good part of it strolling through **Galway City**, seeing the fascinating buildings and monuments and sampling some of its 800 or so years of history. Galway City is 62 miles from Renvyle (you'd want to start early if you're staying at Renvyle House), 57 miles from Letterfrack, 55 miles from Moyard, 40 miles from Cashel and Ballynahinch, and 17 miles from Oughterard. (Two good hotels in Galway City are covered in chapter 13 of this book.)

After you've had a look around, you may want to do some shopping. **The Treasure Chest**, Shop Street, is Galway's best all-round shop for Irish crafts. Certainly it's the place to go if you're pressed for time: Irish apparel for all age groups (including fisherman and Blarney knitwear), pottery, crystal, china, linens, souvenirs, postcards. Other fine shops include **Moon's**, Eglinton Street (department store with Irish apparel, sweaters, pottery, often an attractive July sale); **Taffee's**, William Street (a crazy, dowdy place with literally dozens of friendly dogs darting about but with a vast selection of strikingly handsome Irish knitwear at relatively low prices); **White Gold—The Porcelain Shop**, Mainguard Street (Irish Dresden, crystal, Belleek, handpainted porcelain); **L. O'Donnellan's Craft Shop**, Quay Street (traditional Irish and local Galway handcrafts, knitwear, tweeds, Irish crochet, Carrickmacross lace, Claddagh door knockers, sheepskin slippers); **Frank McDonagh's**, Eyre Square (Irish knitwear, mohair throws, shawls, linens, tweeds, tablecloths, placemats, Irish dolls, souvenirs); **Royal Tara Factory Shop**, Tara Hall (showroom for fine Irish bone china; located in one of the grand old houses of Galway); **Cobwebs**, Quay Lane (small antique items, including jewelry and porcelain); **Archway Antiques**, just off Eyre Square (furniture and a wide variety of other items); **Antiquarian Books**, Cross Street (good selection of Irish-interest and other books, plus well-framed old maps of the area and the country); **Kenny's Bookshop**, High Street (wonderful Irish prints and books, along with a fine selection of Irish landscape paintings); **FallerCraft**, Eyre Square (wonderful new Irish apparel and crafts shop, good sweaters); **The Sheepskin Shop**, Shop Street (clothing and rugs); **K & W**, Eglinton Street (crystal and china); and **The Blue Cloak**, Abbeygate Street (high fashion women's apparel).

Quite likely, you will want to eat in Galway. There are a number of good restaurants, including the **Ardilaun House Hotel** on Taylors Hill (slightly outside the city; intimate, moderate-to-expensive dining room overlooks gardens and serves very tasty dishes; reviewed in chapter 13); the **Great Southern Hotel's Claddagh Room**, Eyre Square (overlooks Galway Bay; excellent but expensive seafood and meat dishes; reviewed in chapter 13); the Great Southern's **Oyster Room** (moderately priced breakfasts, grills, 3-course luncheons and dinners); **O'Flaherty's** (good, inexpensive food in new pub designed in 19th-century style); **Lyndonhouse Restaurant**, Shop Street (old eatery containing many trappings of historic Galway; not terribly romantic but serves good food ranging from hamburgers to sirloins and seafood, quiche to omelettes and Irish stew; open all day and on Sunday from noon to 9:30 P.M.; inexpensive; fast service if you want; wine license; own bakery); **The Cellar Grill**, Williamgate Street (hamburgers, country pâté, grilled sea trout, fried chicken, and sirloin are good); **O'Neachtains**, High Street (very pleasant pub restaurant with excellent meat and seafoods; open every day; full license; inexpensive-to-moderate prices).

If you're interested in pubs, there are plenty here. Try **The King's Head**, High Street (dark, woody, with fireplace; traditional music at 9 P.M. Monday through Saturday and at 8 on Sunday; tasty, inexpensive pub food); **The Lion's Tower**, Eglinton Street (one of the city's finest and neatest; old-style woody pub with velvet settees and trestle tables; good place to sample oysters and stout during Galway's September Oyster Festival; good sandwiches as well as seafood and meat dishes from noon to 3 and from 6 on; morning and afternoon coffee); **The Railway Bar and Lounge**, Great Southern Hotel, Eyre Square (rather plain, but the international set alights here often, making it comparable to the Saddle Bar in Dublin's old Shelbourne Hotel). For the real thing in Irish pubs, go to **Seagan Ua Neachtain**, Quay and Cross streets. You may be greeted by a lively, spontaneous music session or the lonely, plaintive sound of a tin whistle. There's nothing forced or stagy here. You can drift from one group to another to hear fascinating stories of the old days—although some may be told in Irish. *Don't*, however, eat here, especially those strange items posing as sandwiches.

¶ Here is a listing of Galway City's finest in entertainment and annual events:

- **Taibhdheare na Gaillimhe**, Middle Street, is the Irish-speaking theatre founded in 1928, performing regular productions of plays in Irish plus evenings of traditional music, song, and dance.

- **Druid Lane Theatre**, Chapel Lane, was founded in 1965 and holds evening performances with particular emphasis on Anglo-Irish plays, such as those by Synge and O'Casey.
- **The Galway Oyster Festival** in September is the time when you can indulge in plentiful oysters accompanied by creamy glasses of stout.
- **The Galway Horse Show** is held at the end of June, then again at the beginning of July.
- **The Galway Races** (horseracing) is held at the end of July/beginning of August, then again in September.
- **The Claddagh Festival**, held the first week in August, celebrates the traditional fishing village that once rested on the outskirts of Galway.
- **The Galway Bay International Sea Angling Festival**, held in September, is popular among anglers from around the world.

¶ Thirty miles off the coast of Galway are 3 limestone reaches that loom above the waves and form the **Aran Islands**. Their rugged otherworldliness has attracted people from all over the Western world, and a day trip may be of interest. (You can stay there if you wish. See the review of the **Johnston-Hernon Kilmurvey House** in chapter 13.) For centuries, the craggy landscapes have been home for many Irish-speaking fishermen and their families. Before that, the sheer cliffs served as fortresses for brave prehistoric warriors who held out against fleets of invaders. These rugged islands born of the sea—islands that time seems to have forgotten—offer rewards beyond the merely picturesque or scenic. In some circles, the Arans are still considered to be part of the fabled lost continent of Atlantis, which sank into the sea in ancient times. Others say that Aran is really Avalon, the legendary earthly paradise of the Celts, where such heroes as King Arthur were transported after their deaths. A few have maintained that ancient Aran was the Land of Eternal Youth—*Tir-na-n'Og*—and that its secret is still hidden somewhere on the islands. Regardless, the early settlers built such stone forts as Dun Aengus, beehive huts, and pagan places of worship that evolved into Christian churches that still stand today. The islands are the setting of *Riders to the Sea*, John Millington Synge's brilliant one-act play about the fishermen's lives.

There are 2 ways to journey to the Aran Islands—boat and plane. A cattle boat—*Naomh Eanna*—sails daily from June through September (less frequently other times) from the Galway pier to the 3 Arans. This is a 30-mile journey, 60 round-trip, or about 3 hours each way. The 2 smaller islands—**Inishere** and **Inishmaan**—don't have docks that accept the steamer, so curraghs are rowed out to pick up passengers, supplies, and livestock. This can be a rough trip on a stormy day. The boat does dock at **Inishmore**, the largest island. While it is no luxury vessel, it does serve tea, coffee, sandwiches, and drinks (full license). The boat leaves early (and on time—check schedules with C.I.E. Transports at 091-62141), so you may wish to stay overnight in Galway City beforehand. (Two Galway City lodgings appear in chapter 13.)

There's also boat service from Rossaveal, County Galway, to the Arans. This is a 10-mile journey each way. Rossaveal may be closer to your Connemara lodgings. The O'Brien family operates 3 vessels—*Rose of Aran, Dun Aengus,* and *Donemark.* It has frequent sailings to the 3 islands that take about an hour each way. (For information call 091-72273.) Another firm, Aran Ferries, operates the vessel *Queen of Aran* to Inishmore on a frequent basis. (For sailing times, call 091-68903.) But be forewarned: The boats departing from Rossaveal are small, and if the sea is rough, you'll have the ride of your life. The boats seem to almost capsize as waves slosh over the deck. The feeling is not so much of getting seasick as it is of being scared to death. After such a journey, you may wish to stay overnight on the islands, where there are a number of lodgings. (One of them is featured in chapter 13.)

If you decide to fly to the Arans instead of chancing the rough seas or spending the several hours each way required for the boat trip, *Aer Arann* has frequent 20-minute flights at reasonable fares. The planes are tiny, but the flight is usually smooth and the pilots are experienced. The Galway phone numbers are 091-84348/84235. You may also split your trip between the boat and the plane. The plane takes credit cards at Galway *only.*

If your time is limited, visit the largest island, Inishmore. All 3 islands have many historic and prehistoric sites, but Inishmore seems to have the greatest number of them. While the 2 smaller islands remain less in touch with today's world—a factor that may enhance their appeal—they are correspondingly more difficult to reach. Only the *Naomh Eanna* visits them, and it doesn't sail every day. And remember, too, that you must transfer to a curragh to get to them. There are more flights to Inishmore, but there is also service to the smaller islands.

5 THE DRAMATIC SHANNONSIDE/CLARE LODGINGS

Dromoland Castle

NEWMARKET ON FERGUS

For all of you romantics who believe in the power of the beyond, there is the story of Biddy Early, the Wise Woman of County Clare, who to this day (many years after her death) is said to have the power to bless lovers, among others, with very favorable results. Her story begins when the 19th century was young. Rumor began to spread that she had the power to cure not only diseases but all unhappiness, including affairs of the heart. Soon people from all over the county were heading for her doorstep in Feakle village, about 20 miles from Dromoland Castle. Biddy had a heart of gold and took kindly to those in need. She could look at a person and understand his or her troubles before the person could speak a word. She would then look into a strange magic bottle and give the person a message that would summon the cure. As a result, those who could afford to do so paid her in food and drink; thus was her existence. As to Biddy's own love life, she married 4 times. Each man was more dashingly handsome than the previous one. As a lure, she cast an inescapable spell over them. She obtained the last of these young men when she was 80. (If you don't believe this, it's documented in *The Limerick Chronicle* of July 29, 1869.) He was Pat O'Brien of Glonnagruss. Stories go that this match was as feverish as if she had been a woman of 20. But all these men died of the drink, since it was so readily available in her house. Sad as that may be, Biddy Early's ghost is said to wander on summer nights in County Clare, blessing lovers and those good people who are troubled.

▪ ▪

Dromoland Castle, County Clare

Wonderful Dromoland Castle is an enchanting place to stay. It's almost a rustic counterpart to the lavish and much larger Ashford Castle in County Mayo. Not that Dromoland isn't lavish in its own way; it has enormous rooms with high pargeted ceilings, glittering chandeliers, grand oil paintings (enough to fill a museum), wondrous antiques, and impressive suits of armor. Yet Dromoland is more countrified. It's woody (buffed oak and rosewood), and its color schemes embrace earth tones. Floral patterns are emphasized; the plush carpeting is almost grass green. Then there are the warming fireplaces, emitting scents of elm, beech, and ash.

Built on the grounds of an earlier 15th-century O'Brien castle, parts of the current castle stem from the 16th century, with an 18th-century Queen Anne courtyard. An early-19th-century main building, of Gothic style, has 4 massive 80-foot towers. The O'Briens were the Barons of Inchiquin, whose descendants maintained the castle until 1962, when it was purchased and lovingly refurbished by Bernard McDonough, a

West Virginia businessman who opened it as a hotel. It is now owned by the fine consortium that operates Ashford Castle.

Dromoland has 1,500 acres of green lawns and deep forests, as well as a small fishing lake that mirrors its stately beauty. On the grounds near the lily pond is the strange Hermit's Cave. Deep inside, a faint ray of light streaks down into what apparently was a fireplace. While there are many tales, no one seems to know any more about this phenomenon. In the walled rose garden behind the castle is the stone archway from Red Mary and Conor O'Brien's 17th-century Lemenagh Castle, near Kilfenora. Here, during long, warm summer afternoons, Lady Inchiquin held her garden teas.

Dromoland is charming—and very difficult to leave. But before you do, visit the drawing rooms, the marvelously long and artistic first- and second-floor hallways (where you can sit at a period-piece desk and tend to your correspondence), the semicircular bar room (once the Inchiquins' library, with gilded-mirror-over-fireplace, massive carved wooden bar, and full castle windows overlooking the grounds), and the special craft shop where you can purchase (among many Irish items) a finely prepared little booklet on Dromoland and its history by Joe McCarthy. A dramatic new entryway has been added to Dromoland to make it one of the most spectacular entrances of any castle in Ireland.

DINING AT DROMOLAND: The stately dining room is the height of country elegance, with an enormous brass chandelier, dark red flocked wallpaper, oil paintings, and golden drapes. Even though it is almost 100 feet long, there is a pleasant intimacy about the room that's enhanced by the enormous windows overlooking the gentle lake. (If you're fortunate with the weather, you can witness the beauty of a Dromoland sunset from here.) An equal delight is the food. Some of the delicious appetizers are smoked trout with horseradish cream sauce, seafood salad, and pâté with Cumberland sauce. The soup course is equally good—it might be cream of fresh carrot, cream of fresh cauliflower, or clear turtle soup with sherry. There's a sizable selection of entrees. The roast turkey with ham and sausage dressing is superb, as is the thinly sliced rare beef in Madeira sauce. The tender grilled steak and the roast lamb are also rewarding. Seafood selections include baked fillets of sea trout, grilled salmon steak, scampi, and baked whitefish with herb sauce—all perfectly prepared. The desserts are fine, but almost too much after the abundance of food that precedes them. The wine list is good—moderate to expensive. There's often piano music in the bar following dinner, which is from 7 to 9.

A special note should be made of the magnificent Dromoland break-fast in the dining room. It's buffet style and includes fresh fruits, juice, homemade breads, croissants, and preserves, along with the full traditional Irish breakfast (sausages, bacon, eggs, grilled tomatoes). You may have porridge and they'll even broil a fresh fish for you or rush in with a smoked finnan haddie or kippered herring—if your heart is set on it. Breakfast is from 7:30 to 10. Dromoland also serves a full luncheon in the dining room from 1 to 2. For all meals, the dining room is expensive but well worth it. A less expensive lunch is available in the bar, where tasty sandwiches, smoked salmon with brown bread, and pâté are served.

PARTICULARS: Dromoland Castle (061-71144) has the dynamic new manager Elizabeth O'Mahoney, who was previously one of the bright lights of the famous Park Hotel in Kenare, County Kerry. It is open all year and has a full license. It is expensive, and breakfast is not included. AmEx, Diners, Master, and Visa are accepted. There are 71 rooms, including 6 elegant suites, all with bath and phone. (U.S. agent: Ashford Castle Inc.) Sporting facilities abound here. Besides walking and running, there are golfing (18-hole course), cycling, tennis, fishing, and boating right on the estate, and riding nearby. Dromoland is the ideal headquarters for exploring the Shannonside region. Although it's only 8 miles from the airport, it seems a peaceful world away. *Finding Dromoland*: It's on the N18 Limerick-to-Ennis road, just outside Newmarket on Fergus, and it is signposted. *Tip*: You can take a taxi to Dromoland from Shannon for a reasonable (sometimes negotiable) fee and have your rental car delivered there. This is especially helpful if you're nervous about picking up your car at the airport and immediately finding yourself in traffic as you adjust to driving on the left-hand side. At Dromoland, you're away from it all and can practice a little before coping with traffic. And many people feel too sleepy to drive after a transatlantic flight. This arrangement is also a way to avoid the lines at the rental-car desks. *But* if you are going to do this, be sure to make definite arrangements with the rental-car agency before you leave home and *not* after you arrive at Dromoland. The agents at Shannon may think you're a "no show" and give your car to someone else.

Gregans Castle BALLYVAUGHAN

About 15 miles from Gregans Castle, near Kilfenora village, are the ruins of Lemenagh Castle, built as a stronghold in the 15th century and expanded in the 17th century. In the mid-17th century, a most unusual story of love and devotion unfolded here. The castle was the home of Conor O'Brien and his wife, Mary Mahon O'Brien. She was known as *Moira Ruadh*, or "Red Mary," because of her fiery red hair. Conor and Red Mary were deeply in love and completely devoted to their son, Donough. They made a blissfully happy family until Oliver Cromwell came along. Conor was one of the first to be killed in battle. Although Red Mary was heartbroken when she spied Cromwell's soldiers carrying her husband's body back to Lemenagh, she was wise enough to remember her son and know what she had to do for him and for her dead husband. When the soldiers approached the entrance, she refused to accept the body, saying that this was not her husband and that she wasn't even married. She explained her son by saying he had been born out of wedlock and that the father had been an unknown soldier with whom she had had a brief affair. She did all this because her property, which she wanted her son to inherit, would have been confiscated had it been proven that Conor was her husband. Her devotion to her son was so great that she rode off to Limerick City to the Cromwellian garrison and offered to marry any officer who wanted her to lend even more credence to her story. So when one John Cooper, a captain, said he fancied her, she married him. Now there are varying accounts as to what happened. One suggests that they lived together as man and wife for a few months. Then, when Red Mary felt certain she had tricked all, including her new husband, she savagely kicked him in the groin. While he was doubled over, she beat him to death with a weapon and quickly buried him on the castle's grounds, telling everyone that he deserted her as well as the army. Thus, she had saved the property for her son. But another account has it that John Cooper was a tall, muscular man and much too powerful for her to murder in such a manner. This version suggests that the couple lived together as man and wife, but that the Cromwellians still didn't believe her initial tale, so they were dispossessed for about 25 years. During that time, Red Mary stayed with Cooper because he kept petitioning for the restoration of the property and therefore was her only hope. Finally he was suc- cessful, and Red Mary was so thankful for her son's sake that she kept

Cooper as her husband. But it was said that her heart was never in this marriage, and that she lived out her days pining for Conor.

"Let's create a really nice little hotel in an unusual surrounding," said Peter Haden to his wife, Moira, in the early 1970s. And the result was just that. Gregans Castle Hotel is in the *very unusual*, lunarlike region of County Clare—The Burren, near Ballyvaughan village. Sitting at the base of Corkscrew Hill, amid beautiful gardens, this 17th-century Martyn family manor home has been completely refurbished into a delight of cozy country elegance.

"What we wanted to do was to bring together things that are sympathetic to one another and to our ideals," Peter said. The stark gray exterior walls are in harmony with the stony surroundings; yet they're enlivened with bright white window trims and shutters. The interior furnishings are often springlike and floral, to match the many potted flowers on the outside. The very comfortable antique furniture in the public rooms ties in with the sense of the past. There's even a collection of antique brass items in the rustic Corkscrew Bar, with its stone, turf-burning fireplace and beamed ceiling. Here excellent pub food is served, especially homemade soup and seafood quiche. The bedrooms are beautifully done, with spring-bright matching floral bedspreads and drapes. This is truly a house that inspires relaxation. The cordial and concerned Hadens make certain that it is always tidy and spotlessly clean, yet you're never aware of the behind-the-scenes activity.

Gregans is not actually a castle but part of a 3-building medieval complex—2 buildings across the road and this one that is now a hotel. Of the structures across the road, the 15th/16th-century tower house most resembles a castle. Now in ruins, it may be visited, but conservation work is in progress, so beware of electrical fences. It's best to have the Hadens' young son, Alexander, take you on a tour up into the tower.

DINING AT GREGANS CASTLE: The equally harmonious dining room overlooks the gardens and distant Galway Bay. The food is simply prepared but excellent. Starters include fresh hot tomato or cold cream of cucumber soup, courgette (zucchini) stuffed with Irish bacon, and smoked salmon. Entrees include grilled haddock with fresh tomatoes, roast pork, baked stuffed Galway mussels, and baked Aran lobster with drawn butter. While all are good, the latter is absolutely superb. The vegetables are all locally grown and very well prepared. Reports from other diners are that the roast beef and lamb are very good as well. Wines are moderately priced and good. Dinner, served from 7 to 8, is moderate to expensive. Nonresidents should reserve. After dinner, take the time to stroll about the grounds. Most likely you'll be followed by an entourage of lovable kittens. Note the flickering lights far across the bay in County Galway. Then sense the lonely loveliness of this Burren estate lost somewhere amid the gray wash of stone and the whitewash of stars.

PARTICULARS: Gregans Castle (065-77005) is open from the end of March through October and has a full license. It is moderately priced, with breakfast included, and accepts Visa. There are 16 rooms, 12 with bath (those without have a small lavatory with toilet and wash basin). Two rooms are in the pleasant and cozy annex. (U.S. agent: Robert Reid.) Sporting facilities include beaches, swimming, surfing, and sea fishing nearby, plus excellent golfing 25 minutes away. Also possible are hill climbing, walking, and running. Since Gregans is in the heart of The Burren, it's an ideal base for exploring the ancient monuments and remains as well as the Aillwee Cave. *Finding Gregans:* It's outside of Ballyvaughan village on the N67 (or T69), 37 miles (or about an hour's drive) from Shannon Airport.

Suggestions for Your Visit   SHANNONSIDE

¶ Certainly take the time to enjoy your accommodations. In the case of Dromoland, not only will you want to linger in the majestic sitting room, hall, and rustic bar, but you'll be lured into strolling some of the estate's 1,500 beautiful acres, which include a fishing lake.

¶ If you are staying at Dromoland, this is a good area for shopping. Besides the small shop in Dromoland Castle itself, there's the **Ballycasey Craft Workshop** 5 miles away, where the Ennis-to-Limerick road (N18 or T11) branches off for Shannon Airport (N19). At that junction is the Georgian **Ballycaseymore House**. In its attractive courtyard, craftspeople produce a wide range of items, including gold and silver jewelry, fashion knitwear, suede and leather garments, leatherwork products, embroidered items, woven baskets, Aran knits, cut glass, wooden items, cold-cast products, handwoven and handspun items, copper pictures, craft pictures, picture frames, patchwork items. You can watch the craftspeople as they work. They're here Monday through Friday from 10 to 6, and some are open by appointment on Saturday (phone 061-62105). Also here are ample parking, a pottery shop, a tearoom, and restrooms.

Brief mention should be made of the **Shannon Airport Duty-Free Shop**, which you can visit only as you're leaving the country. Here you'll find small selections of many Irish crafts, including crystal, along with duty-free liquor and cigarettes, and Irish groceries (yes, you can bring Irish meats back to America—it's the only country in the world accorded that privilege). Both Irish and American currencies are accepted here, as are all credit cards.

There's also shopping at the **Bunratty Folk Park**, just behind Bunratty Castle on the N18 Limerick road, about 10 miles southeast of Dromoland. Here you'll see the rural heritage of Ireland—basketmaking, cooking, breadmaking, candlemaking, agricultural demonstrations, thatching, farming, and housing (various furnished farmhouses that you can visit). There's also a blacksmith's forge. Purchasable items include candles, forge products, prints, and woven apparel. The Folk Park is very well done, and you may want to spend an hour or so here, because it provides a very valuable insight into Irish rural history. It's open daily, all year round, from 9:30 to 5:30 (until 7 P.M. June through August). There is a very reasonable fee, plus a tearoom.

While here, you may also wish to tour **Bunratty Castle**. It stands on what once was an island on the northern bank of the Ratty River, where it meets the Shannon. Built around 1460 on the site of 3 previous castles, it's located in a vital spot that overlooked one of Ireland's major shipping ports in those days. The road by the castle was once an impassable marsh. Originally it was a MacNamara abode and fortress, but in the 1500s the Kings of Thomond—the O'Briens—took it over. During Elizabeth I's reign, the castle thrived and glittered for the aristocracy. The walls and ceilings were ornamented with resplendent stuccowork, elegant furnishings were installed, and magnificent gardens were cultivated. It is thought that William Penn, founder of Pennsylvania, lived in the castle as an infant. In 1954, Lord Gort purchased Bunratty and, with the assistance of the Irish Tourist Board, authentically restored it to its 15th-century state. Today the castle exhibits one of the finest collections of 15th-to-17th-century art, tapestries, furniture, furnishings, and accoutrements in northern Europe. From the

great banquet hall and the captain's quarters to the kitchen and the
solar rooms, the castle is fascinating. It is open year-round from 9:30
to 5:30—with the last admission at 4:45. There is a moderate entry
fee.

And now a word about food. Bunratty Castle (061-61511) holds
medieval banquets with entertainment twice each evening (6 and 9)
year round. You're ushered up the stone staircase to the great hall and
given the customary mead to sip while you have a look at some of the
castle's wonderful antiques and art. A traditional program of music and
entertainment accompanies the dinner of rather-too-basic Irish food.
Be forewarned that this is a very popular tourist haunt. If you want to
avoid crowds, stay away from the banquets. But if you want to experience it, be sure to reserve early—several days in advance during the
summer season. It is moderately priced and accepts all major credit
cards.

Another dining possibility is in the Bunratty Folk Park, where each
night from May through September the **Shannon Ceili** is held, with
one sitting at 5:45 and another at 9. This is a rural version of the
Bunratty Castle banquet: a sherry reception, a hearty Irish meal, and
a couple of hours of entertainment. At this reconstructed medieval
barn, which resembles a fisherman's warehouse, you sit on benches at
long pine tables and are plied with Irish stew, boiled potatoes, and soda
bread—accompanied by jugs of red wine. This is followed by fresh apple
pie with cream and Irish tea. With the country-style entertainment (tin
whistles, flutes, fiddles, spoons, and accordions), the whole event comes
across as an enjoyable Irish version of an American barn dance. En-
tertainers include a fiddler, a storyteller, and a dancer tapping to the
reel, and hornpipe to boot. Again, be forewarned that this is another
tourist haunt. If you don't mind that, reserve early in the summer season
(061-61788). It's moderately priced.

Next to Bunratty Castle is **Durty Nelly's Pub** (061-74072), reportedly one of Ireland's most popular pubs. The crowds who throng it at
all hours would seem to confirm this. Dating from the early 1600s, it's
thatched outside and dimly lit inside. The crowds have made no impression on the original stone walls, the wooden settees and benches, and
the turf fires. This pub is very much as it was when the castle's guards
used to hustle in for refreshment. Much of its clientele is Irish, indicating
that it's authentic and not just a tourist stop, but make no mistake—
tourists certainly are here. Upstairs, there's a quieter, rustic bar, and
next to it is **The Oyster**, where you can choose everything from a full

Irish meal to sandwiches and snacks. Many select Durty Nelly's for their evening out in Shannon, starting with the meal and staying on for drinks. There are also frequent impromptu sing-songs here. Inexpensive to moderate.

Fast becoming one of Ireland's most popular romantic restaurants, and with good reason, is the wonderful **MacCloskey's Restaurant**, just behind the Bunratty Castle grounds. It only seats 55, and the food is so good that you must reserve early (061-74082). (A review appears in chapter 14, Special Restaurants.)

Another restaurant near here, at **Hurlers Cross**, just before you turn off on the Shannon Airport road, is **Thisilldous**. ("This will do us," said the owners when they were searching for a location for their restaurant and decided on their own intimate living room with fireplace.) The cuisine is a fine blend of Irish/French, emphasizing seafood. The 35-seat restaurant is moderate to expensive and has a wine license. It's open 7:30 to 11:30 P.M. and closed from December 22 through January 22, as well as Sunday and public holidays. All credit cards are accepted.

¶ Just a few miles north of Dromoland, near Quin, **Knappogue Castle** offers another tour. Built in 1467, it was for centuries the home of the MacNamara family, who built 42 such edifices in their extensive domains. In 1966, it was purchased by Mark Edwin Andrews of Houston, Texas, a former U.S. assistant secretary to the Navy. With the assistance of the Irish government, he restored and furnished the castle in authentic 15th-century style. (It also has elements of Georgian and Regency periods.) The castle is open daily from May to October, 9:30 to 5, for a very reasonable fee. There's a souvenir shop in the beautifully restored courtyard. Tea, homemade scones, and soda bread are served.

Like Bunratty Castle, Knappogue has 2 medieval banquets each evening (at 6 and 9), but only from May through October. Knappogue also serves mead before ushering you into a vast dining hall for several hours of banqueting and entertainment. Somehow, though, Knappogue seems a little more spontaneous and less forced about it all. Most people prefer the food here over that at Bunratty, but Knappogue's, too, is the hearty Irish variety and plentiful. Although some of the entertainment verges on the frivolous, there are meaty chunks of Irish history dramatically tossed in as well. Lovely harp music is also a welcome feature. Again, it's touristy, so if you're interested in this sort of thing, reserve as early as possible. It's moderately priced, and major credit cards are accepted.

Near Knappogue is **Craggaunowen Castle** and its *crannog* project, which is held in trust for the nation. The recently restored 4-storied castle is a good example of the fortified homes of the 16th-century Anglo-Irish gentry. Its ground floor houses portions of the Hunt collection of medieval art. (The balance of the collection is at the National Institute for Higher Education [NIHE], at Plassey House on the Dublin Road in Limerick City.) The Craggaunowen Castle grounds contain a reconstructed *crannog* (an island built on an inland body of water to create an easily defended Bronze Age dwelling place) and a ringed fort. Within the latter are reconstructions of 4th-century farmers' houses showing what can be done by human labor unassisted by machinery. There's also a *souterrain* (an underground passage that could be used for food storage or escape). The castle and the project are open daily from March to October, from 9:30 to 5:30.

Six miles northwest of Quin village, on the L31, is the town of **Ennis**, site of **Ennis Abbey** (built in the 13th century with 15th-century additions and consisting of the nave, chancel, and south transept of a church, along with sculptured tombs) and Ennis courthouse (built in the mid-19th century in classical revival style).

Eight miles north of Ennis, on the L53, is the picturesque village of **Corofin**, where you will find the **Clare Heritage Centre**, or **Sinsearlann an Chlair** (literally, "Clare house of ancestry"). Permanent and special exhibits portray different themes of Irish life. Here you may also obtain genealogical advice, and there's a research service available for those with Clare roots. It's open March 17 through October 31, Monday through Saturday, from 10:30 A.M. to 12:30 P.M. and from 2 to 5 P.M. On Sunday, it's open only from 2 to 5 P.M.

NOTE: You may wish to return to Dromoland from here or you may wish to continue north on the L53 another 8 miles to **Kilfenora**, in the strange, lunarlike rocky region called **The Burren**. Here is the **Burren Display Centre**, offering details on the history of the area and its environment. From here you may wish to travel on to the dramatically beautiful **Cliffs of Moher** by heading south on the L53A to Ennistymon, then on the T69 to Lahinch and on around to Liscannor and the cliffs—a distance of 11½ miles. It would be about 32 miles back to Dromoland from here by heading back to Ennistymon and picking up the T70 to Inagh and Ennis, then taking the N18 (Limerick City road) back to Newmarket on Fergus.

NOTE: Both The Burren and the Cliffs of Moher are covered in greater detail below for those of you staying at the more conveniently located Gregans Castle.

¶ Some of you staying at Dromoland may wish to visit **Limerick City**, which is 17 miles away on the N18. It is one of Ireland's oldest cities, but it can be rather dreary. So many other towns and cities in Ireland gleam by comparison. Two interesting buildings here are the 13th-century **King John's Castle**, whose towers and curtain walls have survived the years, and the 12th-century **St. Mary's Cathedral**, with a splendid bell tower that affords you a view of the city. The latter is open daily from 9 A.M. to 1 P.M. and from 2:30 to 5:30 P.M. during the summer months, and from 9 A.M. to 1 P.M. during the winter months.

Also in Limerick is the **Hunt Museum**, at Plassey House, part of the NIHE (National Institute for Higher Education) on the Dublin Road. The museum contains an exhibition of Irish antiquities and European art objects collected by antiquarian and art historian John Hunt. Included are medieval bronzes, ivories, and Limoges enamels. It's open daily from April through September from 9:30 to 5:30.

There are quite a few restaurants in Limerick, including the new **Granary Tavern** at Charlotte Quay. Within a restored period tavern are 2 restaurants—**The Mariner**, serving basic fish, meat, and poultry dishes with sandwiches and pub food available at the bar (inexpensive to moderate; lunch 12:30 to 2, dinner 6 to 10; pub food all day; closed Sunday) and **The Viking Steak House**, which has a nightly cabaret, including a welcome drink, a 5-course dinner, and Irish folk/ballad entertainment from May through October 15 from 8 to 11 P.M. (moderate prices; closed Monday). Both accept all credit cards.

¶ About 16 miles southeast of Limerick City is the **Lough Gur Stone Age Centre**. Take the N21 to Patrickswell, then the N20 through Croom and on to just before Rockhill, where you branch off to the left on the L28 headed for Kilmallock, where the centre is located. The centre, which presides over one of the country's most ancient sites, is designed to give a clear introduction to Neolithic man and his habits. The shores of small, horseshoe-shaped **Lough Gur** are dotted with prehistoric pagan monuments, dolmens, stone circles, ruined fortresses, prehistoric graves, *crannogs* (manmade islands), pottery, weapons, and skeletons, along with the ruins of the Desmond castles. The new building has been constructed of Stone Age replicas and incorporates a tourist office. Modeled after dwellings of the Neolithic period, it features many replicas of material found in and around Lough Gur. In addition to an audiovisual presentation, there are models of stone circles and burial chambers, photographs, and facsimiles of weapons, tools, and pottery. Walking tours to the many interesting archaeological features of the locality are conducted at regular intervals. The centre is open daily from May to September from 10 A.M. to 1 P.M. and from 2 to 6 P.M. (2 to 6 P.M. only on Sunday).

¶ If you are staying at Gregans Castle in Ballyvaughan, you are in the heart of **The Burren**, or *Boirinn* (translated either as "stony place" or "great rock"). Rising from the background of the Cliffs of Moher, it spreads out to form northern County Clare. This strange, lunar 100-square-mile landscape is composed mainly of limestone. Here you'll find (along with the gray rock) megalithic tombs, dolmens, stone forts, caverns, castles, and the most interesting flora in the country. These wildflowers, which also are found in places as distant as the Arctic and the Alps, flourish between the fissured rocks as though they were in cultivated rock gardens. Bloody cranesbill, purging flax, fen violet, columbine, mountain avens, burnet rose, male and female cat's foot, wall lettuce, juniper, foxglove, and fern are only a few examples of what's here. And beneath the rocky surface are spectacular caves and surging streams. Potholes and turloughs (seasonal lakes that appear, disappear, and reappear) are in abundance.

¶ Two miles southeast of Ballyvaughan village is the remarkable **Aillwee Cave**, with 1,000 feet of passages. It was discovered by a farmer in 1944 and opened and developed as a tourist attraction in 1973. You can go on a guided tour for a reasonable fee. The first of the great chambers you'll see is Bear Haven, where bear beds and bones were found. (Bears have been extinct in Ireland for centuries.) The next major chamber is the Great Cascade, with a spectacular 40-foot frozen waterfall. You'll see splendid examples of stalagmites and stalactites. Farther in, a steep slope leads down to an underground river with waterfalls and cascades. The source of this river has never been discovered, even though many attempts have been made. It—like most of The Burren—remains a mystery. The cave is open daily from March 13 through November 13 from 10 to 7. The rest of the year, it's open weekends and by appointment. There's a pleasant terrace restaurant here (bearing the name of the cave) with a magnificent view of the stony Burren and glittering Galway Bay. You can have a whole meal, even wine, or just a snack in the tearoom. It's open all day, but closed January 1 through March 31 and November 1 through December 31. Visa and Master are accepted, as they are in the fine craft shop (which has many books on The Burren). Before you leave the area, take a moment to look around at the mountain of stone, **Aillwee Mountain**, then across the valley to **Cappanawalla Mountain** and **Newtown Castle**

(16th century; 5 stories) and over to Ballyvaughan village and Galway Bay.

In **Ballyvaughan** village, you may be interested in having a look at the **Manus Walsh Craft Shop** (paintings, silver jewelry, and enamels). There's also **Claire's Restaurant** (run by Walsh's wife), an intimate spot with candlelight, a turf fire, and piano music. Serving fine local seafood at moderate prices (Visa, Master), it's open April 1 through September 30 from 6 to 10 P.M. (closed Monday, except in July and August). There are several interesting pubs in the town, including **O'Lochlain's**, a rather quiet one in a mid-1700s whitewashed house. For an Irish pub, it's unusually spotless with a flagstone floor, rustic tables and benches, and an old inlaid mahogany clock. This is a charming place to have a quiet drink.

¶ Some 15 miles south of Ballyvaughan is **Kilfenora** village and **The Burren Display Centre** (described earlier in this section). Follow the T67 for 10 miles south to Lisdoonvarna, then take the L53 southeast for 5 miles to Kilfenora. The unique audiovisual interpretive program, designed to introduce the tourist to the special attractions of this strangely beautiful region, re-creates a microcosm of most of The Burren's many interesting features. It's open daily from March 17 to October 31, 10 to 6 (except in June, July, and August, when it stays open till 7). A tearoom and a craft shop are in the complex.

¶ The awesome **Cliffs of Moher** are about 16 miles from Gregans Castle—via the N67 through Lisdoonvarna and westward to the coast. Rising 700 feet above the sea and extending some 5 miles along the coast, the cliffs are one of Ireland's most popular sights. At the northern end is the **O'Brien Tower**, built by wealthy landowner Cornelius O'Brien in 1835 as a place from which to observe the beauty of the area. On a clear day, you can see the **Aran Islands** off Galway and the purple mountains of Connemara. A new single-story building erected on the original site of O'Brien's coach house and stables is the **Cliffs of Moher Visitor Centre**, where you'll find shops for literature and crafts, light food service, toilet facilities, Irish Tourist Board information, a reservations clerk, and an exhibition area showing some of County Clare's major attractions, including its bird and marine life. Admission is free, and it is open daily from 10 to 6 from early March to late October.

NOTE: Be sure to use *extreme caution* when exploring the Cliffs of Moher; people have slipped to their deaths from here. Also, you may wish to combine this journey with a visit to the Burren Display Centre at Kilfenora, since the 2 places are relatively close.

¶ About 12 miles northeast of Ballyvaughan, on the N67, is **Kinvara**, where the 16th-century **Dunguaire Castle** has weathered the turbulent years in fine shape. It was once the stronghold of the King of Connacht, Guaire Aidhneach. The castle, on the shores of the Galway Bay, derives its name from that of the king—*Dun* ("fort") of Guaire. As the castle changed hands over the years, there were many stirring encounters between warring factions here. It is now open to the public daily from April to September, 9:30 to 5:30.

Dunguaire also holds nightly banquets at 6 and 9 from May through September for a moderate fee. They are somewhat smaller than those at Knappogue and Bunratty, but many prefer this castle for both food and entertainment over the others. Starters include a hearty wine and Galway Bay prawns. Lobster bisque and smoked salmon or trout follow. The entree is a game bird served with a robust salad. You finish with a rich dessert. After the banquet, the staff, including the waiters and waitresses—all dressed in period costumes—present dramatic enter-tainment. This includes the reading of works by famous Irish writers such as Synge, Yeats, O'Casey, and Gogarty (Gogarty owned the castle for a time in the 1920s), along with music and song. This is another popular activity for tourists, so book early.

If you visit Dunguaire during the day, you may wish to continue on 17 more miles (29 miles altogether from Ballyvaughan) to **Galway City** to explore its interesting sights. (For possibilities there, see the Sug-gestions in the County Galway chapter of this book.) To reach Galway City from Kinvara, follow the N67 north to Kilcolgan, where you'll pick up the N18 north, passing through Clarinbridge to Oranmore. At Oranmore, pick up the N6 to Galway City.

If you're hungry en route, watch for a *small* sign in Kilcolgan for **Moran's Oyster Cottage, The Weir**. It's just about a mile off the main road toward the sea. This rustic little cottage has become world famous for its seafood—everything from snacks to full meals. And it *hasn't* become commercialized. (Moran's is reviewed in chapter 14, Special Restaurants.) At Clarinbridge, a little farther down the road toward Galway, is **Paddy Burke's**, known as an old oyster inn with seafood and bar specialties as well as basic Irish meat dishes. (Prices are mod-erate; AmEx, Master, and Diners are accepted.) This place, which is open all day, every day, often is mobbed. It's on the main road and well known for good food. Paddy Burke's is the site of the inauguration of Galway's Oyster Festival each year.

¶ All those who love literature may wish to visit the places associated with Lady Augusta Gregory and William Butler Yeats. These are around

Gort, County Galway—about 22 miles from Ballyvaughan. Take the N67 east to Kinvara, then pick up the L54 (a sharp right) east to Ardrahan, then take the N18 toward Gort. About a mile outside the village, turn left, following the signposts for **Coole Park**. This was the estate of Lady Gregory, the poet/playwright who founded the Abbey Theatre in Dublin. At her home she often entertained the likes of Sean O'Casey, George Bernard Shaw, John Millington Synge, and Yeats. While her magnificent mansion was demolished upon her death (for no apparent reason), the lanes of ilex trees still stand here, as does the great copper beech tree in the garden. On the latter, Ireland's great writers (including those mentioned above) inscribed their initials. After you leave Coole Park, continue along the road for about another mile and then turn right at the signpost for Thoor Ballylee. Follow this narrow road for about a mile. **Thoor Ballylee** is a 16th-century castellated de Burgo tower (still in superb condition) where Yeats wrote during the summer months in the 1920s. He bought the castle for 35 Irish pounds. It's open to the public for a minor fee from May through September, 10 to 6. Also here are a charming little bookshop and a tearoom with excellent homemade baked goods. If you're interested in continuing, it's about 21 miles to Galway City from here.

¶ During the summer months, there are sailings from **Ballyvaughan** to County Galway's **Aran Islands**. These islands are well worth seeing. (They are described in the Suggestions in chapter 4.)

6 COUNTY KERRY'S GRANDEST

The Park Hotel   KENMARE

The loveliness of the place to which they had come was unbounded.
                              —Irish, 14th or 15th century

The harp of the wood plays melody, its music brings perfect peace;
colour has settled on every hill, haze on the lake of full water.
                              —Irish, 9th century

There's music along the river
  For Love wanders there,
Pale flowers on his mantle,
  Dark leaves on his hair.
      —James Joyce
      Chamber Music

Without question, one of the finest lodgings in northern Europe is The
Park Hotel in Kenmare, County Kerry. It has won the prestigious Egon
Ronay award for the finest hotel in Great Britain and Ireland. From its
majestic stone exterior commanding a verdant sweep of hills overlooking
the sea's estuary to the splendor of its richly furnished interiors, this is
the pièce de résistance of the romantic's dream. Built in 1897, the hotel
has more elegantly restored period furniture and oil paintings in both
bedrooms and public rooms than most museums could ever presume to
display. Yet in no way is there any museum stuffiness about The Park.
Instead there is an exhilarating ambience along with an intimate and
almost matchless peacefulness.

Roam about The Park, so called because of its location in an 11-acre park on the edge of a sleepy village at the top of the spectacularly scenic Ring of Kerry. Guests often spend the morning hours darting in and out of other people's bedrooms and suites, gawking at the array of mahogany four-posters, the magnificent matching mirrored cabinets and chests of drawers, the cherrywood bureaus, the overstuffed settees, and the sleek walnut side tables. The public rooms—gleaming with Victorian brass chandeliers, flickering with firelight from massive marble fireplaces—are all overwhelming amid the majesty of late-19th-century furniture and the richness of period portraits and murals. You'll regret leaving any of them, including the charming bar and lounge whose French doors are often open to the gentle, refreshing bay breezes.

It would be easy to write forever about this truly thrilling place and still not do it justice. But one more thing must be said. The place is absolutely immaculate and in perfect condition, even down to the public

Park Hotel, County Kerry

restrooms (which also have beautiful antiques). All of this is due to
the persistent diligence and impeccable taste of The Park's dynamic,
young managing director-owner, Francis Brennan.

DINING AT THE PARK: If this fine lodging deserves so many superlatives
for its furnishings and ambience, it commands even more for its food.
On a typical evening, you'll dress for dinner and stroll down the grand
staircase, often to the accompaniment of soft, romantic piano music
played on the antique grand piano. Then you'll sip an aperitif in the
drawing room as you study one of the most promising menus you'll see
anywhere.

After you've made your selections (and the choices are not easy),
you'll be ushered into the dining room, which overlooks the twilit sea
spread out beneath velvety hills. This room is as stunningly romantic
as the rest of the hotel.

Does the menu live up to its promise? The answer is an unqualified,
overwhelming *yes*. The emphasis is on French haute cuisine. Among
the heavenly starters are ribbons of duck breast with sour cherry sauce,
chicken liver and pistachio nut terrine, thinly sliced salmon and turbot
baked in lemon butter, and hot scallop mousse in creamy watercress puree.

The roast lamb with oyster and walnut stuffing is an absolutely fantastic entree, but then so are the baked salmon in wild herb sauce,
grenadin of veal with scallop mousse (served with fresh spinach and
lobster sauces), roast lamb with honey and thyme, turbot baked with
apples and flamed in Calvados, sole poached in champagne and served
with lobster sauce, and lobster from Kenmare Bay prepared perfectly
any way you choose.

New additions to the appetizer menu include chilled watermelon
soup, cucumber soup, and strips of duckling breast in blackberry sauce.
All these dishes are beautifully prepared by head chef Matthew Darcy
as you're settled at your table by Gerard Browne, one of the world's
finest headwaiters.

Suffice it to say that the desserts and the Irish and continental cheeses
are all beautiful. The wine list is long and wonderful, and the prices
range from moderate to expensive, including some excellent buys from
Chateau Latour. The restaurant is expensive. Lunch is served from 1
to 2 (also good bar lunch) and dinner from 7 to 9. The dining room
is open to nonresidents, but reservations are required.

PARTICULARS: The Park Hotel (064-41200) is open from April through
Christmas and has a full license. It accepts AmEx, Diners, Master, and

Visa and is expensive. (U.S. agents: Selective Hotel Reservations; Robert Reid; David Mitchell; American Wolfe.) There are 50 bedrooms (6 are suites). All have full baths, direct-dial phones, and radio, and breakfast is included. There's a free 9-hole golf course on the grounds, as well as an all-weather tennis court and a croquet lawn. A portion of the grounds near the bay consists of woodlands, where running, walking, and strolling are delightful. Since Kenmare is at the southernmost extreme of the Ring of Kerry, The Park Hotel is the ideal place to begin a tour of the beautiful Ring. On the other side of Kenmare, heading toward Bantry, is the less traveled but very attractive Beara Peninsula, with spectacular mountain roads. Available within the Kenmare region are pony trekking, swimming, waterskiing, boating, sailing, and fishing. *Finding The Park:* It's 21 miles south of Killarney Town, on the N71 or Moll's Gap road. This is a breathtakingly beautiful road, but *please note* that it is narrow and winding. It is virtually impossible to pass other vehicles here. Tourists tend to be so carried away by the beauty that they drive very slowly, so this journey often can take more than an hour. If you're tired or anxious to get to The Park, there is a back route, but it is not nearly as attractive. From Killarney, take the N22 Cork City road until you come to the tiny village of Glenfesk, where you'll see a road to the right signposted for Kenmare. The Park is 108 miles from Shannon Airport and 60 miles from Cork City.

Caragh Lodge   CARAGH LAKE

The softness of your speech
Is like rain, falling
Among parched thoughts.

The lenience of your lips
Is like a cloud dissolving
At the kiss of the wind.

From your deep consideration
Runs the dark stream, nourishing
The lake of my delight.

                    —Bryan Guinness
                      "By Loch Etive"

The setting of a lodging often plays a major role in its appeal to the traveler. Certainly this is true of Caragh Lodge, which is just a mile off the famous Ring of Kerry and only about 15 miles from the beginning of the beautiful and much more secluded Dingle Peninsula. Overlooking Caragh Lake, one of the loveliest lakes in Ireland, and with the backdrop of some of the country's highest mountains, this 19th-century estate is a charmer. Its 9 acres of gardens—which include rare and tropical shrubs as well as rhododendron, azaleas, and palm trees—are so striking that they have won national gardening awards.

Inside, the 2 delightful sitting rooms and the dining room are furnished with the finest antiques from many different periods and European countries. They blend beautifully and are well worth taking some time to enjoy. Likewise, the bedrooms in the main house (there is a more modern annex) are traditionally furnished. Ask for one of those, especially one overlooking the beautiful lake.

DINING AT CARAGH LODGE: The new proprietors, Ines and Michael Braasch, daughter and son-in-law of the previous genial owners, have carried on the tradition of combining fine French and German cuisine. Yet there's a strong emphasis on simple fresh seafood dishes here. Poached salmon, bass, and trout are menu standards, and they are superb. The owners even smoke their own salmon in a specially designed smokehouse. Among the meat dishes are excellent beef, lamb, and pork roasts. Special mention should be made of the superbly prepared vegetables from the estate's own garden and greenhouse. There are good desserts as well. The dining room is moderate to expensive and open evenings from 7:30 to 8.

PARTICULARS: Caragh Lodge (066-69115) is open from March to mid-October, has a full license, and accepts Visa and Master. (U.S. agent: Robert Reid.) There are 10 moderately priced bedrooms, all with bath. Full breakfast is included. There's a fine library here. Lake swimming is excellent, with a private sauna at shoreside. There's also an all-weather tennis court. The quiet of this locale lends itself to many pleasant walks and offers an excellent area for running. *Finding Caragh Lodge:* It's on the N70, a few miles south of Killorglin, which is the northernmost point of the Ring of Kerry and a few miles south of the southernmost point of the Dingle Peninsula. Thus, this is an ideal touring location for both the Ring and Dingle.

Suggestions for Your Visit   COUNTY KERRY

¶ There are many fine excursions from The Park Hotel and back that can be made comfortably, but one that may *not* be made from Kenmare without reaching a state of total exhaustion is to the Dingle Peninsula. It is too far away and too demanding. This is better for those staying at Caragh Lodge or at one of the closer County Kerry lodgings reviewed in chapter 13. A comfortable Dingle Peninsula itinerary follows the one for Kenmare below.

¶ If you're touring the **Ring of Kerry** from Kenmare and back on the N70, be sure to save an entire day (starting early) for this beautiful, seascaped route. The complete circle, and return to Kenmare, is about 112 miles of often narrow, winding roads heavily traveled by tourists. If you feel this is too much, it is better to do a portion of it, take the time to savor the beauty, and then cut back.

Principal scenic points are: **Kenmare** (where the Roughty River flows into the Kenmare estuary and eventually Kenmare Bay; some of the finest mountains and hills in the country); **Sneem** (where the Kenmare River meets the sea); beautiful **Parknasilla** (magnificent beaches, boating, sailing, swimming, surfing, waterskiing, and the **Parknasilla Great Southern Hotel**, reviewed in chapter 13); **Waterville** (magnificent seascapes and hills); **Cahirciveen** (off of which lie **Valentia Island** and the dramatic **Skellig Rocks**); **Glenbeigh** (which arches into Dingle Bay and has a fine backdrop of horseshoe hills). These are followed by **Windy Gap** and the **River Caragh** to **Glencar** and **Killorglin**, the end of the Ring.

On this journey, you might like to pack a picnic lunch or stop at one of the little wayside restaurants, such as **Stone House** in **Sneem** (good basic Irish food; wine license; all credit cards; open for lunch 12 to 3 and dinner 6 to 10, April through September; moderate); **The Huntsman** in Waterville (good seafood, meat, and poultry at moderate prices; wine license; all credit cards; open for lunch 12 to 4 and dinner 6 to 10; closed November to mid-March); **Smugglers** in Waterville (moderately priced beachside restaurant; strong on seafood but good meat and poultry as well; wine license; all credit cards; open daily 12:30 to 10 except November through February; great view); **Butler Arms Hotel** in Waterville (good seafood, moderate to expensive; inexpensive pub food; AmEx, Master, Visa, Diners; full license; open for lunch 12:30 to 2:30 and dinner 7:30 to 9, except November through April);

Chez Marie in Waterville (good bistro serving fresh fish and vegetable dishes, steak, Irish stew, homemade soups; wine license; moderately priced; Master, Visa; open noon to 9:30 daily); **Waterville Lake Hotel** in Waterville (moderate to expensive; fancy restaurant specializing in seafood; full license; all credit cards; lunch 1 to 2:15 and dinner 7:30 to 10; closed November through mid-April); **Teach Culainn** in Cahirciveen (inexpensive traditional Irish fish and meat dishes; full license; open daily all year from 10:30 A.M. to 11:30 P.M.); **Old Schoolhouse** in Cahirciveen (good seafood, steak, and home baking; in old schoolhouse; moderately priced with wine license; open daily from noon to 9:30, except November through February); **Towers Hotel** in Glenbeigh (inexpensive to moderate; specializing in seafood, especially shellfish; full license; AmEx, Master, Visa, Diners; open daily from 7 A.M. to 9 P.M.; closed November through March); **Ross Inn** in Glenbeigh (good seafood and steak restaurant overlooking beach; full license; inexpensive; Master, Visa; open evenings 6:30 to 9, but closed mid-September through May).

On the **Ring of Kerry**, there are a number of interesting craft shops, including **The Homestead Craft Shop** and **Barbara O'Connor's**, as well as **Marshall's** and **The Sneem Craft Workshops. Gleann Bhride Handweavers** is in Waterville; **Human Clay Pottery and Gallery** is in Cahirciveen, and **Sheeog Irish Handcrafts** and the **Teapot** are in Killorglin.

¶ You might enjoy the scenic 21-mile drive over the narrow, twisty Moll's Gap road into **Killarney Town**. There are many reasons for visiting Killarney, any of which can easily take a half day to a day, so it's best to decide what you want to do in advance. If your stay at The Park Hotel is an extended one, you may wish to make several trips. Remember that Killarney is popular with tourists, so if you have an aversion to this sort of thing, it may affect your plans. But the town is attractive and very good for Irish craft shopping. (**Threads and Clay at The Old Granary, Serendipity,** and **Antiques Etc.** are all on College Street; **The Artist Gallery** and **White Heather** are both on Plunkett Street; **Inisfallen Gift Shop** and **Mayberry of Killarney** are on High Street. And there are so many more to discover.)

Besides shopping, you might enjoy a visit to either **The Laurels** (an attractive Tudor-style pub that often has a pleasant sing-song in the evenings) on Main Street or **Foley's** (a wonderfully old Victorian pub where early-1900s ballads are played on a tinkly upright piano) on High Street.

If you're in Killarney and you're hungry, there's one place where you *must* go to eat. **Gaby's** on High Street ranks right up there with the world's best seafood restaurants. This gleaming little Mediterranean-style cafe is reviewed in chapter 14, Special Restaurants.

¶ There are many ways to do some serious exploring of the **Killarney** area. One half-day journey goes through the breathtaking **Gap of Dunloe**, on the outskirts of the village. This tour can be accomplished by pony trap or by a very arduous, mostly uphill, 4-mile hike between the **Purple Mountain** group on one side and the **Macgillycuddy's Reeks** range on the other. The scenic area, except for the path, has been left untouched since the Ice Age. Along the way, you'll pass Black Lough, an icy-cold glacial tarn that legend claims has no fish because St. Patrick drowned the last Irish serpent in its waters. From the top of the Gap, the unspoiled panoramic views encompass staggering mountains, the Upper Killarney Lake, and the Cummeenduff ("Black Valley") rolling into the hills. The sense of being immersed in romantic wonder, far from the real world, is greatest here. (Unfortunately, you may have to share it with many other tourists if it's a busy day.)

Descending from the Gap to the shore of the Upper Lake, you'll see an old hunting lodge called **Lord Brandon's Cottage**. This is a wonderful area for a picnic lunch. From this point, you'll probably want to return to the outskirts of Killarney via pony trap (you can climb aboard and get off whenever you wish, and don't have to make the entire journey on the same trap). You can walk back if you still have the energy, but you'd need a marathoner's stamina to do so.

If, however, you started early enough to go through the Gap (i.e., fairly early morning), you could pick up a boat tour on the shores of the Upper Lake that will take you through hauntingly beautiful scenery amid isles steeped in ancient history. The tour passes through the Upper, Middle, and Lower Lakes of Killarney, takes another half day, and leaves you at **Ross Castle**, where jaunting cars will take you back to Killarney Town. If you drove those few miles to the beginning of the Gap of Dunloe tour, remember that you'll have to return those same few miles once your trap drops you in Killarney. Or else ask a trap to take you back. If you are planning to do the entire day's tour, it might be advisable to park your car in Killarney in the morning and do everything by pony trap. Prices? By American standards, they're minimal. Trap drivers will vie for your business, and prices may vary slightly, so pick and choose. Even if you are determined to avoid tourist meccas, it would be a terrible shame to miss this spectacular area.

¶ Another half-day tour of the Killarney area takes in the **Muckross**

Estate, including Muckross Abbey, Muckross House, and the Torc Waterfall. This journey, too, may be made by car or pony trap from Killarney Town. Three miles outside of town on the Kenmare Road is the entrance to **Bourne-Vincent Memorial Park**, which takes you via the Lower Lake shore to Gothic Muckross Abbey. (If you are driving a car, some walking is required.) The abbey was founded in the early 15th century and has a history well worth researching for those interested in the Elizabethan period.

Slightly down the road is **Muckross House**, a truly impressive 19th-century manor with a Portland stone exterior. Here you'll see exhibits of Kerry folklife, including ancient forms of harvesting, cobbling, and printing, as well as such crafts as stone carving, basketweaving, pottery, and weaving—to say nothing of the hand-carved period furniture. The splendid subtropical gardens and the nature walks offer a fine example of the beauty and serenity of the area. From here, you'll come to the sweeping, 60-foot Torc Waterfall, fed by the Devil's Punch Bowl on Mangerton Mountain. If you follow the road upward a little farther, you'll come to Ladies View, offering a majestic vista of the Killarney lakes. Continue on this road, if you wish, and you'll arrive back at Kenmare.

¶ A third classic half-day tour is to **Aghadoe Hill**. Traveling from the center of Killarney Town, you take the Tralee Road a short distance until you see a sign for the **Aghadoe Heights Hotel**. Take this road until you reach the hotel, on Aghadoe Hill. Opposite is one of Killarney's most breathtaking panoramas. The village, the lakes, the mountains—all can be seen from this prime and less tourist-ridden vantage point. It has been said that if you have only one moment to spend in the Killarney area, you should spend it here.

In pagan times, Aghadoe Hill was allegedly where lovers met because it was the birthplace of all beauty. Only those who worshipped the gods and goddesses of pure love could survive here. Legend has it that whoever falls in love at Aghadoe will be blessed for a lifetime.

If you're doing this tour, continue on from Aghadoe to the shore of Lower Lake and **Ross Castle**, a well-preserved 14th-century ruin and onetime residence of the O'Donoghue family. Across from the castle is **Ross Island**, a beautifully wooded peninsula that is accessible by road. There is also a road around the island, plus a network of paths that take about an hour to walk and provide beautiful views of the lake. The road from the Ross Castle area back to Killarney is clearly marked. From there, you can return to Kenmare.

¶ Another tour from Kenmare—and a far less touristy one—heads to the south and the less-traveled **Beara Peninsula**. Take the Bantry Road from Kenmare and after a few miles, you'll turn left on the Tim Healy Pass road. This will bring you onto the peninsula, at which point you must decide whether to do the entire circle of Beara (which is 84 miles back to Kenmare) or to cut across the spectacular but arduous **Tim Healy Pass** (which cuts the journey roughly in half). Either way is most interesting and very beautiful, but many feel the Tim Healy Pass is one of the wonders of Ireland. Certainly if you like mountain scenery—with no other signs of life except for a few other cars on the road—then this is for you. It's also a fabulous place for a picnic. There are no restaurants or petrol stations here. If it's a misty day, skip this trip. Not only won't you see anything, but you'll be in for one of the most hair-raising drives of your life on these narrow, twisty, and barrierless roads.

¶ If you want just a short drive from Kenmare, take the Bantry Road once again. But this time, when you come to the turnoff for the Tim Healy Pass, do *not* take it. Instead, continue straight up into the mountains to the **Turner's Rock Tunnel**. It's only about 8 or 9 miles from Kenmare, but you'll feel as if you're the only people in the world. Here you can practically reach up and touch the sky or look down the verdant miles of empty, cavernous valleys. It's a memorable sight. On a good day, this is an ideal place for a picnic. There's even a convenient roadside turnout before you come to the tunnel.

¶ If you wish to extend the above journey, you can continue on to **Glengarriff**, 17 miles from Kenmare. This is a pleasant little resort community located in a lovely wooded glen. Here there are some enjoyable little walks, including one to **Poulgorm** ("Blue Pool"), which is just a couple of minutes' walk by a path west of the post office. If you're interested in botany, **Garinish Island**, or Ilnacullin, is a short boat ride from the village harbor. Some 60 years ago, this once-barren island was transformed into a garden paradise, with plants, flowering shrubs, and trees from all over the world.

¶ Now if you still want to continue, you may want to take the road on into **Bantry**, which is 28 miles from Kenmare. Here you'll find the historic **Bantry House**. Built in 1750 on beautiful Bantry Bay, this palatial estate was formerly the home of the Earls of Bantry. The mansion has a fabulous display of furniture and art, much of it from the 18th century. Of interest are fireplaces from Versailles, tapestries made for Marie Antoinette, Russian icons, and tiled panels from Pompeii. The house and gardens, open daily all year, are definitely worth a visit.

Admission is inexpensive, and there's a pleasant tearoom and craft shop.

In **Ballylickey**, the town next door to Bantry on the Kenmare side, is the **Ballylickey Manor House Restaurant**. Part of the Ballylickey House cottage complex, it has a very attractive poolside dining room serving gourmet cuisine. (See chapter 13 for a review of the lodging and its dining room.)

¶ There are many fine walks of varying durations in the Kenmare area, including one that takes you across the Roughty River Bridge to **Sheen Falls** and back—about 4 miles. Across the road and a little farther down from Sheen Falls is **St. Finan's Holy Well**, known not only for its supposed healing powers but also for its aphrodisiacal powers.

¶ Finally, take a little time to stroll about the beguiling village of **Kenmare** (or An Neidin, which is Gaelic for "Little Nest"). The pleasant shops are worth a visit—**Kenmare Homespuns**, **The Craft Shop**, **T. A. O'Shea** (crafts), **Marie's** (lovely children's clothes), **M. T. O'Sullivan** (crafts), **D. J. Cremin** (Irish crystal and crafts), **Finnegan's** (crafts), **Quills Woolen Shop** (enormous variety of Irish woolen goods). Lacemaking is done at the **Poor Clares Convent** here. And if it happens to be a Fair Day (when local farmers come to town to sell their cattle), there will be sidewalk displays of clothes and antiques (especially little brass items). One new shop that's a must is **Cleo's**, with elegant wool, linen, and handknit apparel for women and a few menswear items as well. (The shop has a larger branch on Kildare Street in Dublin, near the Shelbourne Hotel.)

Besides the outstanding Park Hotel, there is a good French restaurant in Kenmare—**The Lime Tree**. It's a small romantic place that's moderately priced and has a wine license. It's open for dinner from 7 to 10, but is closed Sunday and from November through March. Visa is accepted. Now if you're looking for a simple little coffee shop with very good snack fare, there's **An Leat Pinguin**. It's inexpensive and open from 9 A.M. to 6 P.M., but closed Sunday. Also in Kenmare is **Hawthorne House** on Shelbourne Street, very near the Park Hotel. It's a bed-and-breakfast that also serves delicious, moderately priced dinners and has a wine license. An extremely pleasant couple, Ann and Gerry Browne, run the establishment. Gerry is also the maitre d' at the Park. If you're interested in staying at Hawthorne House, it has 7 rooms with bath, is inexpensive, and doesn't accept credit cards.

¶ If you are staying in **Caragh Lake**, you can tour all or part of the **Ring of Kerry** in reverse. (See the itinerary earlier in this section.)

But one more memorable and far less traveled tour is that of the **Dingle Peninsula**. Round trip, it's about 130 miles, so you will need a day to do it. Here again, if you feel this is too much, you can do a portion of it and cut back.

Start by traveling north up the N70 to Killorglin (the end of the Ring of Kerry) to Castlemaine, about 15 miles. From here, you can drive south down the L103 the 24 miles to Dingle Town. On your right will be the striking Slieve Mish mountains; and on the left, lovely Castlemaine Harbor. Soon you will come to **Inch Strand**, a spectacular shoreline. Sweeping out from the mainland 4 miles into Dingle Bay (which it separates from Castlemaine Harbor), this is a dazzling white sandbar backed by towering sandbank hills. At peak season quite a few tourists swim in its azure waters, but in the off season, the strand is virtually abandoned. Take a stroll here with the glittering sea before you, the soft purple mountains of Kerry behind, and the vast expanse of sky above. It's no wonder that David Lean chose this setting for some of the scenes in his movie *Ryan's Daughter*. Earlier, it was the setting for the film version of J. M. Synge's *Playboy of the Western World*. Here at Inch you might enjoy pondering a literary mystery, as many do. Expertly engraved on the wall of a very old stone-and-cement beach shed is this verse: "Dear Inch must I leave you, I have promises to keep, Perhaps miles to go to my last sleep." Where have you heard something similar before? The writings of American poet Robert Frost. Remember: "The woods are lovely, dark and deep. But I have promises to keep, And miles to go before I sleep, And miles to go before I sleep." Who wrote the former? Which was written first? Supposedly Frost never visited Ireland, but he did befriend W. B. Yeats, whose verse he admired. Yeats had visited Kerry and was very fond of the terrain. There are some who feel that the Kerry verse was written by young Yeats and that Frost borrowed the idea.

From here you'll want to journey on to the wonderful, hilly fishing village of **Dingle**, one of Ireland's most picturesque spots. There are 2 superb seafood restaurants here—**Doyle's** and **The Half Door**, side by side on John Street. (For reviews, see chapter 14, Special Restaurants.) Another fascinating little restaurant here is **An Cafe Litearta** on Dykegate Street. In front is a fine bookstore with Irish records and tapes as well. In back is a cafe, where you can get everything from morning coffee to good snacks, sandwiches, salads, and full meals at inexpensive prices. If you're particularly hungry, try the leg of lamb with fresh basil sauce. Also good are the fresh salmon and fresh trout. It has a wine license, accepts all credit cards, and is open Monday through Saturday 11 to 9 and on Sunday from 11 to 6. It's closed from mid-January through mid-March.

Dingle Town provides a field day for the shopper. On Green Street, which goes straight up an extremely steep hill, are **Commodum Craft Centre, Irish Crafts and Gifts, Mitchell's, Oliver McDonnell**—all fine shops for Irish clothes and crafts. On Strand Street are **Arts and Crafts** and **Leac a Re Crafts**.

Three lodgings in the Dingle Town area—**Skellig Hotel, Milltown House**, and **Alpine House**—are adequate; they are covered in chapter 13.

From Dingle, you have a choice. You may wish to cut 30 miles from your journey by heading east across the **Conor Pass** and proceeding to **Tralee** (the end of the Dingle ring 30 miles away), or you may proceed west to see the entire Dingle Peninsula. This latter choice eventually will include crossing the spectacular Conor Pass. If you are touring westerly Dingle, proceed on to Milltown and Ventry. (Those not doing this should skip ahead to the next reference in this itinerary to the Conor Pass.) At **Ventry**, with its own harbor and lovely beach, is **An Bradan Fease Potaireacht**, which translates from the Gaelic as "The Salmon of Knowledge Pottery." Its pottery pictures famous Irish legends. There's a tearoom here as well.

From here, pass through Fahan to **Slea Head**, with spectacular seascapes and views of the 7 **Blasket Islands**, now uninhabited. Then move on to the village of **Dunquin**, with its rocky cliffs and sandy coves. Here you'll find interesting **Dunquin Pottery**, with its own cafe. The slope of Croagh Marhin, above Dunquin, was the site of the movie town Kirarry, built especially for the film *Ryan's Daughter*. Once the film was completed, the set was destroyed, in accordance with Irish law. You might like to stop here for a drink at **Kruger's Pub**, whose claim to fame is that it's the closest Irish pub to America. Don't expect to find anything remotely like the Oak Room at New York's Plaza Hotel. It's pretty gloomy, but it's one of the few pubs in the area, and it *does* have local color. Incidentally, this area is one of the country's last strongholds of the Gaelic language.

The road from Dunquin passes spectacular seascapes, then cuts inland and north to **Ballyferriter**, site of **Potadoireacht na Caoloige** for fine handweaving and the Louis Mulcahy pottery. From here, you'll simply head up the coast and switch back to Dingle to pick up the road for the breathtaking **Conor Pass**. This is not the world's safest road to navigate, so proceed with caution. On a clear day, the views from the 1,500-foot summit reveal much of the Dingle Peninsula. To the south, you'll see all of Dingle Bay and Dingle Town (4½ miles away). In the valley directly below are the Dingle lakes. To the north are Brandon and Tralee bays and the sandy peninsula, **Rough Point**, that separates them. You may have gathered that this is one of Ireland's finest sights. The pass road ends at Stradbally, and from here you continue on up the coast to Tralee, the end of the Dingle circuit.

¶ You might, however, like to consider an optional detour off the main route from here to **Tralee**. If so, at Stradbally, take the signposted road to the town of Castlegregory, a tiny village at the base of Rough Point. There are beautiful sights around this area, including the lonely, less-traveled **Brandon Head**, a lovely place to have a picnic or just to pause and enjoy the dazzling sea. At Castlegregory, there's an oddly appealing lodging called **Aisling House**. (See chapter 13 for a review.) In this area, too, is the fine **Tomasin's Craft Shop**.

At **Tralee**, you might like to check out these fine Irish craft and apparel shops: **Browse, Cabell's, Quilters, Monica's, Siamsa Shop, Tralee Gift Shop**.

For food, you might like to try the intimate **Cordon Bleu**, which boasts a tasty smoked marinated fillet of Dingle herring. Also excellent are the sole, salmon, trout, and meat dishes. Wine license; moderately priced; Diners, Master, and Visa accepted. Open for lunch 12:30 to 2 and dinner 7 to 10:30, closed Sunday and Monday. Then there's an excellent, moderately priced seafood restaurant (especially good shellfish) called the **Ocean Billow**. It's open for lunch 12:30 to 2 and dinner 7 to 9:45, but closed Sunday; wine license. **The Mount Brandon Hotel** has a pleasant enough coffee shop and a dining room, and the range of foods (snacks to full meals) isn't bad. Both of these hotel restaurants are open from noon to 9:45, and they accept all credit cards. Four miles west of town, in the scenic Spa section, is **The Oyster Tavern**, with good fresh fish and shellfish. It has a full license, is moderately priced, and is open for lunch from 1 to 2:30 and for dinner from 7 to 10:30. Also in this area is a very quaint and basic-but-interesting old inn called **Seaview**. (See the review in chapter 13.)

Tralee is also a center for entertainment and special annual events: **Siamsa Tire**, the National Folk Theatre of Ireland, Godfrey Place (23055), is a program based on Ireland's heritage of music, folklore, and dance—the heart of which is the Irish language. Mid-June to the end of June on Monday and Thursday; July and August on

Cliffs, Slea Head, County Kerry

Monday, Tuesday, Thursday, and Friday. September 1 through September 9 on Monday and Thursday. Curtain time is 8:30.

- **Teach Siamsa** is the rural version of **Siamsa Tire**. This theatre workshop is held in Finuge (3 miles from Listowel off the main Tralee-Listowel road; Listowel is 17 miles from Tralee). Performances are Wednesdays during July and August. Curtain time is 9 P.M. Another workshop is at Carraig (6 miles from Dingle Town, between Muirioch and Feothanach; Dingle is 30 miles from Tralee). Curtain time each Friday during July and August is 9 P.M.
- **Listowel Writers' Week.** Seventeen miles from Tralee, in Listowel, is an annual working convention, with fun as well, attended by writers from all over the world. (It's usually the first week in June.) The fiction workshops cover everything from poetry to short stories, novels, and playwriting.
- **The Rose of Tralee Festival** is a 6-day merrymaking event in Tralee in late August and early September. It should be avoided by all connoisseurs.

1

THE BEGUILING HOMESTEADS
OF COUNTY CORK

Ard na Greinne   SCHULL

In his 1978 book, *The Wind That Round the Fastnet Sweeps*, Irish writer John M. Feehan described an experience he had while viewing beautiful Cape Clear Island off the Cork coast near Schull:

While I was enjoying breakfast out on the deck I had a rather intriguing experience. On the island, somewhat west of where *Dualla* was anchored, there is a very well-kept and roomy Youth Hostel, which in the past was a Rectory and which is now used mainly by young hikers, mostly in their late teens or early twenties. They generally arrive in couples and stay for a few days but for those in the first flush of love there is one big stumbling block. There are two large dormitories and the males are strictly separated from the females so that the Romeos and Juliets find this something of an unreasonable strain. To overcome such a serious drawback to a gay holiday they stroll after breakfast, by way of no harm, up the side of a heather-covered mountain sloping down to the sea, east of the hostel. When they believe they are well out of sight of roads and houses they get down to the task of expressing their Christian devotion for one another. So on this lovely summer's morning I saw four or five young couples hastily moving into position on different parts of the mountain which rose straight out of the sea directly in front of *Dualla*. Now they made one rather serious miscalculation. It did not seem to dawn on them that they were visible from the sea, so sitting unobtrusively in the cockpit of *Dualla* I had a Dress-Circle view of a most realistic Irish version of *Oh! Calcutta*, and judging from the various

acrobatics and gymnastics I saw it occurred to me what a great pity
D. H. Lawrence had not spent some of his youth on this holy island
of St. Kiaran. If he had, then *Lady Chatterley's Lover* might have
been a much more enjoyable, humorous and less depressing book. I
think it was the great Catholic writer Hilaire Belloc who said that if
sex can make you laugh everything is alright but if it does not make
you laugh there are dark problems on the horizon.

Discovering the tiny fishing village of Schull in a remote southwestern
arm of County Cork is much like finding Brigadoon. As you wend
around Mount Gabriel while afternoon shadows lengthen, it comes as
a complete surprise when the foothills part and there emerges a most
entrancing sweep of valley with a town and seascape too endearing for
words. Fishing boats and sailing ships bob and dance on the blue-green
frothy water. Wind whips and swirls down the hills and in from the
waves, infusing the sleepy old village with a sea-scented, mountain-
scented bliss. Just a short distance from the town to the west, up a very
narrow road, sits Ard na Greinne ("Height of the Sun"), overlooking
the famous Fastnet Rock lighthouse. The Rock has long been a sig-
nificant symbol—the last Irish soil seen by an emigrant leaving for
America during the famine years and up into the 1900s.

Ard na Greinne, a quaint 1800s farmhouse gleaming in its soft pink
wash, is a wonder. From the moment you enter, you feel at ease, with
a sense of belonging. A delicious peace descends and remains with you
throughout your stay. So wonderful is the feeling that it's almost painful
to leave. And this, of course, is the true test of any vacation lodging,
but especially a romantic one. Responsible for this are owner-managers
Frank and Rhona O'Sullivan. The charm of the O'Sullivans matches
the charm of their establishment.

Converted into an inn some years ago, it is beautifully furnished,
mostly with rustic antiques. Besides the finely appointed bedrooms (many
with fine antiques), you may choose to relax in the cozy second-floor
residents' lounge and browse through old books and magazines. Or you
may wish to visit the appealing bar, with its stone fireplace, flagstone
floor, and rough-beamed ceiling. Have drinks on the garden patio in
fair weather.

DINING AT ARD NA GREINNE: The very romantic dining room—with
fireplaces, beamed ceilings, and intimate candlelit tables—is one you
won't want to leave. And that's without mentioning the food—which
is superb. Quietly, simply, the O'Sullivans prepare meals with such

subtle care that their cuisine has won much acclaim. They take obvious starters such as avocado stuffed with prawns, country pâté, and smoked salmon and prepare them so deftly that you feel you've never tasted them before. The superb entrees include rich crabmeat gratin, succulent black sole on the bone, tender yet hearty steak, and delicious pork. Vegetables—such as wonderfully prepared scalloped potatoes with a hint of nutmeg, and broccoli with freshly made béarnaise sauce perfectly touched with the right balance of lemon—are worth crossing the ocean to sample. The homemade desserts are equally memorable, as is a tasty Cork-produced cheese called Gubeen. The wine list is fine and reasonable. Breakfasts are excellent. Dinner is served 7:30 to 8:30; prices are expensive. The dining room is open to nonresidents—*but* reservations are vital.

PARTICULARS: Ard na Greinne (028-28181), open from Easter to the end of October, has a full license. AmEx, Diners, and Visa are accepted. Moderately priced, it has 7 bedrooms, all with bath, and breakfast included. Because the inn is so small, it is often fully booked, so reserve early. (U.S. agent: Robert Reid.) Deep-sea fishing, boating, and sailing may be arranged through the inn, which is located in the heart of beautiful western Cork. *Finding Ard na Greinne*: The inn is located a mile west of Schull, and the route is marked with blue-and-white signs.

Longueville House   MALLOW

Tongues in trees, books in the running brooks,
Sermons in stones and good in everything.
            —An 18th-century writer of the
                  Blackwater River area

Living short but merry lives,
Going where the devil drives;
Having sweethearts but no wives—
      Live the rusty Rakes of Mallow.
            —Ned Lysaght

(Lyrics written about turn-of-the-century Mallow when it was the "in" thing to spend a season at its spa. Bacchanalian revelries of beautiful women and gallant men took precedence over the Mallow waters.)

Longueville House, County Cork

Near the Town Park of Mallow, scene of the famous Glenanaar hurling matches, in the lower Mallow Castle grounds, is Jephson's Rock, or Crown Point, rising sheerly out of the waters of the Blackwater River. Here, in centuries past, it became known as Lovers' Leap. Its first tragedy, which was in the 16th century, occurred when 2 lovers, unable to avoid the pursuit of their vindictive parents, made love for a final time here and flung themselves into the black, still-deep waters below.

Many guests who return again and again to Michael and Jane O'Callaghan's Longueville House in Mallow, County Cork, remark that it's just as if they've come home. The O'Callaghans have the special knack of making you feel you've known them all your life and that they're welcoming you into their home as old friends. And what a home for such a welcome.

This splendid Georgian estate, on a hill overlooking the rich Black-water River Valley, is one of the finest lodgings in the Irish Republic. Whether you are sipping a drink in front of a carved wood fireplace in a sitting room elegantly appointed with comfortable antique divans and chairs, or having coffee at twilight in the Victorian conservatory (a more recent addition), or strolling by moonlight over some of the estate's 500 acres, you'll experience a feeling of peace and pleasure here.

Try to obtain one of the front-facing antique-furnished bedrooms, from which you can look down the sweep of hill and across to the ruins of Dromineen Castle, the ancient home of the O'Callaghan family overlooking the Blackwater River. The castle is flanked on either side by majestic oak trees planted in the formation of the English and French battle lines at Waterloo. Watching a sunset over this area is unforgettable.

The manor was built in 1720 by the Longfield family, on land granted by Cromwell, who had snatched it from the O'Callaghan family when he attacked Dromineen Castle in the 1600s. When Richard Longfield was dubbed Baron Longueville in 1795 and granted a huge sum of money by the British Parliament for his support of the British Act of Union, he dropped the house's original Gaelic name, *Garamaconey*, in favor of Longueville House and began renovating in the grand Georgian tradition.

Two enormous wings were added on either side of the house, along with marvelous stone parapets and a pillared porch. Other features still visible are the dramatic hall-door entrance with a beautiful fanlight, the Portland-stone-floored entrance hall, the ornately decorated plas-terwork ceilings, the white marble Adam fireplace with a carved relief of Neptune, the massive inlaid mahogany doors, and the grand staircase. In 1866, the genteel conservatory was added, complete with a white wrought-iron façade and curved glass panels. Today the house glitters with a fine collection of antique Irish silver, old Waterford chandeliers, excellent oil paintings of Irish patriots and presidents, and some memorable landscapes, including a stunning pastoral scene of haystacks and lime-green fields.

The fascinating thing about Longueville is that after years of dis-placement, the O'Callaghan family remained attached to its beautiful landscapes. Senator William O'Callaghan, father of the present owner, purchased the property back from its illegal heirs in 1938. The present owners have turned the estate into a wonderfully romantic spot—complete with its own maze, vineyard, and farm. Another great asset is that the O'Callaghans truly love what they do. They care about the people who visit Longueville—and help them plan their itineraries in great detail. And since they seem to know every section of the country, their assistance is invaluable.

DINING AT LONGUEVILLE: There would be enough reason to stay at Longueville just to enjoy the furnishings, the hospitality, and the great sense of peace. But, delightfully, there's an even greater reason—the food. The grand President's Restaurant—so named because it is decorated with stately portraits of Irish presidents—is a treasure. Chef Jane O'Callaghan uses meats, vegetables, and fruits from the estate's own farm to prepare luscious dishes.

Creamy salmon mousse pâté, fresh baked Blackwater trout with almonds, terrine of pork with gooseberry chutney, veal terrine, avocado filled with prawns, and farm-fresh vegetable soup are among the most addictive appetizers. Among the entrees, you'll be forced to choose from crispy duckling with port sauce, escalope of salmon in cibolette (chive) sauce, roast leg of Longueville lamb and rack of lamb (the best in the country), heavenly black sole on the bone, succulent pink trout baked in herbs, escalope of veal in Stilton sauce (most rewarding on a chilly night), veal kidney in mustard sauce, poached salmon hollandaise, pickled ox tongue with parsley sauce, apple-stuffed pork roast, fresh turbot in prawn sauce, prawns in garlic butter, and sweetbreads in wine sauce. All of these are excellent choices, but there are many more. Desserts are also superior, as is the cheese tray. The wine list is a good one—and modestly priced. It includes some white wines produced from the Longueville vineyards.

For breakfasts at Longueville, specially prepared homemade honey, breads, fruits, and fruit salads abound. These are followed by fresh fish and/or eggs, homemade sausages, and bacon. You may even have specially prepared porridge if you wish.

This is a memorable dining room, partly because Jane darts off in the slow season to bone up at places such as London's Cordon Bleu and France's Moulin de Mougins, while Michael travels in search of new wines. The prediction: Once you've spent an evening here, you may well want to revise your plans so you can stay longer. It is moderate to expensive—but well worth it. Dinner is served from 7 to 8:30. The dining room is closed Sunday and Monday to nonresidents. Nonresidents must have reservations on the other evenings.

PARTICULARS: Longueville House (022-47156) is open from Easter through December 20, has a full license, and accepts Master, Visa, and Diners. (U.S. agents: Robert Reid Associates; Selective Hotel Reservations; David Mitchell.) There are 18 bedrooms (all with private baths), moderate to expensive, with the marvelous breakfast included. There's a free 18-hole golf course 4 miles away in Mallow Town, and excellent riding facilities are nearby. If you're a fisherman, Longueville offers 3 miles of its own salmon and trout waters on the Blackwater River. Indoor billiards and table tennis are also available. Longueville House is 22 miles from Cork City, making it an ideal base for touring that fine old city. It is 40 miles from Kinsale, one of the most beautiful little harbor villages in Ireland, with excellent little cafe-restaurants. It is 42 miles from Killarney Town, with its quaint shops and beautiful lakes. Blarney Castle and the Blarney Woolen Mills and shops are only 16 miles away. Shannon Airport is 64 miles (over good roads) away, so you can drive directly to Longueville from the airport if you like—or check out of Longueville in the morning and still have time to catch an international flight. *Finding Longueville*: It is 3 miles west of Mallow town on the N72 Killarney Road, and it is signposted.

Assolas Country House   KANTURK

During the 1600s, there were 2 armies in this part of Cork. One, called The Irish Troops under General Taaffee, was billeted at what is now known as Assolas Country House. It was superior in numbers and cavalry. The other, called The Regulars and led by Lord Inchiquin, was stationed in nearby Mallow and had far more artillery. Both armies were subjects of the British Crown and as such had a similar goal—to suppress rebellious groups longing for a free Ireland. Members of the armies should have cooperated for a joint effort, but jealousy prevailed. The 2 leaders became bitter enemies. Stories vary as to why this occurred. Brief accounts tucked away in old histories of the area suggest that Lord Inchiquin and General Taaffee were involved with the same sultry or angelic woman (opinions varied greatly as to which sort she was), who played one against the other for various reasons.

A different version—which, because of the greater number of details, seems more likely—suggests that a dashing Scottish officer named Allistair McDonald and employed by General Taaffee fell passionately in love with an "ethereal Irish beauty" whom "pompous" Lord Inchiquin longed to have as his own. Their splendiferous affair proceeded to enrage Inchiquin. Regardless of which story is factual, history seems to concur that there was a needless battle near Assolas in the Dunhallow Valley and that the initial victor was the lithe young Scottish soldier, who completely outmaneuvered Inchiquin and his troops. But fate was against this soldier, and as he was riding away from his field of conquest and crossing the Assolas River, he was stabbed through the heart by an Inchiquin loyalist. The story goes that McDonald's Irish love rushed to his side and in anguish planted a farewell kiss as he drew his last breath. The spot where he fell is known as The Chieftain's Ford, and it is very near Assolas House. The other Irish troops who fell with McDonald were buried around Assolas in a wooded area known as The Soldier's Grave.

Driving through the grounds of Assolas, with its own gentle Merryvale River, its sweeping lawns and cheery gardens, its ancient yew trees and striking Queen Anne demesne, you'll be enveloped in a lovely warmth— which often is not the case with the more austere old Irish estates. This warmth is so strong that it prompts the visitor to fantasize about spending a Christmas holiday here. It's easy to imagine strolling the grounds on a brisk December day, or perhaps taking one of the boats for a row on the river, or doing a little horseback riding. Then you could enter the manor and warm yourself with a sherry before the fire as the wondrous scents of Christmas dinner drifted in from the kitchen. Alas, that's not to be, for the Bourkes, who own and manage Assolas, reserve that pleasure for themselves. But the good news is that the manor is open to guests during the summer months.

Lovingly outfitted in period antiques, the front part of the house, built in 18th-century Queen Anne style and containing the sitting room with a log-burning fireplace and the dining room, carries the aura of grand (yet comfortable) country elegance. The back section of the house, which was built in the 1600s as a tower house (now truncated) of Jacobean design, contains the more rustic antique-furnished bedrooms.

It is interesting to note that the manor's stone out-offices, with still visible castings of sealed windows, suggest that Assolas once was a monastery, which probably was outlawed during the reign of Elizabeth I. In the early 1700s, a lonely Protestant minister named Reverend

Gore lived at Assolas Country House. So anxious for company was he that each night for the 34 years of his residency, he hung a lighted lantern high on the walls of Assolas to guide travelers who had to ford the river. In doing so, he saved people from drowning when the river was swollen, and he prevented many highwaymen from robbing poor innocents. So many of them became his friends that this became known as "The House by the Ford," or, in Gaelic, *Ata Solus*, meaning "The Ford of Light." (The anglicized version evolved into Assolas.)

Assolas is located in the beautiful vale of Dunhallow. Here, in the 1500s, poet Edmund Spenser came with his young bride to Kilcolman Castle. "Our love shall live, and later life renew," he wrote, and then went on to be so inspired by his view of the vale that he composed *The Faerie Queene*, his poetic hymn to Queen Elizabeth I. Since Spenser advocated Irish genocide because he felt the beauty of the land was wasted on the Irish, infuriated locals set fire to the castle's interiors, killing one of his children, and despoiled the lands. A year later, Spenser died of starvation in London.

DINING AT ASSOLAS: The charming dining room—with intimate mahogany tables adorned with fresh flowers and a grand oval center table—overlooks the lawns, gardens, and river. Here Mrs. Bourke offers a brief but fine menu of delectables, and all the vegetables and dairy products come from the manor's own farm and garden. Guests may choose from 3 starters, 2 soups, and 3 entrees each evening. Starts may include braised lamb kidneys in Cognac, prawn and trout rillette, avocado mousse, cottage walnut pâté, and honeydew melon cooler. Among the soups, chilled lemon is a favorite. Among the entrees might be roast pork with spiced peach sauce, whole sole meunière, beef Burgundy with rice, beefsteak and kidney pie, and poached plaice with asparagus cream sauce. Desserts are beautifully homemade, and there's a cheese trolley. The menu changes frequently. Prices are moderate and wines are reasonable and good. Dinner begins at 7:30. Nonresidents may drop by, but *only* if they have reservations.

PARTICULARS: Assolas (029-50015) is open from mid-April through October and has a wine license. No credit cards are accepted. There are 10 bedrooms (9 with private bath), with breakfast included. Prices are moderate to expensive. Make reservations well in advance. (U.S. agent: Robert Reid.) Salmon, trout, and coarse fishing, as well as boating (be sure to look out for the friendliest swans ever), tennis, and croquet (perfect for Assolas) are available on the estate. Nearby golfing and horseback riding for experienced riders may be arranged. *Finding Assolas:* The manor is about 3½ miles east of Kanturk village on the L186 or the Buttevant Road, and it is signposted. Assolas is about 60 miles from Shannon Airport, 30 miles from Cork City.

Ballymaloe House   SHANAGARRY

It was on a summer's day during the late 1800s that the population of Ballycotton, which is just a short distance from Shanagarry and Ballymaloe House, spotted in the dazzling sea off the local fishing pier an island where none had existed previously. So hauntingly beautiful was the island—with rugged mountains, silky glens, and a glitter seemingly from velvety lakes—that dozens of local young fishermen, enchanted by this beauty, took to their boats and sailed off toward the mirage. At the time, there was still much talk of *Tir-na-n'Og*, the Land of Eternal Youth in Gaelic folklore. Here everyone is eternally young—and blissfully, romantically happy.

As the boats approached the island, it seemed to recede slowly into the horizon, and most of the youths accepted the then-current belief that such islands sail around the world like boats popping up here and there and then move on. The feeling was that no mortal, even though sighting such an island, would ever be allowed to set foot on it. Yet, when the boats returned to the Ballycotton pier, not only had the new island vanished but also one of the boats that had sailed out to seek it.

Since the day was serenely calm, it was unlikely that the vessel had capsized. Time would tell, the villagers thought. And it did. According to later accounts, there were constant reappearances and sudden disappearances in Ballycotton of the young fisherman whose boat had disappeared. He was said to return because of his love for his mainland folk, whom he longed to have join him on this enchanted island. Each time he returned to Ballycotton, he looked as young as—if not younger than—the previous visit. His tales, still part of eastern Cork legends, tell of a gorgeous red-haired woman who snatched him from his boat, sinking it at the same time. Almost like a mermaid, she drew him to

Ballymaloe House, County Cork

this enchanted island—as the old locals tell it. She drew him into a life of incomparable beauty and sensuous delight—a life he would live forever. His only remorse was that his fishermen friends couldn't join him in such endless pleasures. He was the chosen one.

Finding Ballymaloe House in Shanagarry, County Cork, is a little like searching for one of the Seven Cities of Gold or the Fountain of Youth. So hidden away is this unspoiled Irish estate—which is part 14th-century Geraldine (owned by the Fitzgerald family) castle and keep, part 18th-century Georgian country manor, and part 19th-century Regency—that you feel it doesn't exist. But be patient, because once you do find this lost, lonely place, you'll treasure it.

Ballymaloe's exterior is perhaps the most photogenic of the lodgings in Ireland. Set amid 400 peaceful, rolling acres of rich farmland, it boasts vine-covered stone walls, vast multipaned gleaming windows, and a rustic flagstone courtyard. The interior is not overrun with antiques, and it has a charmingly simple farmhouse atmosphere (without any loss of amenities). There are 26 bedrooms. Fifteen are in the main manor and 11 extremely cozy rooms surround the old coachyard, beside the manor. Connected to the latter is the small, 16th-century gate-house. This is the epitome of a romantic European setting. Actually, there's also a French provincial feeling about it, with a small entrance hall and quaint bath followed by a steep wooden-staired incline into the narrow, intimate bedroom quarter. This is like a dream—but one you should book well in advance.

In addition, a half-mile from the manor and courtyard buildings is The Gate Lodge accommodation. This is a Victorian structure with a small, but romantic, bedroom with bath and a kitchen/living room. Here you can settle in and cook your own meals if you don't want to go out. Or, if you'd rather, you can dine at the Ballymaloe House.

DINING AT BALLYMALOE: There are 4 interconnecting dining rooms here. Two are painted deep purple, 2 red/pink. All are very simple but with candlelit intimacy, and all are hung with modern Irish paintings, including some of the best works of Jack Yeats, brother of William Butler Yeats. The food served here is remarkably good, partly because all the ingredients are locally grown (except for the fish, which comes from nearby Ballycotton Bay). Fish chowder, French peasant soup, turnip and bacon soup, oysters in champagne sauce, hot crab pâté are fine starters. Main courses include lobster served in the shell, an even more succulent hot buttered lobster, casserole of roast pork in mustard sauce, crisp duckling with sage and onion stuffing, roast ribs of beef béarnaise, rack of lamb, Ballymaloe bacon chop with an unusual and hearty whiskey and caramel sauce, and a tarragon calf's-liver dish sautéed in Irish whiskey. You can't go wrong with any of these dishes. The chef extraordinaire here is Myrtle Allen, who has won countless culinary awards and has written a very popular cookbook—*The Ballymaloe Cookbook* (published by Gill & Macmillan, Dublin). Since its debut in 1977 it has become a best-seller in Ireland. It's available in some American shops. Besides Ballymaloe, Mrs. Allen and her husband, Ivan, operate the charming **Ballymaloe at The Crawford Gallery** in Cork City. (See more on this under Suggestions for Your County Cork Visit.)

Myrtle Allen also has opened a cooking school at Ballymaloe with weeklong courses. (For details on this see chapter 18.)

The Ballymaloe restaurant has a very good selection of moderately priced wines, as well as a fine selection of expensive ones. Desserts are excellent and are all freshly baked. Lunch is from 1 to 2, dinner 7 to

9:30. The restaurant is open to nonresidents, but reservations are required. It is moderate to expensive.

PARTICULARS: Ballymaloe House (021-652531) is open all year, except for three days at Christmas. It has a full license and accepts AmEx, Visa, Master, and Diners. Accommodations are moderate to expensive—30 bedrooms with phone (29 with bath), and breakfast is included. (U.S. agent: Robert Reid.) Facilities include a heated, outdoor swimming pool, tennis court, riding, stables, golf course (9-hole), and a trout pond. The sea is a few miles away—for swimming and fishing, which may be arranged. River fishing is also available. A wonderful craft shop in a charming separate old stone building on the premises is a must. It offers great Irish clothing and Myrtle Allen's homemade relishes. If you're at Ballymaloe in the off-season or off-hours, be sure to ask Mrs. Allen's daughter Wendy to open the shop for you. The people here are very accommodating. *Finding Ballymaloe:* While this is not easy, it's about 20 miles east of Cork City and 2 miles outside the village of Cloyne, on the Ballycotton Road. If you have any difficulty, ask—and be prepared for a Corkman or woman to grab the opportunity to enlist you in a long (but charming) one-way conversation.

Suggestions for Your Visit COUNTY CORK

While many visitors use these marvelous County Cork accommodations as headquarters for touring the Ring of Kerry and the Dingle Peninsula, the distances are actually too long for comfortable touring. A jaunt to either of these places and back would leave one exhausted. However, there are many rewarding journeys of shorter duration.

¶ Cork, a city more than 800 years old, is about 22 miles from Longueville House, 30 miles from Assolas Country House, and 20 from Ballymaloe House. It's well worth a stroll about to see its fascinating buildings and drink in its history. After you've done that, if a little Irish craft shopping is in order, consider **The Cork Craftsmans Guild** in the Savoy Centre, Patrick Street; **James Mangan**, Patrick Street; **The Queens Old Castle Shopping Centre**, Grand Parade and Patrick Street. Just behind Patrick Street where it meets Grand Parade is the exciting new **French Quarter** shopping and restaurant area. The quaintly designed buildings and cobblestoned streets here are fascinating. Some of the shops include a number of high-fashion Italian and French women's boutiques; **Heritage**, a lovely little specialty shop with crafts and quilts; **Anne McCarthy Antiques** (china, linens, silver, brass, copper); **Mills Antiques** (very old Irish paintings, glass, china); **Collins Book Shop** (excellent selection of Irish interest books); **Pinocchio** (toys). But perhaps the finest shop here is **Stephen Pearce**. One of the reasons is because its top quality Irish craft items seem fresher and far more compelling. Here you'll find individual handcrafted glass and pottery items that quite likely you will never see in stores in any other part of Ireland, such as Jerpoint Glass hand-blown by Keith Leadbetter from Stoneford, County Kildare and European country pots designed and made by Michael Roche from Kiltrea Bridge Pottery in Enniscorthy, County Wexford. The shop has many other exclusives from jewelry to furniture. Do seek it out. There are also a few good snack-y cafes and pubs here, including **Bully's Wine Bar and Restaurant** and **The Huguenot**.

For antiques, try the antiques market on **Tuckey Street**, especially **Parade Antiques**. You'll find more antique shops on the side streets in this area.

You may be interested in dining in Cork City, where there are several very fine restaurants. These are the **Arbutus Lodge** in the hilly Montenotte section, **Lovett's Restaurant** on Churchyard Lane in the Douglas section (closed Sundays), and **Ballymaloe at Crawford Gallery**. For the first two it's important to make reservations and best to taxi to them from city center, as they're difficult (although rewarding) to find. (Lovett's and the Arbutus are reviewed in chapter 14.) The Ballymaloe restaurant is operated by Myrtle and Ivan Allen of the wonderful Ballymaloe House in Shanagarry. Located in the Crawford, a peaceful 18th-century, red-brick building containing exquisite examples of 20th-century Irish landscape paintings, the Ballymaloe offers superb nibbles of Irish cuisine—a suggestion of the culinary grandeur you'll savor if you travel to Ballymaloe House. You may just wish to drop in for tea and a home-baked pastry—and a linger over a gorgeous Irish oil landscape. The Crawford is on Emmet Place, not far from Patrick Street. The Ballymaloe restaurant is open from 9:30 to 5:30 daily and has a wine license.

If you're interested in visiting a pub, you might like to try **The Gateway** on Barrack Street, which is Cork's oldest—dating back to the 1600s; **Le Chateau** on Patrick Street, a grand old bar established in 1793; or **Rearden's Cellar Bar** on Washington Street, dating from the 1800s.

Here is a listing of Cork City's finest in entertainment and annual events:

- **The Cork International Choral and Folk Dance Festival** is held in May and draws choirs from many Western countries.
- **The Cork Jazz Festival**, held in late October, is a relatively new but popular event.
- **The Opera House**, Emmet Place (20022), stages operas and ballets by the Irish Ballet Company.
- **The Everyman Playhouse**, Father Mathew Street (26287), emphasizes Irish plays.
- **The Entertainment Centre**, Grand Parade, in back of the Irish Tourist Board (23251), presents lunchtime theatre during July and August. Monday through Friday: one-act plays by Irish writers. A light lunch is served from 12:45, the performance begins at 1:10. Very inexpensive. The centre also presents evening programs Monday through Friday during July and August. Different events each night include **Oíche Chéilí**—an evening of Irish music and dance in which the audience rises to perform with the cast; **rinceoil chorcaí**—traditional musicians play a wide range of Irish music and do some **céilí** dancing. Curtain is at 8:30 or 9, depending on the program. Phone in advance. Very inexpensive.
- **The Mall Room**, Imperial Hotel (965333), holds folklore discussions June through August, Tuesday and Thursday, 5:30 to 6:30.

¶ About 18 miles south of **Cork City** is the charming little 18th-century coastal village of **Kinsale**, sited on the slopes of a hill. Here you can wander the delightful Old World streets, visit the shops (especially **J. Cronin** and **The Craft Shop** at Commercial Hall), and above all sample the wonderful little cafe-restaurants (especially **The Blue Haven**, Pearse Street) that have made the village renowned as a gourmet's paradise. The **Kinsale Gourmet Festival** is held each year in early October. (See chapter 14 for restaurant reviews.) If you're interested in a drink, the **Spaniard Pub**, on the edge of the village, is a fascinating fisherman's pub. The Kinsale area is excellent for swimming, fishing, boating, beautiful coastal drives, picnicking. Unfortunately, although there are lodgings in the area, they are not terribly romantic. If that's not a concern, the **Blue Haven Hotel**, Pearse Street, and **The Folk House**, Guardwell, have a few rooms. **Acton's**, Cork Road, is a major hotel. **Ardcarrig**, on Compass Hill behind the Trident Hotel, has become a popular bed-and-breakfast because of its unusual (for Ireland) breakfasts and its cordial American owners, the Gilmores. There are only 3 moderately priced bedrooms with baths in this Georgian townhouse that sports a charming library with fireplace and antiques. But its breakfasts include Irish cheese omelettes, tomato and mushroom crepes and even eggs Benedict. It's open April through December, is moderately priced, and doesn't accept credit cards.

NOTE: If you're staying at Longueville House, Assolas Country House, or Ballymaloe House, do *not* attempt to fit in Cork City and Kinsale on the same day. Both warrant leisurely days of their own. If you don't have time to do both, it's better to choose just one of them.

¶ Another relatively short journey is to **Blarney Castle** and **Blarney Woolen Mills** on the L69 (about 21 miles from Assolas, 16 miles from Longueville, 25 miles from Ballymaloe, and 5 miles from Cork City). Many think **Blarney** is a tourist trap because busloads of people go there to kiss the famous **Blarney stone**. But nobody forces you to participate. It is of more interest that parts of the castle date back to the 15th century—and this is a very dramatic castle indeed. The grounds, the groves, and the caves around the castle have a fascinating, eerily romantic air. The other reason for visiting here is the Blarney Woolen Mills (established first in 1824), where there are weaving and kiltmaking demonstrations. There are also many good shops here featuring fine Irish crafts. The mill is open every day throughout the year. There's a restaurant attached; a pub and shops are in the nearby small town.

¶ Still another short journey from Cork City (14 miles), on the T29 Cork-Killarney Road, is the internationally reputed **Dripsey Woollen Mills**. Here you can buy tweed and fine wool fabrics just as designers such as Cardin, Saint Laurent, and Kenzo have done. There is a wide array of colors from which to choose. Since Dripsey does its own dyeing, spinning, and weaving, the prices are lower than you will find at most other woolen mills in Ireland.

¶ If you are staying at Ballymaloe House, there are several interesting little trips in the area around **Shanagarry**. In Shanagarry itself are several pottery makers. **Stephen Pearce Pottery** offers demonstrations Monday through Friday throughout the year and has a shop that's open every day. **The Pottery** is a shop open Monday through Friday, all year, but there are no demonstrations.

A few miles away, at **Ballycotton**, you can watch the fishermen land their catches and sell them. Along the nearby coastline, you can find ideal spots for water sports or for picnicking.

About 20 miles north of Ballymaloe is the charming coastal village
of **Youghal**, well worth a visit. The town dates back to the 14th century,
with still-visible town walls from the 15th century. There are many
fine examples of period architecture, including the very prominent 18th-
century Clock Gate. There are a few interesting shops (also visit **Youghal
Pottery** on Quarry Road), but, *more important*, one of Ireland's finest
seafood pub/restaurants—**Aherne's**—is here, on North Main Street.
It has won European cuisine awards and is open every day all year for
lunch and dinner, except during the winter season, when it's closed on
Monday. (See chapter 14, Special Restaurants, for a review.) Youghal
is where John Huston shot his classic 1956 film, *Moby Dick*, with
Gregory Peck and Orson Welles.

¶ If you are staying at **Ard na Greinne**, all of the above suggestions
are too far off course, but there are some magnificent journeys in southwestern Cork. Closest at hand is a tour around the **Mizen Head** peninsula, with spectacular seascapes. Once you've done that, you can
circle up and tour the northern peninsula (Sheep's Head or Muntevary)
above it. Here you'll transit the breathtaking, mountainous **Goat's Pass**,
affording magnificent vistas, including the largest of Cork's peninsulas—
Beara—to the north. There are several restaurants on Sheep's Head,
including the wonderful **Blairs Cove** near Durrus, which serves gourmet
cuisine in a 250-year-old stable. (See chapter 14 for a review.) **Killeen
North Restaurant** at Kilcrohane serves candlelit dinners in an 18th-
century cottage each evening throughout the year. There's even a lovely
Japanese restaurant, **Shiro**, at Ahakista, for dinner. This area is also a
good one for picnics. It's easy to spend a day on this drive.

¶ If you're interested in touring the larger **Beara Peninsula**, with its
staggeringly beautiful, yet arduous-to-drive (steep, winding, narrow roads)
Tim Healy Pass, you'll need to save a day (a clear one at that) to
travel from Ard na Greinne and back. It's a good idea to take along a
picnic lunch. Although there are restaurants on this peninsula, they
tend not to be as good as those on Sheep's Head.

Another charming town to visit is **Ballydehob** on Roaring Water
Bay, about 10 miles southeast of Ard na Greinne. There are many
craftworker shops here specializing in weaving, pottery, furniture, sculp-
tures, wooden toys, and handmade scrolls. **Kilcoe Castle**, built by the
McCarthy clan, also is here.

During the summer months, there is a ferry to beguiling **Cape Clear
Island**, 7 miles off the Schull pier. The boat leaves every day at 2:30
P.M. and allows you 3 hours to enjoy the romantic walks, including

Bantry House, County Cork

one to a lake about 15 minutes from the dock. The 150 or so inhabitants speak the Gaelic tongue. The island is considered to be the birthplace of its patron saint, St. Kiaran, said to have preceded St. Patrick by 30 to 100 years. Here you'll see **St. Kiaran's Well** (many claim it's the earliest Christian relic in Ireland and Great Britain), **St. Kiaran's Stone**, the ruins of the **Castle of Dunanore** (stronghold of the O'Driscoll family and built in the 13th century), and the old lighthouse. From the latter and from the elevated road, the views are spectacular. To the north, you can see Mount Gabriel, and the mountains of Kerry beyond; to the east, hundreds of little islands; and to the west, Mizen Head, the Bull Lighthouse, and Fastnet Rock. And of course everywhere the dazzling, turgid Atlantic. It's interesting to note that a telegraph station here received the first European news of the outbreak of the American Civil War. **Cape Clear Pottery** and **Harpercraft Enamel Designs** are interesting craft shops here.

¶ About 16 miles north of Schull, overlooking beautiful Bantry Bay, is the more sizable town of **Bantry**. Here you'll find one of Ireland's great historic treasures—**Bantry House**. Built only yards from the bay in 1750, this dramatic estate was formerly the home of the Earls of Bantry. Much of the furniture and art displayed here is 18th century. The house and gardens, open daily all year, are definitely worth a visit. Admission is inexpensive, and there's a pleasant tearoom plus a craft shop.

At Bantry's Wolfe Tone Square, you'll find **The Irish Scene Factory Knitwear Shop**. It offers pure wool picture sweaters, including scenes of Irish farmhouses and those of houses along Dublin's River Liffey.

Three miles north of Bantry, on the T65, is **Ballylickey**, with **Ballylickey Manor House** (cottages and fine gourmet restaurant). Next door to it is the **Sea View Hotel**, a lovely 1890s house with a very good restaurant. (For further details on these, see chapters 13 and 14.)

¶ If you're interested in botany (if not, skip it), **Garinish Island**, or Ilnacullin, is a short boat ride from the coastal village of Glengarriff, which is 27 miles from Schull and 11 miles from Bantry Town. This once-barren island was transformed into a garden paradise with classical pavilions some 60 years ago. Here, in a temperate climate, grow plants, flowering shrubs, and trees from as far away as China, Tasmania, Japan, South America, and the Himalayas. George Bernard Shaw wrote part of his famous play *St. Joan* here. Boats operate on a frequent daily basis throughout the year.

¶ About 33 miles from Schull, or 17 miles from Bantry Town, is an area known as **Gougane Barra**. Its romantic lake, which is the source of the River Lee, lies amid magnificent mountains with stark, brooding cliffs and foaming streams. In the middle of the lake is an island, now reached by a manmade causeway. At its entrance is St. Finbar's Well, named after the patron saint of Cork. In the 7th century, he established a hermitage here, along with a nearby monastery, but nothing remains of these structures. On the island are the remains of an 18th-century church. Above the lake is the **Gougane Barra Forest Park**, with many fine and signposted nature trails—another ideal spot for a picnic.

In one of the houses near the lake lived the marvelous Irish storyteller Timothy Buckley, a tailor by trade. During the late 1930s and early 1940s, he and his wife, Ansty, held court at their fireside with such notable local authors as Frank O'Connor and Sean O'Faolain. Under the name of "The Tailor," Buckley wrote daringly about the humorous aspects of the sex lives of the Irish country people. This was in easier

times—before the establishment of the English language in this part of
the country. Once the Irish Free State and the Church became firmly
entrenched, the compilation of "The Tailor's" fireside chats was translated and banned. Two puritanical priests forced the Buckleys to burn
the manuscript in the hearth that had kindled so many cheery—if
earthy—tales. Even today, many say that this was the cruelest adventure
of the embryonic Irish Free State. Shortly after 1943, when Buckley
and his wife died in disgrace, this wonderful book was miraculously
resurrected and released to the general public. It became—thankfully—
an enormous success.

¶ Besides car journeys, there are many fine walks in the Schull area.
The **Colla**, or Coast Road, offers many special seascapes and is about
7 miles from Schull and back. For those even more adventurous, there's
the spectacular **Mount Gabriel** to climb. (Try to ignore the 2 unat-
tractive white domes at the top. They track the Concorde on 500 miles
of its flight.)

Before leaving Schull, be sure to visit its craft shops—**Batik by
Teresa, Pat Connor** (pottery and sculpture), **Phyllis O'Meara's** (a few
miles west of Schull and specializing in knitwear). Schull also has the
quite fascinating **Mizen Bookshop**, next to an equally pleasant little
candlelit restaurant called **The Courtyard**, which specializes in seafood
and is open Monday through Saturday for dinner during the summer
months (from 7:30 to 10; full license; moderate to expensive; AmEx,
Visa, Master). Schull has become an artist's community, where you are
quite likely to see Irish writers and artists during the summer months.
They do not dominate; they only enjoy—as you will—this wonderful
paradise.

8 COUNTY TIPPERARY'S GRANDE DAMES

Cashel Palace Hotel

Royal and saintly Cashel! I would gaze
  Upon the wreck of thy departed powers,
  Not in the dewy light of matin hours,
Nor the meridian pomp of summer's blaze,
But at the close of dim autumnal days,
  When the sun's parting glance, through the slanting showers,
  Sheds o'er thy rock-throned battlements and towers
Such awful gleams as brighten o'er Decay's
Prophetic cheek. At such a time, methinks,
  There breathes from thy lone courts and voiceless aisles
A melancholy moral, such as sinks
  On the lone traveller's heart, amid the piles
Of vast Persepolis on her mountain stand,
Or Thebes half buried in the desert sand.

> —Sir Aubrey de Vere
> *The Rock of Cashel*

Around the early 12th century, King Cormac of Munster erected Cormac's Chapel on the Rock of Cashel as a testament to his conversion from paganism to Christianity. Unfortunately, according to legend, his bride suffered the consequences. Upon becoming devout and taking the vows of king-bishop, he banished her passionate presence to a nunnery, no less, because one of his vows promised celibacy. Every time he felt sexually aroused, he brutally flagellated himself in the chapel.

■ ■

129

"Tranquility in an age of change" is the description of the Cashel Palace Hotel in Cashel, County Tipperary, in its brochure. Quite frankly, that statement does a terrible injustice to this wondrous Queen Anne estate built in 1730 and still maintained magnificently. It is a breathtakingly beautiful lodging with some of the most romantically furnished bedrooms in the country that are equipped with Regency four-poster canopied beds, spectacular antique wardrobes, and lavish settees, along with individual thick white terrycloth bathrobes.

This splendid mansion was built as the Protestant Archbishop Theophilus Bolton's palace, and a supreme palace it was. It still is—poised dramatically at the base of the awesome Rock of Cashel ruins, the seat of the kings of Munster more than 7 centuries ago. According to legend, St. Patrick compared the Trinity to the three leaves of the shamrock in a sermon atop the Rock, thus giving Ireland its national symbol. Many of the bedrooms of the Cashel Palace look toward the summit area where the saint supposedly spoke.

The south façade is of red brick faced with limestone, while the north side is stone-faced. The extravagant interior contains a sweeping

Cashel Palace, County Tipperary

entrance hall with red pine paneling and carved wood Corinthian pillars. The magnificent reception and sitting rooms off the entrance hall are resplendent with antiques of the Queen Anne period. One of Cashel's finest features is its great red pine staircase with twisted balusters and intricate foliate carvings.

This is one of Ireland's exceptional lodgings and well worth a few days' stay.

DINING AT THE CASHEL PALACE: The Four Seasons dining room at Cashel has an intimate, Old World atmosphere with cozy but elegant tables, candlelight, and chandeliers. The food here is truly haute cuisine. Marvelous starters include roast quail in mulberry game sauce, avocado and mussel salad, goat cheese and Brie flambé in breadcrumbs and brandy, hot oysters beurre blanc, and terrine of rabbit with plum salad. The succulent entrees are beautifully prepared. Notable among them are salmon poached or grilled in sorrel sauce, escalope of veal with orange sauce, sole meunière with mussels and caraway, turbot and angler poached with fennel, rack of lamb with fresh thyme, and côte de boeuf. There's a fine cheese tray, plus a dessert trolley. Meals are moderate to expensive; wines are good and moderately priced. Dinner is served from 7 to 9:30. Reservations are strongly suggested for nonresidents. Cashel also has a charmingly casual basement dining room called the Bishop's Buttery. Open from 11 A.M. to 11 P.M., it serves light meals, steaks, and leisurely snacks. It has an enormous roaring fireplace, flagstone floors, chunky wooden tables, and captain's chairs.

PARTICULARS: The Cashel Palace (062-61411) is open all year and has a full license. It has 20 expensive bedrooms, all with bath; breakfast is not included. It accepts AmEx, Master, Visa, and Diners. (U.S. agents: Robert Reid; Selective Hotel Reservations.) Just behind Cashel Palace, in sight of many of its bedrooms and reached by a short stroll along the Bishop's Walk, is what many consider one of the wonders of the world—the Rock of Cashel. Nearby scenery includes the Glen of Aherlow and the Galtee and Slievefelim mountains. The River Suir, 4 miles away, provides excellent trout fishing. Riding schools are plentiful, and the famous horseracing track, The Curragh, is nearby. The region is also famous for its shooting facilities. Walking and running conditions are ideal. *Finding Cashel Palace:* It's very easy to find, since it's right in the middle of charming Cashel village on route N8.

Dundrum House   DUNDRUM

About 20 miles southeast of Dundrum is Slievenamon, a 2,368-foot mountain that in ancient times was called *Sliabh na mBan* or "The Mountain of the Women of Feimhinn." It was so named for the women of the area who wooed and enchanted Fionn (the greatest legendary hero of Ireland) and his Fianna warriors with their great beauty and sexual dexterity. The most attractive of these was said to be Grainne, who won Fionn as her husband by beating the rest of the nubile beauties in a race to the top of the mountain. But once the honeymoon was over, so the story goes, Grainne realized that her victory was a deceptive one. For Fionn was far more attracted to his achievements as a warrior than to romantic and sexual pursuits. So it was that as the neglect worsened, Grainne began to fall hopelessly in love with Diarmaid, one of Fionn's leading warriors. Obviously, Diarmaid had time for both areas of endeavor, and soon they had passionately consummated their love. Lean and strong, Diarmaid was of such superior masculine beauty that Grainne became possessed of him—and likewise he with her luminous, voluptuous being. So they realized they had no choice but to elope. They did, and were to spend many blissful years in hiding, raising 4 sons and a daughter. One day, however, Fionn was able to settle the score. He met up with Diarmaid, who had been wounded by the poisonous bristles of a wild boar. Fionn, who had healing powers, refused to exercise them, leaving Diarmaid to die and Grainne to mourn her lover forever.

There are many versions of this legend, but the basic elements remain the same. And to this day, there are various flat rocks and megaliths throughout the country known as The Beds of Diarmaid and Grainne. To approach them is to summon extreme aphrodisia and fertility.

It takes a tremendous effort to restore a centuries-old estate to the caliber that allows it to rank as one of Ireland's finest lodgings. The time involved—to say nothing of the vast amounts of money (enough to make a bank manager go gray overnight)—is staggering. Well, Austin Crowe and his family had such overwhelming determination, fed by their love of the Irish past, that they mustered the tenacity to suffer through it all. And their efforts are our reward.

In 1978, the Crowes took over Dundrum House in Dundrum, County

Dundrum House, County Tipperary

Tipperary. In 1981, after extensive interior renovations and a full-scale
search (still in progress) for Irish period antiques, the house had been
transformed into a stunning hotel.

In 1730, the Norman Maude family built Dundrum in the midst of
2,400 wooded acres that had once been owned by the Irish chieftain
O'Dwyer family. Philip O'Dwyer was dispossessed of the lands during
the Cromwellian confiscation of Ireland. In 1641, he had led an attack
against Cromwell's armies and was sentenced to death for the deed. In
1909, the house was put on the market and acquired by a religious
order. Later it became a retreat house. Today the acreage is reduced to
100, but they are notably spectacular and peaceful, being adorned with
majestic trees and a gentle, clear, trout-filled river. The magnificent
interiors now boast splendid bedrooms. And the antiques (mostly wonderful Victorian pieces) are everywhere. The sitting room and entrance
hall with its fireplaces, crystal chandeliers, and oil paintings are worth
a visit on their merit alone. But there's so much more to enjoy.

DINING AT DUNDRUM HOUSE: In the intimate dining room with its price-less carved white marble fireplace, Austin Crowe's son Michael deftly handles the duties of chef. While dishes here are pretty much of the basic Irish sort—beef, salmon, lamb, turkey, and ham—the special touches transform them into far-above-the-ordinary dishes. For in-stance, a tender, beautifully tasty sliced sirloin of beef became outstand-ing in a light Irish-whiskey-and-cream sauce. Likewise, a fresh hollandaise sauce added immeasurably to the fine poached salmon. The entrees and desserts here are equally sprightly. Prices are moderate and wines are also reasonable and good. AmEx, Master, Visa, and Diners are accepted. Dinner is served from 7 to 10. The dining room is open to nonresidents, but reservations are recommended.

PARTICULARS: Dundrum House (062-71116) is open all year and is 47 miles from Shannon Airport. It has a full license; accepts AmEx, Mas-ter, Visa, and Diners; and is moderately priced, with breakfast included. The hotel has 36 bedrooms with baths and an elevator to all floors, making access easy for the handicapped. (U.S. agent: Reservations Systems.) The River Suir runs through the estate grounds, providing trout fishing and lovely walks along its banks. Dundrum has its own stables, so horseback riding, jumping, and pony trekking are available to guests. There's an outdoor tennis court and table tennis indoors. Golfing is available nearby, as is mountaineering. Running is excellent here. Dundrum is close to such scenic wonders as the Rock of Cashel, the Glen of Aherlow, the Galtee and Slievefelim mountains, Cahir Castle, and Holycross Abbey. *Finding Dundrum House:* The hotel is on the Cashel-Dundrum Road (L111), about a mile from the village of Dundrum. It is signposted, making it easy to find.

Suggestions for Your Visit   COUNTY TIPPERARY

¶ This is Ireland's largest inland county, and its fertile landscapes provide a variety of scenery—from mountains and hills to lush plains and river valleys. But the main reason most tourists visit Tipperary is the awesome ruins on the **Rock of Cashel**. They tower over Cashel Town, are within walking distance of the Cashel Palace Hotel, and are 6 miles from Dundrum House. You can easily spend a morning or afternoon here.

Moving off for a day's hunting from the Rock of Cashel, County Tipperary

The Rock itself is of limestone and rises some 200 feet out of the plain. This alone would have been dramatic, but with the ruins, it becomes a spectacle. The focal point of these is a 13th-century Gothic cathedral, which is now roofless, allowing dazzling shafts of sunlight to play on its walls and floors. Camera buffs will love this. Another must—if you're strong of limb but not faint of heart—is to climb the 127 steep stone steps to the pinnacle of the thick walls and then follow them around. On a clear day, you can seemingly see all of Tipperary from here—and perhaps glimpse forever as well.

Also of interest on the Rock are the remains of the early-12th-century **Cormac's Chapel** (said to be one of the finest examples of Romanesque architecture in Europe), the 15th-century **Hall of Vicars Choral**, and the plain, though majestic, 92-foot **Round Tower** (a splendid example of 11th-century architecture in perfect condition.)

From the 4th to the 12th centuries the Rock of Cashel was noted as the headquarters of the kings of Munster. It was visited and blessed by St. Patrick in the 5th century, when King Aengus, ruler of the time, accepted Christianity. From that event, its religious significance grew. In the early 12th century, King Muirchertach presented the Rock to the Church. Nothing remains of the earliest of the Rock's ruins.

¶ There are also several other buildings of interest in Cashel Town, including the 13th-century **Dominican Friary**, 15th-century **Quirke's Castle**, and 19th-century **St. John the Baptist Cathedral**.

While you're in Cashel, you might like to do some shopping. Some shops worth checking out are **The Gift Shop, Padraig O Mathuna** (jewelry, silver), **Rossa Pottery**—all on Main Street; **Sarah Ryan Ceramics** on Ladyswell Street; **Shanagarry Weavers** on Cahir Road. Besides the fine dining at the **Cashel Palace Hotel**'s 2 dining rooms (described previously), the town has another restaurant called **Chez Hans**, which serves dinner from 7 to 10 year-round, except Sundays and Mondays. (A review appears in chapter 14, Special Restaurants.)

¶ There is a pleasant day's journey from Cashel Town and back that is about 100 miles (add 10 more miles for those staying in Dundrum) and takes you through some beautiful pastoral scenery. Drive to Tipperary Town and leave it via Bridge Street, following the signs that will take you south on the scenic route through the Glen of Aherlow. The road winds between the Galtee Mountains and the Slievenamuck Hills, and the views are spectacular in this area where many an ancient battle was fought and where outlaw Irishmen once hid.

From here, carry on through Bansha village to Cahir. In the center of this town is **Cahir Castle**, a splendid (mainly 15th-century) structure with the only working portcullis (sliding gate) in Ireland. The castle, formerly a Butler family fortress, is the largest medieval castle in the country. It has been fully restored and is open daily from April to September, and from Tuesday through Sunday the rest of the year.

From Cahir, head west on the N8 Mitchelstown Road. After about 10 miles, you'll come to a left-hand turn signposted for Ballyporeen. Along this road are the **Mitchelstown Caves**, containing some of the finest natural subterranean configurations in Ireland. The chambers are vast. Open daily, all year, they must be explored with a guide, who lives near the entrance. One of the caves is accessible only by a rope ladder. During the 1921 War of Independence, the caves became the hiding places of Irish rebels.

Continue on to the tiny village of **Ballyporeen** ("Small Potatoes"), whose claim to fame is that it was the birthplace of Ronald Reagan's great-grandfather. (The president visited the village in 1984.) From

Ballyporeen, head east to Clogheen, then south through "The Vee" to **Lismore**. On a clear day, "The Vee" is awesomely beautiful. The road zigzags through to Knockmealdown Gap (about 1,115 feet above sea level) and then descends to the charming little village of Lismore, on the south bank of the Blackwater River in County Waterford.

Of interest here is **Lismore Castle and Gardens**, positioned dramatically on a cliff jutting out over the river. Built in the early 12th century by King John, it occupied the site of an earlier, large monastic settlement. Later the castle became the property of the Dukes of Devonshire, who restored it in the early 1800s in Gothic style. The riding house, which connects with the upper and lower gardens, was built in 1631. Save a little time to stroll through the walled woodland gardens, which feature camellias, dogwood, magnolias, and flowering shrubs. There's also a special **Yew Walk**. Here it is said that (as with many places in this part of the country) Edmund Spenser wrote a portion of his *Faerie Queene*. It is open daily from early May to mid-September— except Saturday. You can also stay here if you wish, but it is *very* expensive. It's owned by the Duke of Devonshire, whose brother married Adele Astaire. They lived here and were often visited by her brother, Fred. (See chapter 15, Special Holidays.)

From here, proceed east to **Cappoquin** village. Near here, **Affane** was the birthplace of Valentine Greatrakes, who, during the 17th century, gained the nickname of "The Stroker." It was said that if he stroked the diseased portion of a person's body, that person would be cured. Some accounts suggest that Greatrakes occasionally became carried away with his faculty, especially when dealing with beautiful women. He would beguile them into believing they were suffering from depression and then proceed to stroke it away in the most caring and passionate of ways.

After Cappoquin, you must decide whether you wish to proceed the 11 miles east to Dungarvan Town or whether a few miles from Dungarvan you wish to make a left-hand turn and head north for Clonmel and then on back to Cashel or Dundrum. If you go into Dungarvan, you will have to pick up this road again anyway in order to return to Cashel or Dundrum.

Points of interest in **Dungarvan** are **Dungarvan Castle** (built in the 12th century under King John's rule and very much changed over the years—but still interesting); parts of the ancient town wall and the remains of a 13th century **Augustinian priory**. The town and some of its structures were saved from complete annihilation by Cromwell in the mid-17th century when a very beautiful Irishwoman drank to his health in front of all at the town gate and then in secret disdain surrendered to his sexual advances—or so the story goes.

Leave Dungarvan by backtracking on the same road by which you came. Follow it a short distance to the right turn for **Clonmel**. This will take you up through the beautiful **Nire Valley**. In the center of the valley is **Ballymacarberry Town**. From here, you can hire ponies or horses and even a guide to allow you to climb some of the spectacular mountain trails in this area where the Comeragh Mountains meet the Monavullagh Mountains.

Leaving here, you follow the road to Clonmel Town (or "Honey Meadow," as it translates from the Irish). Some of the 14th-century town walls still exist. In the mid-17th century, the town garrison, commanded by Hugh O'Neill, gave Cromwell the strongest resistance of his Irish campaign. The town's **West Gate** was repaired in the 19th century and is still intact.

From here, you can follow on back to Cashel or Dundrum.

NOTE: Now for a word about food. For this journey, if the weather is good, a picnic lunch is an excellent idea, since there are so many panoramas and pastoral settings. There are restaurants along the way, but most of them are less than spectacular. Worth a mention (although you may not be in these towns when you want to eat) are **Knocknagow**, a basement restaurant on Main Street in Tipperary Town (relatively good food at moderate prices; open every day for lunch and dinner); **The Gold Coast Restaurant**, outside of Dungarvan at Ballinacourthy on Dungarvan Harbor (good for seafood; moderate prices; open all year, 10 A.M. to 11 P.M.; Visa, Master); **Seanachie**, 5 miles south of Dungarvan on a beautiful hilltop on the N25 Cork Road (delicious traditional Irish seafood and meat dishes; inexpensive to moderate prices; open every day except Sunday—for lunch from 12:30 to 3 and dinner from 6:30 to 9:30). Perhaps the best known of these is the **Seanachie**, which is Gaelic for "The Old Storyteller." This traditional bar and restaurant is housed in the renovated buildings of an early-19th-century farm. In the old kitchen, with its inglenook fireplace, are many of the cooking utensils used in the old days. The barn, which houses the restaurant, has one of the finest Georgian dressers in Ireland, along with a superb collection of early Belleek pottery. Nearby is a graveyard, where victims of the Great Famine were brought from Dungarvan and buried. The farm served as a short-term hiding place for President Eamon de Valera during the final days of the Irish civil war in 1923.

(While this is a very pleasant place that has won all sorts of awards, it does attract tour buses, so it may not be for you.)

¶ Another day trip convenient from your County Tipperary lodgings is the 35-mile journey from Cashel to **Kilkenny** (or 41 miles from Dundrum to Kilkenny). Kilkenny hosts an exceptional **Arts Week** at the end of August each year. Although this city dates from the 6th century, when St. Canice founded a monastic settlement and a church here, it is important today as the finest example of a medieval city in Ireland—with narrow, winding streets, old buildings, and a superb castle. The 13th-century **Kilkenny Castle** stands breathtakingly above the River Nore and has undergone a meticulous restoration. It is open every day, June through September, and closed Monday in the off-season. The fee is embarrassingly modest, and guides are available. The basement houses an art gallery, and the castle's stalwart old kitchen is now a plain but very charming snack restaurant. There are many interesting features of this castle, which is still being restored, but don't miss the double fireplace of Carrara marble in the Great Hall (as though you could).

In this town, on Parliament Street, is **Rothe House**. Now a museum, it was once the house of Elizabethan merchant John Rothe. Built in 1594 and preserved as it was, it gives a splendid idea of how such a merchant lived. It is open all day, Monday through Saturday and Sunday afternoon from April through October. From the end of October to April, it is open Saturday and Sunday afternoon. Fees are minimal.

In Kilkenny as well is the **Kyteler's Inn**, on St. Kieran Street. This weird old building, dating from the early 14th century, not only serves relatively good pub lunches and meat and seafood dishes nightly, but on Friday evenings the inn goes to town with its famous **Witching Banquet** and **Seanachai** ("storytellings"). A witch greets you at the door with a glass of mulled wine and ushers you into the courtyard. Later, you'll dine in the scary, dungeonlike basement area by the light of flickery candles (4-course meal with tasty meat and fish entrees). Then you'll move to the inn's Tudor Room for an evening of traditional Irish music and storytelling, topped by a complimentary Irish coffee to ward off the ghostly chills. The moderately priced dinner is served from 6 P.M. on, but if you're interested, make reservations (056-21064).

Why the witching here? Well, there's a good reason. It's the intriguing story of Dame Alice Kyteler. Dame Alice's family was of the prosperous money-mad Anglo-Norman ilk. Her father died when she was a young woman, leaving his banking business to her. It is said that he had taught her well the value of power and money—so well that she developed an insatiable desire for both. This and her voluptuous beauty would prove to be her downfall. Many powerful men were drawn to her doorstep, and she was attracted to 4 of them in turn. After whirlwind courtships and brief marriages, 3 of these wealthy men widowed her—painfully and mysteriously, as it was said. When she married the fourth, still building her fortune, gossip and envy flared. Dame Alice had become the largest moneylender in the land, and while masquerading as deeply concerned for the needy, she raised her rates of interest to usurious heights. When a fourth husband began sliding toward oblivion, public outcry reached epidemic proportions, and Dame Alice's Waterloo was close at hand. By now she had become so jaded and self-involved that she scarcely noticed the case building against her. Idleness had led her to the proverbial devil's work. In fact, at about the time her first husband was expiring, she began worshipping the devil in the form of a great black dog. It was later surmised that her desire for money far outweighed her attraction to this man or any other. A few witches' potions laced with poison brought on a slow (she didn't want it to look like murder), agonizing death and another inheritance. It is said that after each death she took to the ritual slaughter of animals. Her innocent servant girl, Petronilla, believed her tale that the animals were diseased, just as she had believed in and joined Dame Alice's mourning. But the townspeople and the Bishop of Ossory were not to be tricked. A longtime foe of her moneylending practices, the bishop now demanded that she be tried for witchcraft. Even though Dame Alice's powerful friends, led by the seneschal (estate steward) Arnold le Poer, had the bishop imprisoned, he was a determined man. Soon released, the bishop insisted on the trial, at which the dame's children by her first 3 husbands testified against her. Found guilty, she was sentenced to burn at the stake. But through the aid of her friends, she fled the evening before her scheduled execution, leaving humble Petronilla to be the scapegoat who would rid the town of the devil and the witches' curses summoned by Dame Alice. Dragged screaming through the streets of Kilkenny, Petronilla was set ablaze at the spot where the old *Tholsel*, or Toll House, now stands, and she went to her death praying. To this day, her spirit is said to haunt the Kyteler's Inn and the streets of Kilkenny.

As you stroll through the city, you'll find many quaint and interesting shops. Besides the Kilkenny Design Shop, there are **Rothe Crafts**, Parliament Street; **Peter Mulhern** (handweaving), Michael Street; **Ru-**

dolf Heltzel Gold and Silversmith, Patrick Street; Liam Costigan (fine silver jewelry), Colliers Lane off High Street; Roberts' Books (including antique books), St. Kieran Street, just under the Kyteler's Inn. Aside from the Kyteler's, there are other restaurants here that are acceptable but not great. A short distance outside Kilkenny, on the Castlecomer Road, is the Newpark Hotel, where there are 2 restaurants open all year for lunch and dinner (AmEx, Visa, Master, and Diners are accepted). One is a relatively inexpensive grill room, the other a more fanciful intimate European dining room with quality meat and seafood dishes at moderate prices. An interesting pub is Tynan's Bridge House, 2 Horseleap Slip, off John's Bridge in town. This pub exudes antiquity— a carved marble-topped bar with brass-globed oil lamps, gilt mirrors, spice drawers, and anachronistic bar trappings. Other interesting features are an ancient clock, a fine front snug for intimate conversations, brass scales, and wonderful impressionistic Irish landscape paintings that are almost Monet-like. Don't mistake it (or miss it); this is one of Ireland's finest old country pubs.

Teehan's (run by Gay and Helen Teehan), on Parliament Street, is an interesting pub if you like traditional Irish music. People just drop in here off the street and start playing and singing. But they're good, sometimes very good. Also about a half-mile outside of the town on the Carlow-Dublin N9 road, you'll find Lacken House. It's an inexpensive B&B type of place (9 rooms, 2 with bath) that's open all year. But the key feature here is the dining room where owner-chef Eugene McSweeney holds forth. His superb Irish cooking has won him several major culinary awards. The moderately priced dinner is served from 7 to 10:30; the dining room is closed for dinner Sunday and Monday. All major credit cards are accepted, and there's a wine license.

¶ If you're staying at the charming Dundrum House and have fallen in love with owner Austin Crowe's antiques, you may dream of owning such treasures yourself. Well, dream no further. Austin's source is an antiques dealer par excellence located 35 miles to the north in the Tipperary township of Roscrea. The shop is Malt House Antiques & Restoration, Valley Place.

Also of interest in Roscrea are the ruins of the 12th-century St. Cronan's Abbey, of Hiberno-Romanesque design. Near the ruins and still intact is a 60-foot round tower. It once was 20 feet higher, but it was shortened to make room for a cannon in the 19th century. The 15th-century remains of the Franciscan Friary with its belfry have been partly incorporated in St. Cronan's Catholic Church. The gate tower,

2 other towers, and the curtain walls are remainders of the 13th-century **Ormonde**, or St. John's Castle, in Roscrea.

Here as well is the 18th-century **Damer House**, rescued from demolition in 1974 by the Irish Georgian Society. It's open daily from Easter through September for a modest fee. There is interesting Georgian country furniture here, plus a craft shop. If you want to eat in Roscrea, a moderately priced hotel and restaurant called **The Tower** serves basic food.

If you're interested in hiking or walking, Roscrea is the center for climbing the **Slieve Bloom** and **Devil's Bit Mountains**.

9

THE SPLENDOR
OF COUNTY WEXFORD

Marlfield House

A beautiful game most delightful,
They play sipping at luxurious wine
Men and gentle women under a bush,
Without sin, without crime.
   —from the 8th-century Irish *Voyage of Bran*
      (telling of *Tir-na-n'Og*, Land of Eternal Youth)

If you arrive at Mary Bowe's magnificent Regency mansion in the mid-afternoon when the guests are away touring, you may think you've happened upon a movie set. So glitteringly perfect is this house that you'll have difficulty imagining it as a lodging, or even someone's home. For sheer elegance, Marlfield House stands above all the grand Irish country houses. Situated amid 35 tranquil acres of woodlands and splendid gardens, the house has been decorated with the finest antiques and oil paintings.

   Once you walk into its majestic drawing room, with its mahogany bar, white marble fireplace, gold mantel clock, and sparkling old Waterford chandelier, you'll be reluctant ever to leave. Then there's the sweeping curved staircase, which leads to the spacious bedrooms as opulently furnished as the rest of the house. Here you'll find half- and full-tester beds as well as beautifully appointed bathrooms.

   A Mary Bowe inspiration is the house's relatively new conservatory, patterned after the precise detailings of early Victorian cast-iron curvilinear conservatories. In gleaming white with windows overlooking

Marfield House, County Wexford

the rolling lawns and the lovely gardens, it now houses one of the country's most romantic restaurants.

DINING AT MARLFIELD: Here in this room that literally shimmers with glass and mirrors and evening candlelight, you'll be as rewarded as you were in the rest of the house. The decor is a sea of pure whiteness offset by beautiful cut and potted flowers. As if this were not enough, the food is wonderful too. Served on Wedgwood china by friendly waitresses who zip about (unobtrusively) in creamy pink and pale green dresses, there's quite a variety from which to choose. The fresh Kilmore crab salad, served with homemade mayonnaise, is a favored starter. It's so good that many wish Mary Bowe would offer a larger portion as an entree. But of equal stature are the smoked salmon quiche, chicken liver mousse (light but memorable), quenelles of smoked trout with melon and port, veal sweetbreads with walnut salad, and pigeon pâté.

For entrees—all truly delicious—diners can choose from plaice stuffed with crabmeat, lemon sole with a sauce lightly laced with Stilton cheese, chicken breasts with port and sorrel sauce, sirloin steak with mustard and Burgundy sauce, simply prepared black sole, poached sea bass with ginger, fillet of pork with honey. The house wine, a 1981 Château de Tracy Pouilly Fumé, is a pleasant and moderately priced accompaniment to the fish dishes, but there are equally fine moderately-priced reds to support the meat dishes. If you prefer, there are many fine vintage wines here. Lunch is moderately priced, but dinner verges on the expensive— with justification. Lunch is served from 1 to 2:30, dinner from 7:30 to 9:30. Nonresidents must reserve.

PARTICULARS: Marlfield House (055-21124) is open all year and has a full license. Its rooms are expensive, but breakfast is included. No credit cards are accepted. The 11 rooms all have bath and phone. (U.S. agents: Robert Reid; David Mitchell.) The amenities include an antiques shop, a tennis court, and a croquet lawn. Two miles away are wonderful bathing strands. Nearby are deep-sea fishing, freshwater angling, shooting, and riding. Gorey is the perfect headquarters for touring both beautiful counties of Wexford and Wicklow. *Finding Marlfield House*: It's just outside of Gorey village, on the L31 Gorey/Courtown Road.

————

Suggestions for Your Visit   COUNTY WEXFORD

¶ You could spend several days just enjoying Marlfield House and its grounds. Do plan to spend some time here. A little farther afield, the sea and beautiful seascapes are just 2 miles down the road. You might like to spend a morning at the beach, venturing back to Marlfield for a leisurely lunch around 1. Or you might prefer to take along a light picnic lunch and save yourself for one of Marlfield's splendid evening meals.

¶ A very beautiful pastoral journey from here is to **Glendalough** in County Wicklow, 33 miles away. Take the N11 north 11 miles to Arklow. Then take the T7 northwest 13 miles to Rathdrum, passing through Woodenbridge and Avoca, where the famous Meeting of the Waters occurs. From Rathdrum, take the T81 9 miles northwest to Laragh, and on into Glendalough. (For details on these sights, plus shops, restaurants, and other Wicklow journeys, see Suggestions in chapter 10.)

¶ Another excursion from Gorey leads south 19 miles on the N11 to quaint Enniscorthy and then 15 miles farther south on the N11 to Wexford town, passing through Ferrycarrig.

Enniscorthy is a hillside village on the banks of the pleasant River Slaney. It figured in many conflicts with the Anglo-Normans, including the Rising of 1798, when it was taken for several weeks by Irish patriots. In late June and early July, the annual (and enjoyable) **Strawberry Fair** is held here. Besides the main winding street with its fascinating old buildings, there's **Enniscorthy Castle**, which some historians believe was built by Raymond de Gros, a key leader of the Anglo-Norman invaders who landed in the 1170s. Others contend that it was built in the 13th century by the Prendergasts. One of the castle's square towers had to be rebuilt in 1586, and it is still in such perfect condition that it houses a museum. Here there are many items dealing with the Rising of 1798, along with others from the Easter Rising of 1916. There's also an old-fashioned still of the type a farmer might have used to make *poteen*, the illegal Irish brew. It's open June through September, 10 to 6 Monday through Friday and 2 to 6 on Saturday and Sunday. The rest of the year, it's open daily from 2 to 5:30.

Near the base of the hill is a fascinating old pub called **The Antique Tavern**, which is filled with curiosity items and serves good, inexpensive pub grub. It's open every day. Across the street is **Louis Kerr**, for old jewelry and crystal.

Ferrycarrig, where the River Slaney surges into a narrow gorge, feels like the middle of nowhere—a very peaceful nowhere. On the north bank of the river is **Ferrycarrig Castle**, one of the Normans' earliest Irish castles. There's a walkway to the base of the castle with appointed picnic spots where you can enjoy a dramatic view of the Slaney as it gushes into Wexford Harbor and the sea. There's fabulous fishing here, as well as a wonderful pub—**The Oak Tavern**. The **Ferry Bar** within offers quite acceptable pub grub and excellent, inexpensive French wines (even half bottles). It's open every day from 12:30 to 9:30 and affords a beautiful view of the river. Also in The Oak Tavern is the **Ferry Restaurant**, with charcoal-broiled steaks at very reasonable prices, good seafood starters, salads, and homemade desserts. It's open from 7 to 10 P.M., except for Monday. And if you just want local color, you can attend the **Front Bar**, which the locals frequent and which houses an open fire and a piano. Do seek out this place—if only for a drink.

Wexford is a beautiful town hovering on the banks of a gentle estuary and harbor. Now almost a city in size, this is one of Ireland's special places. Its history goes back into prehistoric time. Artifacts unearthed in the area—flints, stone axes, and more—indicate that a community (or communities) existed here around 2000 B.C., and the inhabitants grew barley for trading. About 150 A.D., the Egyptian geographer

Ptolemy marked this area on his map as Menapia (or *Lough Garman* in Gaelic). In the 9th century, Viking sailors were so smitten with the locale that they claimed it as their own. Hating the native name, they changed it to *Waesfjord*, or "the Harbor of the Mud Flats." Actually, it was then 2 villages: the Viking stronghold with its own barracks, churches, and burial grounds, and the completely separate Gaelic community living in crowded dwellings around Selskar Abbey, their center of worship in both pre-Christian and Christian times.

Certainly you will want to spend a couple of hours strolling past the ancient buildings and interspersing this with a little shopping, dining, or a visit to a pub. For restaurants, there's **Captain White's** on George's Street. The emphasis is on good seafood—salmon, black sole, turbot, trout. Food and wines are moderately priced here, and there's a full license. AmEx, Diners, Master, and Visa are accepted. It's open all year for lunch from 12:30 to 2:30 and dinner from 6 to 9:45.

Another dining possibility is the Tudor-style **Tavern Bar** in the Talbot Hotel on Trinity Street. They serve an excellent hearty homemade pâté with brown bread. Try the Kilmore crabmeat sandwich (enormous and delicious). The menu has still more to offer: mussels, oak-smoked salmon, Rossmore oysters, trout mayonnaise salad, and Kilmore lobster mayonnaise salad or sandwich. There are a few nonseafood entries, along with a succulent rhubarb cream pie. Lunch is from 12:30 to 3 and dinner from 6 to 9, weekdays and Saturday. On Sunday, lunch ends at 2:45. Meals are inexpensive to moderate: AmEx, Diners, Master, and Visa are accepted.

If you're looking for a coffeehouse, try **Nagle's Coffee Dock** on North Main Street. This is the Wexford version of Bewley's (Bewley's being Dublin's grande dame of coffee-based dining places—see chapter 14) with its bustling activity and wonderful homemade cakes and baked goods. Like Bewley's, this establishment also serves good, hearty meals— roast ribs of beef, chicken, ham, ham salad, plaice, rainbow trout. All are served with an array of vegetables. This is *not* posh, intimate dining by any means. It's included here because it is one of those unusual places that capture your attention. It's also a good spot for observing a cross section of Wexford town (and environs) life. Amazingly inexpensive, it's open from 8:30 to 6:30 every day but Sunday. It does not have a liquor license or accept credit cards.

Interesting pubs include **The Crown** on Monck Street. A onetime stagecoach stop, it is among the country's oldest pubs and is still owned by the Kelly family. Drift into one of the rear lounges for a pint, and you'll be captivated by the array of memorabilia, including all sorts of military equipment (rapiers, dueling pistols, pikes from the Vinegar Hill massacre, gun collections, Norman armor) and some excellent old prints. During quiet hours, the place is more like a museum than a pub, but it should be seen.

Andy Kinsella's pub on South Main Street, with its frosted windows, old brass lamps, and massive mahogany bar, is another of Wexford's oldest, as is **The Thomas Moore Tavern** on Cornmarket Street. Done in Tudor fashion with 2 floors, it was the birthplace of the poet Thomas Moore's mother and is very popular with the young set. **The Cap Con Macken** at the Bull Ring is a unique establishment in that it combines an old pub with a grocery store, a spirit shop, and a funeral parlor. If you want to eat and drink yourself to death, this is the ideal place to be.

For shopping, try the **Crafts Center** on North Main Street (Wexford crafts, woven baskets, *sugán* (traditional rope and wood) chairs, ornaments, Irish food products, coffees); **Lowney Antiques**, South Main Street (antique furniture); **The Book Shop**, Charlotte Street (good selection of books on Ireland and especially County Wexford); **F. J. Hynes**, South Main Street (Irish glass, silver, Claddagh rings); **Joyce's China Shop**, South Main Street (fine selection of Waterford crystal, especially glasses); **Barker's**, South Main (Irish crafts, woolens, sheepskins, souvenirs); **Wexford Art Centre**, Cornmarket Street (young Wexford artists sell their own paintings here, as well as coffee and lunches); **Martin Doyle**, Lower Rowe Street (handmade gold and silver jewelry, some with gems, by a talented young designer who works here in his tiny shop); **Diana Donnelly**, Bull Square (elegant women's wear, silk dresses, in salonlike shop); **Chic**, South Main Street (elegant women's country clothes, tweeds); **Sunset Antiques**, South Main Street (small, interesting old items).

Wexford's entertainment and annual events include:

- **The Wexford Art Centre** (23764) does concerts, dance, dramatic performances.
- **The Wexford Mussel Festival**, inaugurated in 1980, is a 3-day event held at the end of August to celebrate the home of Ireland's mussel industry. Events include a fishing competition, a tennis tournament, speedboat racing, paragliding, waterskiing, and a dance.
- **The Wexford Opera Festival**, held each year at the end of October (for about 10 days), has become world famous since its inception in 1951. Its policy is to produce rarely performed classical operas with the finest performers. Make reservations early (053-22144), as the Theatre Royal is small and this is one of Ireland's leading

cultural events. Check with the Irish Tourist Board for exact dates. If you plan to be here during the festival, make your lodging reservations well in advance.

One final—and very romantic—Wexford suggestion: If you happen to be here in the evening, stroll down either Monck Street or Charlotte Street to the waterfront. Then take the short walk across New Bridge (preferably at sunset). When you turn back, you will see the gentle harbor all shimmering in crimson. Beyond that is Wexford, with its hills, old buildings, and quaint quayside. This soft-hued vision is an impressionist painting come to life. It's the epitome of what a European harbor town ought to look like—radiant and peaceful and imbued with the past. Too many waterside towns today have had the past torn out of them and replaced by lifeless modern architecture. Take some time to enjoy this setting. If you can't do it at night, go during the day, but don't miss it.

¶ Another southern journey is to **New Ross**, which is 39 miles from Gorey. Take the N11 for 19 miles to Enniscorthy and then the N79 southwest for 20 miles into New Ross, one of the county's oldest towns. It dates from the 6th century, when a monastery was founded here. New Ross is one of those neglected towns that most travel guides forget to tell you about because it's on the way to a more important destination—namely, Kilkenny or Wexford or Waterford. It's a lovely hillside town that slopes to picturesque Dutch-style buildings along the River Barrow, just south of its junction with the River Nore. During the summer months, you can take a very pleasant river cruise for lunch, afternoon tea, or dinner. (For details and a review of **Galley Cruising Restaurants**, see chapter 14.) Also, one New Ross shop has been touted by some to be worth a visit—**Brooks Jewellers & Gifts Shop** on Charles Street.

¶ If you're particularly energetic and time permits (it won't if you've taken the restaurant cruise), you could drive the 27 miles northwest through **Thomastown** (another attractive River Nore town that is the headquarters of the **Kilkenny Hunt**) and on into **Kilkenny**—one of Europe's most fascinating medieval cities. (For Kilkenny details, see Suggestions in chapter 8.) Remember, however, that Kilkenny is 66 miles from Gorey. Although the roads are good, you will have to travel back the same distance if you're staying at Marlfield House. There is so much to see in Kilkenny that you might be smarter to explore it from the suggested County Tipperary lodgings (chapter 8), which require half the mileage.

10
THE GRAND AND QUAINT LODGINGS OF COUNTY WICKLOW

Tinakilly House

O, unto the pinewood /At the noon of day
Come with me now,/Sweet love, away.
　　　　　—James Joyce
　　　　　　Chamber Music

A short distance from Rathnew to the east is Glendalough, the splen-
didly beautiful valley of 2 lakes. Here, in the 6th century, St. Kevin
came seeking solitude and communion with Christ. Immediately he
knew he had come to the right place. Young and stalwart, he lived
here for years as a hermit, sleeping in the hollows of trees and the
curvatures of rocks. In time, word spread about his sanctity and the
sheer peacefulness of his locale. Soon students and scholars from all
over Europe came to join him, establishing one of the most famous
monastic settlements of the day. But it was during the early days when
people first heard of St. Kevin's venture that a beautiful young woman
named Kathleen came to Glendalough seeking the spiritual heights
Kevin had reached. Not only did she quickly climb to these heights,
but she also fell madly in love with the handsome Kevin. She visited
him so often at this retreat that Kevin, being a man, began to feel the
same urges himself. When he realized that if he succumbed to her
beauty it would negate his religious teachings and the life he had so
strongly believed was right, he quickly took refuge on the shelf of a
cliff overlooking Glendalough's upper lake. Here he lived at peace once
again, until one day forlorn Kathleen, wandering through the valley

150

below, came across Kevin's faithful dog, who led her to his latest retreat. Partially awakening from a deep sleep, Kevin saw her exquisite form as if in a dream. Before he was fully awake, passions flamed. But just as they were on the verge of consummating their relationship, Kevin realized that this rush toward ecstasy was no dream, nor was it a new religious experience. Desire soon switched to rage, as Kevin believed this had been a ruse, and he pushed Kathleen over the cliff and into the lake, where she drowned. (The famous Irish poet Thomas Moore wrote a poem about this legend.)

Entering the foyer of Tinakilly House (don't let the name fool you; it's a mansion), you are immediately swept away by its overwhelming grandeur. Yes, *sweep* is most definitely the operative term here. Every-

Tinakilly House, County Wicklow

thing is sweeping—from its regal halls, sitting room, and majestic stair-case to its priceless antique artworks, fireplaces, and audaciously romantic bedrooms. Perhaps the surprise factor here fuels and enhances the en-joyment. Somehow, from the outside, the building seems incapable of housing such palatial interiors. Not that it's not an outstanding building on gardened acreage overlooking the Irish Sea—it just doesn't lead you to suspect just how many wonders are in store.

All of this is somewhat of a miracle that would have been impossible without the concerted efforts and vast financial outlay of its present owners, William and Bee Power. Several years ago, when this enter-prising couple took over Tinakilly, they found it in a state of decay, riddled with dry rot. The woods used in the 1866 construction of the house—pitch pine, bird's-eye maple, and mahogany—had been im-ported from many parts of the world. William Power set out to replace painstakingly each piece of wood—a goal he has now achieved. And this is to say nothing of the rest of the renovation and the beautiful antiques that fill the mansion.

The 7 acres of gardens here show the precision of Victorian garden-ing, with fine stands of beech, evergreen oak, and eucalyptus. There are giant California redwoods at each end of the tennis court. The gardens were originally planned for the visit of Queen Victoria in 1893.

DINING AT TINAKILLY: The intimate yet elegant candlelit restaurant, with its fireplace and shimmering chandelier, is perfect. It's hard to imagine a room more dreamily romantic. The menu here is extremely ambitious, offering such starters as pigeon breast salad with a raspberry vinaigrette, lamb kidneys panfried in butter and olive oil with a light Dijon mustard, terrine of the season's vegetables served with a fresh tomato coulis and herb sauce, salmon tarts with fresh herb cream, melon marinated in honey and sugar water and served with a julienne of smoked salmon. Entrees include roast quail served in its own sauce with fresh chervil, roast Wicklow lamb in honey and thyme sauce, fresh poached salmon in watercress and herb cream sauce, escalope of veal in lime and honey sauce. The sauces here are all extremely good and freshly prepared. The wine list is fine, reasonable, and extensive, with 77 bins in the Tinakilly cellar. The emphasis is on the classic Burgundies and the more complex Bordeaux wines. Dinner, moderate to expensive, is served from 7:30 to 9. Nonresidents are accepted, but reservations are required.

PARTICULARS: Tinakilly House (0404-69274) is open all year, except for Christmas Day and the month of January. There are 14 moderate to expensive bedrooms, all with bath. A full breakfast is included. (U.S. agent: Robert Reid.) Tinakilly is near the beautiful Wicklow mountains and beaches. Golfing is available at the nearby Wicklow and Blainroe golf clubs, tennis at the Wicklow Tennis Club, horseback riding at Broom Hall Equestian Centre. Fishing, hiking, canoeing, running, and mountaineering are all within easy reach. *Finding Tinakilly*: The estate is signposted and located on the main road between Rathnew Town and Wicklow Town—the T7.

Hunter's Hotel   RATHNEW

As leader of the Irish Nationalist Party, Charles Stewart Parnell often held small rallies at Hunter's Hotel during the 19th century. About 9 miles from here is Avondale, his former estate, with its magnificent 18th-century homestead. Parnell became famous for his fights in Westminster for Irish home rule and land reform. In his short lifetime, he took his fellow Irishmen's dreams of freedom and turned them into an attainable goal. Sadly, his career was marred by his love affair with Katie O'Shea, a married Irishwoman. It became the scandal of the time—and is talked about to this day.

It began on a July day in 1880 at London's House of Commons, to which the 34-year-old Parnell, a Protestant, had been elected to represent Ireland. During a land reform debate, this tall, handsome, but gaunt (from overwork) man was summoned from the assembly by a woman who had come expressly to meet him. She was sensuous, curvaceous Katie O'Shea. For months, she had been trying to lure Parnell to dinner parties she conducted for the purpose of advancing the career of her husband, Captain William (Willie) O'Shea.

Parnell's rage at having been called from the assembly suddenly vanished upon seeing her. It is said that from then on, he was hopelessly in love with her, and she, if not in love, was strongly attracted. It wasn't long before they embarked on a passionate affair. Captain O'Shea, a weakling, was unable to advance in any career without the aid of his wife and her rich aunt, who was their benefactress. Because of this, O'Shea was thrilled to see that his wife and Parnell were getting along so well (just how well, he didn't know).

Hunter's Hotel, County Wicklow

At this point, Parnell wanted Katie to divorce her husband, since she, too, was a Protestant. But she refused, knowing that her aunt would then disinherit her. In the spring of 1882, while Parnell was in Ireland, Katie had his first child. Somehow she was able to convince her husband that the child was his. Still trying to advance her husband's political career to keep him happy, she invited Parnell to visit them while they vacationed at Brighton. But instead of its achieving her purpose, it brought the love affair into the open. When Katie and her husband retired to their bedroom one evening, Parnell stormed into the room, lifted Katie from the bed, and carried her off to his own room, where he boldly made love to her.

Later, realizing how foolish he had been, Parnell tried to appease O'Shea by helping him get elected as the party's representative for Galway. It worked for a time. But when Katie's aunt died, Parnell and Katie decided they were free to live together. Willie became so furious that he sued for divorce in 1890. The scandal of the trial and the adulterous affair ruined Parnell's career. Although he struggled to stay in politics, traveling back and forth to Ireland, he became weak with exhaustion, contracted a fever, and in October 1891 died in Katie's loving arms.

"The belladonna lilies are in bloom," confided Maureen Gelletlie in a whisper as she peered over her James Joyce spectacles while puffing on a cigarillo and arranging a floral display in her lounge. "They are so beautiful," she trilled, and paused to admire them before offering tea beside an inlaid mahogany fireplace. The light of late afternoon sprinkled in through the trees and glittered across the high gloss of the thickplanked bare floor, catching in the brass of the turf scuttle. In the garden, a fine hand-lettered wooden sign read: LADIES AND GENTLEMEN WILL NOT, AND OTHERS MUST NOT, PICK THE FLOWERS. In the dim hallway, a look at the registry book revealed an entry for Charles Stewart Parnell, 19th-century Irish freedom fighter, and a reference to a gathering he had arranged here at Hunter's Hotel.

At this stage, you might look around and suddenly wonder if you have stepped into some mysterious time warp. The silence adds to the feeling. Even the voices of staff members seem to be coming from a distant age—so gentle and soft-spoken they are. This aura is all part of the natural wonder of Hunter's—one of the most unusual and interesting of all Ireland's lodgings. Everything about this place—from Mrs. Gelletlie to her staff to the furnishings, even the style of gardens—seems to be an anachronism.

When Mrs. Hunter opened this coaching inn in 1830, she believed its immediate success was due to "the courtesy and civility of the staff," said Mrs. Gelletlie. "And that's what we've maintained ever since." Now in the fifth generation of the same family, it was once the first night's stop for the stagecoach out of Dublin (32 miles away) on the southern route. The carriage trade didn't include "every Tom, Dick, and Harry but was the type of clientele who traveled with nannies and nursemaids," Mrs. Gelletlie noted, then went on to revel in the memories of what must have been. "In later years, they came by train. And in the Twenties, when cycling was in vogue, cycling clubs would stay here. Then there were the groups of serious walkers. They were lawyers and Trinity professors and that sort. Fine people. They'd walk from here to Glendalough [18 miles away] or the reservoir at Roundwood [a more modest 10 miles] to view the wildflowers and then return in the same day for their dinner. Oh, those were wonderful times." And wonderful they still are at Hunter's, with its evocative bar and lounge, hallways filled with memorabilia, and priceless garden sitting room.

DINING AT HUNTER'S: THERE IS NOTHING WHICH HAS YET BEEN CON-TRIVED BY MAN, BY WHICH SO MUCH HAPPINESS IS PRODUCED AS BY A GOOD INN. This quotation from Dr. Samuel Johnson appears in the rustic old dining room at Hunter's and underscores the pleasure of the time spent here. But it should be said right away that you don't come here if you expect haute cuisine. No, Hunter's, true to itself, offers you a hearty, truly wonderful, old-fashioned coaching-house meal—one that you will remember. Don't struggle over what to order. If you've had enough of oak-smoked trout or salmon in your Irish travels (although it is excellent here), try one of the best chicken liver pâtés ever, or sautéed calf's liver in sherry, or poached egg Florentine. The fresh vegetable soup with sweet corn (the corn is tender, sweet, and very fresh—unusual for Ireland) is a special treat.

As for entrees, there are those who rave about Hunter's poached salmon, insisting it's the finest in Ireland. A strong statement that, and unfortunately the author cannot attest to it, because it is not always on the menu. But other selections are notable. Codling and haddock are remarkably fresh and beautifully prepared. It's a toss-up among grilled minute steak (tender and succulent), unforgettably tasty roast chicken stuffed with Irish bacon, and pork cutlets (although they lose something in their unfortunate breaded state). If you want something to remember, try the basic-but-wonderful roast side of Irish lamb. Nothing detracts from its true majesty, and that's what a real coaching inn's dinner is all about. Afterward, savor the homemade caramel ice cream, although you probably will be torn between that and the fresh (from their own gardens) blackberry or apple tart. Meals are moderate to expensive, and wines are reasonably priced and good. Dinner is served from 7:30 to 9:30, lunch from 1 to 3. Afternoon tea is also served. Nonresidents are accepted, but reservations are suggested.

PARTICULARS: Hunter's (0404-40106) is open all year, has a full license, and accepts AmEx, Visa, Master, and Diners. Moderate in price, it has 17 bedrooms (7 with private bath) and breakfast is included. (U.S. agent: Robert Reid.) Hunter's modestly claims that it has all the Wicklow mountains at its feet, along with the wondrous sandy beaches of the Wicklow coast. But within these are opportunities for walking, climbing, driving, fishing, running, cycling, tennis, golf, horseback

riding. This is probably the most remarkable area of eastern Ireland—
one you could spend days savoring and not begin to see. *Finding Hunter's:* The inn is slightly (only slightly) north of the village of Rathnew
on the Dublin Road. If you're approaching from the south, there's a
turn to the right. If you blink, you'll miss it. It's signposted for Hunter's
Country House, and is just a short distance down that road. The hotel
is 36 miles from Dublin Airport.

Suggestions for Your Visit COUNTY WICKLOW

¶ You may have chosen one of the Rathnew lodgings for its proximity
to Dublin. The city is 30 fast miles on the N11 from Rathnew, making
it possible to travel back and forth with relative ease. Thus, you can
have both country and city. (For city touring ideas, see Suggestions in
chapter 12.)

¶ Don't think that the only attraction in this part of the country is
Dublin. Remember that County Wicklow is known as the Garden of
Ireland. Yet its sweeping woodlands, verdant glens, high granite mountains, and distant passes combine to make it one of the most remote
areas of Ireland. Other than the main Dublin Road (N11), most of the
county's roads, while paved, seem to transport you to a bygone age as
they wind narrowly through sparsely populated—often completely un-
populated—areas of extreme beauty.

One of the treasures of this county, and indeed of Ireland, is the
breathtaking valley of 2 lakes—**Glendalough** (16 miles from Rathnew).
Here, amid graceful mountains and the remarkable 6th-century remains
of St. Kevin's retreat and later monastic settlement, a sense of peace
descends. While there are a few tourist shops and often quite a few
tourists, you can escape them all—and you should, because that's what
Glendalough is all about. It's a wonderful place for strolling, hiking,
rock climbing, or just enjoying the remarkably refreshing quiet. It's also
an ideal locale for a picnic. There is a nonimposing hotel here, but the
food is undistinguished, so plan to carry a picnic if you're going to be
there at lunchtime, because there's little else around.

¶ Depending on how much time you spend in Glendalough, you
may want to return to Rathnew or you may want to tack on another
30 miles or so by taking the adventurous (narrow and lonely) but

Powerscourt House Gardens, County Wicklow

spectacularly beautiful high-mountain Military Road (L94), up through Sally Gap and on to Glencree. At Glencree, turn right for the pleasant little village of Enniskerry, with some interesting Irish fashion shops. Slightly south of here are the magnificent **Powerscourt Gardens and Waterfall**, with **Great Sugarloaf Mountain** as a backdrop. A fine 18th-century mansion was formerly part of the estate, but it was gutted by fire in 1974. The gardens, considered the finest in Ireland, are open daily from Easter to the end of October, 10 to 5:30. From here, follow the road to Roundwood, passing along the River Cloghoge, which links Lough Tay and Lough Dan. This is a moodily romantic drive. From Roundwood, take the road back to Rathnew.

¶ Another excursion from Rathnew is to the famous **Vale of Avoca**—14 miles to the south. On the way, you'll pass through the village of Rathdrum. One mile to the south is the **Avondale** estate and forest plantation—the birthplace in 1846 of the man dubbed the "uncrowned king of Ireland," Charles Stewart Parnell. This home was built in 1777 and is open daily from May 1 to August 30 from 2 to 6 and during September on Friday through Monday only from 2 to 6. A curator will point out the ornate ceilings, the furniture, and other articles associated with Parnell. The 523 magnificent forested acres have 2 nature trails that you may follow. And the Avonmore River rushes by, making this an ideal place to spend a couple of tranquil hours.

Continue on to the Vale of Avoca. Thomas Moore, the 19th-century Irish poet, wrote these immortal lines about the place:

> There is not in this wide world a valley so sweet
> As that vale in whose bosom the bright waters meet.

Moore was extolling the place where the rivers of **Avonbeg** and **Avonmore** meet to form the **Avoca River**. While the area is somewhat corrupted today by a restaurant and tourist shops, you can still sense the feeling of solitude that attracted Moore to this region.

In and near Avoca village are a number of craft shops that may be of interest. **Avoca Handweavers** weave wool and make it into garments and home furnishings before your eyes. Most of the finished items are for export, but the remainders are available for purchase. **Glenwood Crafts** is an interesting craft shop, and **Nicole Delahay** at Bank House does handweaving.

A couple of miles south of Avoca village is **Woodenbridge**, where there's another meeting of the waters. This time it's the Aughrim and Avoca rivers, and this is much more attractive than the spot immortalized by Moore. Imagine a sequestered valley with the blossoming wild fruit trees of early spring, mountains around it, gushing waters, the whistle of wind through the vernal landscape, and the scent of nature in bloom—then you have it. If you're hungry, the old **Woodenbridge Hotel**, with a quaint bar and an enormous stone fireplace, provides hearty traditional Irish lunches at inexpensive prices all year long.

From here, you can return to Rathnew the way you came or you can continue 5 miles into coastal **Arklow** and then take the N11 back to Rathnew. Arklow is famous for the **Arklow Pottery** factory, which produces fine china and earthenware (for sale in its warehouse shop).

NOTE: If you wish, you can combine the tours of Glendalough and the Vale of Avoca.

Luggala, County Wicklow

¶ Another journey (a relatively short one) from Rathnew is to go through Wicklow village (2 miles away) and take the coastal road (beautiful seascapes) to Wicklow Head (2 miles), then go on to Silver Strand. In 8 miles, you'll come to Jack's Hole (excellent for swimming), and just beyond is Brittas Bay (a 3-mile stretch of beach). From here, continue on to Mizen Head, then on the short distance to Arklow and back to Rathnew on the N11. (You could do this tour in connection with the Vale of Avoca rather than as separate journeys.)

¶ An even shorter journey is to **Mount Usher Gardens**, 2 miles north of Rathnew on the main Wicklow-to-Dublin Road (N11) at **Ashford**. Here there are 4,000 different species of trees, flowers, and shrubs from many parts of the world. The gardens are arranged handsomely on the banks of the River Vartry, with a spacious tearoom overlooking the river. You can visit here from March 17 through September, Monday through Saturday from 10:30 to 6, and Sunday from 2 to 6. The fee is inexpensive.

11
A MANOR IN
COUNTY KILDARE

Moyglare Manor

Irish history and legend are rife with stories of romance that are as varied as the Irish landscape. Certainly one of the strangest was one about Jonathan Swift (the onetime dean of Dublin's Protestant St. Patrick's Cathedral and author of *Gulliver's Travels*) and 2 very different ladies of his time. The results were tragic and left an eerily designed mansion in Celbridge (just a few miles down the road from Maynooth and Moyglare Manor) to be haunted to this day.

Dublin-born and educated in the city's Trinity College, Swift, by 1689 (when he was 22), had become secretary to an influential Englishman in Surrey, England. Here he met 8-year-old Esther Johnson and became her tutor. Wise beyond her years and quite charming, she formed a friendship with the idealistic young Swift that would bloom over the coming years. It was during this time that Swift was having a consuming affair with a beautiful woman his own age named Varina. With her, he shared his dreams and innermost thoughts, and he asked her to marry him. But, being the socal butterfly that she was, Varina moved on to other beaus, luring them to offer her their all and then dropping them. So crushed was Swift that his idealism began to crumble. Cynicism and bitterness began to shape his character.

In 1694, Swift was ordained and sent to serve in various areas of Ireland for the next 7 years. Unbearably lonely and still shattered, he wrote to his friend Esther Johnson, now a teenager. Esther was melancholy herself, and having just received a sizable inheritance, Swift suggested that she move to Ireland—never thinking that this woman, whom he was to call "Stella," would fall in love with him. But she did. And Swift, who had vowed never to have anything more to do with love, refused it, insisting that only friendship prevail.

During the early 1700s, Swift spent much of his time in England promoting the Tory party in hopes of currying favor to receive a more prestigious church appointment. It was during this time that his overwhelming sexual urges drew him to another Esther. This one was the beautiful and very sensual Esther Van Homrigh, whom he was to call "Vanessa"—perhaps to avoid confusing the 2 Esthers in his life. The pair embarked on the most passionate of sexual unions (from which letters still remain).

It is said that Swift felt the relationship was purely sexual. Vanessa, clever in knowing what her lover wanted, never revealed that it was anything but pure ecstasy. When he was appointed dean of St. Patrick's, Dublin, in 1713 (which greatly disappointed him, because he wanted something even grander), Vanessa followed him, using the ruse that she had to manage her deceased father's estate in Celbridge. Here she lived alone with her servants in what is today known as Celbridge Abbey (now it is the residence of the Hospitaller Brothers of St. John). This spooky, Gothic-style mansion, where Swift and Vanessa resumed their sexual activity, may be visited today. The rooms are weirdly shaped and thoroughly ominous. They meander, belying the enormous size of the building when viewed from the outside. There are still reports that the place is haunted. Why? From this point, the story becomes cloudy. Sifting through the various accounts, we learn that over the years Vanessa's love became more apparent as she realized that she would have to share Swift with another woman—Stella. As for Stella, she was far stronger emotionally than her Celbridge counterpart, and far more devout. Stella could accept a chaste relationship with Swift while knowing about his dalliances just a few miles from the city, because she lived from day to day and was grateful that Swift was a part of her life and her best friend.

Unfortunately, Vanessa spent her days away from Swift writing him passionate letters. He answered many of them, and even though he continued their irresistible affair, it never seemed enough for Vanessa. Eventually Swift became bitter, and when Vanessa made desperate advances, he tried to arrange a marriage for her with a neighbor. Ironically, this wounded her as deeply as Swift had been wounded with his first love affair. But Vanessa's escape was alcohol. Her melancholy deepened, and, even though she was in her mid-thirties, youth fled.

She slipped further and further from reality in that mansion in Celbridge. Then one warm early summer's day in 1723, Swift ended their affair.

Why? No one seemed to know, after so many years of compromising. One feasible answer is that Vanessa, who had never had any contact with Stella, wrote her a rambling letter expressing her undying passion for Swift and the fear that her depression, caused by Stella's existence, was killing her. Regardless of whether or not this account is true, a month after her separation from Swift, Vanessa died of a broken heart. Some years later, Swift's faithful Stella, whom he never allowed himself to love, also died. In 1745, slightly mad and also senile, Swift died and was laid to rest beside Stella in St. Patrick's Cathedral, Dublin.

There are 2 important features of **Moyglare Manor** that should be mentioned immediately. First is its proximity to Dublin. Only a 30-minute drive from Dublin, in Maynooth, County Kildare, this stately 18th-century Georgian home surrounded by 16 acres of pastoral grounds seems a million miles from the big city. So if you only have a few days and you want the country as well as the Dublin experience, this lodging is ideal.

Second, it's a cultural education to go to Moyglare. There are probably more antiques here than in most museums. For all its priceless wonders, however, the place is warm and human. And it has a marvelous restaurant to boot.

Built by the Tuttle family in the Georgian era, it passed from owner to owner, and in recent times had fallen into a state of disrepair. Onto this scene came hoteliers Norah Devlin and her daughter and son-in-law, Anne and Shay Curran. Even though they realized that the entire interior would have to be refurbished and furnished, they marveled at how wonderful it would look filled with superb Irish antiques. So they decided to sell their Barberstown Castle Hotel in Straffan, County Kildare, and begin anew.

Amazingly, within a year of rushing around the country to auctions, farmhouses, and antique shops, they filled Moyglare to overflowing with precious divans, overstuffed chairs, mahogany tables and cabinets, velveteen settees, old china, oils, and watercolors. The palatial bedrooms contain baths as large as most people's sitting rooms. The four-poster, tiered-canopy beds, the Regency wardrobes, and the cozy and plush armchairs set by the marble fireplaces will remain forever memorable.

After soaking in a spacious tub and drying with an enormous bath sheet, lounge in the giant bed, and watch the glitter of the turn-of-the-century crystal candlesticks in the soft pink glow of the room.

DINING AT MOYGLARE: There are exceptionally fine seafoods here in this intimate room, presided over by chef Jim Cullinannon. The prawns and the salmon seem to have leaped from the sea to the plate. The poultry and meats are especially good—particularly the tender steaks. And the sauces—above all the hollandaise—are so delicious that they taste as if they're prepared after the order is taken, and most likely are. Vegetarians could easily make a superb meal out of the splendid offerings of potatoes, turnips, celery, baby carrots, and crispy salads. The lovely fresh fruits and the cheese board are very worthwhile. As a matter of fact, it's worth eating here even if you're not able to stay. But be sure to make a reservation, because this grand Old World dining room, with its romantic candlelit atmosphere, is very popular and intimately small. Prices are moderate to expensive and there's a fine wine list. Dinner is served from 7 to 10, lunch (Sunday only) from 12:30 to 2:15.

PARTICULARS: The good news here is that Moyglare Manor (01-286351) is open year-round. It has a full license and accepts AmEx, Visa, and Diners. It's expensive—with 11 bedrooms, all with bath and breakfast included. (U. S. agent: Robert Reid.) Traditional music is provided in the basement lounge on weekends. Because of Moyglare's proximity to Dublin, its romantic appeal, and the fact that there are so few bedrooms, it is frequently fully booked, even in the off-season, so reserve early. Freshwater fishing is available nearby, and hunts may be arranged through the manor. There are several famous racecourses nearby—including Punchestown, Naas, Phoenix Park, The Curragh, and Fairyhouse— plus riding facilities in the area. The flat terrain makes it ideal for running or long walks. *Finding Moyglare:* From Dublin, take the T3— Dublin-Sligo Road. In about 30 minutes, you arrive in Maynooth. Drive through the village and follow the main road to the right. From this point, proceed straight ahead. This will take you off the T3 and onto the narrower Moyglare Road. In 2 miles, you will reach the manor.

Suggestions for Your Visit   COUNTY KILDARE

¶ With Moyglare's closeness to **Dublin**, certainly you will want to spend a day (or perhaps several days) touring this splendid European city. (For guidance, see Suggestions in chapter 12.)

¶ You don't have to feel that you must spend every waking moment in Dublin while you're staying in Maynooth. There's much of interest in the environs. First of all, if you do nothing more than sit by the marble fireplace in the manor's lounge, inhaling the aroma of limewood logs and sipping a sherry or a cup of Irish tea, you will have found one of Moyglare Manor's richest rewards. Leave plenty of time to enjoy the stunning array of antiques and the finely pargeted ceilings. A stroll around the grounds and down the tree-lined entry road is refreshing and peaceful.

¶ Venturing out a couple of miles into Maynooth village, you may want to visit the remains of **Maynooth Castle** and the neighboring **St. Patrick's College**. In ancient times, Maynooth was one of the seats of the Geraldine/Fitzgerald family. The castle has a 2-story keep that dates from the 13th century. It acquired towers in the 15th century, but they were destroyed by the O'Neills, who stormed the Geraldine stronghold in 1647. The gate tower still remains as a fine example of the original edifice.

Beside the castle is the college, which was established in 1795 and occupies the grounds of an earlier college founded by the Earl of Kildare in the 16th century. The college now is part of the **National University of Ireland**. Of both Renaissance and Gothic design, it is regarded as one of the greatest Catholic seminaries in Europe.

On the grounds of St. Patrick's College, in what is known as the House of Rhetoric, you will note references to the Room of Death. This was Room No. 2, on the second floor, where so many uncanny events occured during the 1840s that the priests and young seminarians came to live in terror. It all began when a despondent student who occupied this dormitory room committed suicide by slashing his wrists with a razor. The reason? There are those who said he had the mind of a genius and found he could not resolve his inner conflicts with the Catholic doctrine. Others suggested that he had fallen in love with a beautiful local girl and that after their relationship had been consummated, his mental anguish over abandoning his religious principles drove him over the brink. Two other sins-of-the-flesh versions allege that he was having an affair with a fellow seminarian and that he was involved sexually with both the seminarian and the local girl.

After the young man had gone to his grave, a new student was assigned to this room. Soon thereafter, he began to feel himself under a spell. Priests and fellow students insisted that it was his imagination, but imagination or not, the possession became so beguiling that he ceased talking about it and began to withdraw. Then one day he committed suicide in the room by slashing his wrists. Naturally, officials were most anxious to cover up this tragedy and suppress speculation, so they maintained it was a coincidence.

While many doubted this, there was no question that something was wrong when a third student was assigned to the room and came under the same irresistible spell. On the verge of slashing his own wrists, he summoned enough strength to throw himself out the window. Though injured, he saved his life and brought far more attention to the matter. Priests then kept vigil in the room and reported the appearance and disappearance of bloodstains on the walls and floor. One priest who spent a night in the room refused to comment on the happenings, but his hair turned snow white by dawn.

After this, college trustees insisted that the front wall of the room be removed and that the room's interior be transformed into an Oratory of St. Joseph, which may be visited to this day. Whether or not this intended exorcism worked, some say the area still remains haunted.

¶ Also in Maynooth is the early 18th-century **Carton House**. Originally it was built in the 17th century by the Talbot family, who leased the land from the Fitzgeralds. Years later, the Fitzgeralds acquired the house and employed architect Richard Castle to rebuild the house completely into the stately mansion it is today. The sweeping exterior, with bays and Venetian windows, and the interior with its splendid rooms, including a saloon with an intricately pargeted ceiling, make this one of Ireland's finest homes. Queen Victoria once slept in its ground-floor Chinese bedroom, and Lord Edward Fitzgerald, leader of the United Irish Movement, spent much of his childhood here. The house is open to the public Sunday afternoon during the summer months.

¶ A few miles down the road from Maynooth is **Celbridge** village, site of **Castletown House**. This magnificent Palladian-style mansion, with twin pavilions, is considered one of Ireland's largest and most architecturally important houses. It was built for William Conolly, the speaker of the Irish House of Commons, and designed by Italian architect Alessandro Galilei, who strove for beauty, serenity, and ro-

Carton House, County Kildare

Castletown House, County Kildare

mance. Construction began in 1715. The interior contains the finest reception rooms in the country. The earliest ones are wood paneled, while the later neoclassical ones, decorated by Sir William Chambers, contain geometric plasterwork ornamentation. The grand staircase, made of cantilevered stone with a dramatic brass balustrade, was erected in 1760. The entire house is magnificently furnished with 18th-century furniture and art. It is open to the public (for a very small fee) April through September (Wednesday, Saturday, and Sunday from 2 to 6) and October through March (Sunday from 2 to 5). Tea and homemade scones are served during the afternoon in The Old Servants Dining Hall. If you wish to return in the evening for a more romantic dining experience, the **West Wing Victorian Kitchen Restaurant** (01-288502) is open for your pleasure. This original kitchen once produced meals for the Conolly family and their guests, as well as the more than one hundred servants. Here you sit by open fires in candlelight and listen to a harpist as you're served good Irish fare. Dinner is served from 8 to midnight, and the restaurant has a wine license. Reservations are advised. AmEx is accepted and prices are moderate.

Also in Celbridge is **Celbridge Abbey**, built in the latter part of the 17th century by shipping entrepreneur Bartholomew Van Homrigh, a Dutch immigrant. Here, at this weird, mazelike mansion and its adjoining grounds, Jonathan Swift and Van Homrigh's daughter, Esther (whom Swift called "Vanessa") engaged in their torrid, tragic love affair—a story detailed at the beginning of this chapter.

12 PAST/PRESENT—
THE ELEGANT LODGINGS
OF DUBLIN

The Shelbourne Hotel
DUBLIN CITY

He was alone. He was unheeded, happy and near to the wild heart
of life. He was alone and young and wilful and wildhearted, alone
amid a waste of wild air and brackish waters and the seaharvest of
shells and tangle and veiled grey sunlight and gayclad lightclad figures, of children and girls and voices childish and girlish in the air.

A girl stood before him in midstream, alone and still, gazing out
to sea. She seemed like one whom magic had changed into the like-
ness of a strange and beautiful seabird. Her long slender bare legs
were delicate as a crane's and pure save where an emerald trail of
seaweed had fashioned itself as a sign upon the flesh. Her thighs,
fuller and softhued as ivory, were bared almost to the hips where the
white fringes of her drawers were like featherings of soft white down.
Her slateblue skirts were kilted boldly about her waist and dovetailed
behind her. Her bosom was as a bird's soft and slight, slight and soft
as the breast of some darkplumaged dove. But her long fair hair
was girlish: and touched with the wonder of mortal beauty, her
face. . . .

—Heavenly God! cried Stephen's soul, in an outburst of profane
joy.

—James Joyce
A Portrait of the Artist as a Young Man

Without question, The Shelbourne Hotel is Dublin's grande dame and
has been so ever since it opened back in 1824. Ideally located overlooking magnificent St. Stephen's Green, this stately and imposing
structure of red brick and gleaming white trim was created to attract

visiting landed gentry from the country as well as the crème de la crème of European society. Many of these came to love the Shelbourne, thinking of it as quaintly romantic and imparting a sense of rustic elegance.

During the Easter Rising of 1916, British troops garrisoned the hotel and forced the guests to sleep in the halls. A far happier day came in 1922, when the constitution for the Irish Free State was drafted in a sitting room here.

In 1842, the famed English writer William Makepeace Thackeray (*Vanity Fair*) stayed here for six shillings and eightpence a day, which he considered very moderate. For this, he commented, he was provided with "a copious breakfast in the coffee room, a perpetual luncheon is likewise there spread, a plentiful dinner is ready at six o'clock; after which there is a drawing room and a rubber of whist [card game] with *tay* and coffee and cakes in plenty."

Shelbourne Hotel, Dublin

While the prices could hardly remain the same today, the 19th-century charm of the Shelbourne remains. Rebuilt in the late 1800s with a strong Victorian flair, and with a pair of Nubian princesses guarding its entrance, it has expanded since to include the neighboring Georgian townhouses. Its first-floor public rooms—the Horseshoe Bar, the Shelbourne Restaurant, the drawing room, and the splendid, newly renovated foyer—still attract a cross section of high society. But it's the drawing room that so strongly reflects the Old World elegance of the hotel. This very spacious, high-ceilinged room—with its Waterford chandelier, oversized gilt mirrors, marvelous clusters of settees, over-stuffed lounging chairs, antique tables, enormous windows overlooking the green, and waiters in constant, though unobtrusive, attendance—epitomizes luxurious indulgence and is perfect for a leisurely afternoon tea. It looks much the same as it did when the poet Yeats held court with his friends. Recently the rest of the public rooms, including the entrance and reception area, were lavishly refurbished in the grand Georgian style with fireplaces, marble, and fabric.

The bedrooms at the Shelbourne vary from large to small, from antique-filled to modern (in the newer wing). Of course, the most desirable are those furnished with antiques and facing on the green, so you would do well to request those in advance.

DINING AT THE SHELBOURNE: The Aisling Restaurant is the city's grandest old dining room. It's a high, molded-ceilinged room with another fine old chandelier. The walls are dark-flocked and adorned with enormous Victorian oil paintings. Each evening, a pianist plays soft, unobtrusive, yet romantic music, which enhances the grace of the room. Here you'll find superbly prepared meals. Recommended are the seafood appetizers, especially the zesty shellfish ones. As for the entrees, especially good are the crab dishes, baked scallops, veal, and Tournedos Shelbourne. Lunch is served from 12:30 to 2:30, dinner from 6:30 to 10:30. It is expensive, with excellent moderate to expensive wines.

PARTICULARS: The Shelbourne Hotel (01-766471) is open all year and has a full license. It is expensive, and breakfast is not included. All major credit cards are accepted. There are 166 bedrooms, all with bath and phone, as well as some suites. (U.S. agents: Trusthouse Forte [Ireland]; Utell International.) The hotel has a garage, a barbershop, and a small but helpful gift shop (good for small items and books of Irish interest). *Finding the Shelbourne:* It faces St. Stephen's Green and is Number 27.

The Berkeley Court Hotel   DUBLIN CITY

If I give you a golden ball,
To play with the gypsies in the hall,
Will you marry, marry, marry, marry,
Will you marry me?
     —Anonymous
        Dublin children's street chant

. . . O and the sea the sea crimson sometimes like fire and the glo-
rious sunsets and the figtrees in the Alameda gardens yes and all the
queer little streets and pink and blue and yellow houses and the rose-
gardens and the jessamine and geraniums and cactuses and Gibraltar
as a girl where I was a Flower of the mountain yes when I put the
rose in my hair like the Andalusian girls used or shall I wear a red
yes and how he kissed me under the Moorish wall and I thought
well as well him as another and then I asked him with my eyes to
ask again yes and then he asked me would I yes to say yes my mountain flower and first I put my arms around him yes and drew him
down to me so he could feel my breasts all perfume yes and his heart
was going like mad and yes I said yes I will Yes.

                                        —James Joyce
                                          Ulysses

    The late P.V. Doyle was Ireland's leading hotelier. Some years ago,
he reached the conclusion that what Ireland did not need was just
another new hotel—the type that could be dropped into any of the
cities in the Western world and blend right into the area. Instead,
Doyle's idea was to create a grand hotel in the Old World manner,
maintaining a graceful ambience while at the same time offering modern
amenities. The Berkeley Court, which opened in 1978, is his creation,
and it certainly is not just another hotel.
    From the moment you walk into its vastly spacious lobby, with its
emphasis on white marble, strikingly beautiful period furniture, enormous antique brass planters, chandeliers, and plush carpeting, you'll
sense its grand-hotel qualities. You could spend a good deal of time
lounging in this palatial ground-floor elegance. Pause for a drink in the
stately yet comfortable Royal Court, with its rich, dark paneling, fireplace, and caned chairs. Or try the summery Conservatory Bar, with

plants and curved-panel glass walls overlooking the trees and flowers adorning the grounds.

The bedrooms and suites are furnished with some antiques and copies of period furniture, such as half-canopied beds and wing chairs. In a recently added wing, there are 5 suites, 3 with Jacuzzi baths and king-sized beds.

DINING AT THE BERKELEY COURT: Ornamented with pastoral oil paintings, The Berkeley Room achieves serene elegance yet retains a sense of intimate dining. Tables covered in white Irish linen and set with white gold-rimmed china and vases of flowers, and cozy, antique tapestry-backed chairs help achieve this mood. Fine foods are in abundance here. The avocado stuffed with Dublin Bay prawns is a favored starter. Popular seafood entrees are fresh seafood platters of prawns, oysters, and mussels; wine-poached sole; and cider-baked plaice with mushroom puree. The fillets of beef, either plain or with a rich red-wine sauce, are very good choices. The wine list is good and moderate to expensive, as are the meals. Lunch is served from 12:30 to 2:30 and dinner from 6:30 to 10:30.

Also here is the new and extremely attractive Conservatory Grill, with its Victorian style and garden atmosphere. Here you can order Irish smoked salmon, roast ribs of beef, roast duckling, and fresh seafood dishes—all good and at moderate prices. It's open from 7:30 A.M. (for hearty Irish breakfasts) to 11:30 P.M.

PARTICULARS: The Berkeley Court (01-601711) is open year-round and has a full license. It is expensive, and breakfast is not included. There are 262 rooms, all with bath and phone. It accepts all major credit cards. (U.S. agents: Doyle Hotel Group; Leading Hotels of the World Group—one of the two Irish hotels listed by this select association; Loews Representation International; Utell International.) The hotel has an indoor heated swimming pool and sauna, as well as the Berkeley Shops, an arcade complete with an elegant jewelry store, a craft boutique, and men's and women's hair stylists. There's a garage as well as a car park. *Finding the Berkeley Court*: It's in the Ballsbridge section of Dublin, just behind Jurys Hotel, on the secluded and eminently Victorian Lansdowne Road.

The Westbury Hotel   DUBLIN CITY

Play on, invisible harps, unto Love
Whose way in heaven is aglow
At this hour when soft lights come and go
Soft sweet music in the air above
And the earth below.
                    —James Joyce
                    Chamber Music

Often in the evening when the stars were still pale in the sky, the boys would see the girls skipping at the other end of the street, as many as ten or fifteen of them jumping gracefully over a regularly turning rope. The boys would slink up nearer and nearer to the skipping girls, the girls would occasionally glance disdainfully at the boys, but in their hearts they wished them to come closer. With a defiant shout, weakened with the tones of a shy shame in it, a boy, bolder than the rest, would jump in merrily; the rest would follow him, and joyous faces of boys and girls would shine out of thin dusty clouds raised out of the road by the beating of skippers' feet dancing in the way of peace.

Tired of skipping, someone would suggest a ring; and boys and girls, their shyness gone, would join hands in a great ring. . . .

Shy, grey-eyed Jennie Clitheroe, with her curly head hanging, stood before Johnny. He wished she hadn't picked on him, for a lot in the ring knew he was gone on her, and had seen his uncovered eye often seeking her out as she sat on the seat opposite in the Sunday school; and his face went scarlet as he heard the titters of the ring.

Chase him all round Dublin, chase him all round Dublin,
    chase him all round Dublin,
As you have done before.

Johnny made off round the circle of players, dodging in and out under the upraised arms, with Jennie hotfoot after him. For a while he kept well in front, then slowed down so that she could catch him, but dodging her at the last moment so that she had to fling an arm round him. Pretending to struggle, he managed to give her girlish body a sudden and affectionate pressure, releasing her at once when the ring shouted Oh Johnny, fie for shame!

So in a cute and gentle way, this play and these songs touched the time when the girl would long to let him kiss her with kisses of his mouth and his banner over her would be love.
                    —Sean O'Casey
                    I Knock at the Door

Having accomplished one major feat—The Berkeley Court Hotel— Ireland's major hotelier, P.V. Doyle, set to work on another, and completed it before his untimely death. The Westbury, while quite different from The Berkeley Court, was designed on the same principle of Old World, grand hotel ambience and was opened in 1984 in the romantic heart of Dublin just off St. Stephen's Green.

Don't be misled by the façade of The Westbury, which looks too modern for its environs. The opulent interiors feature long foyers of cream and soft red marble filled with antiques, period reproductions, and glittering chandeliers. A popular gathering spot is the elegant Terrace Room and Polo Bar, with period reproduction furniture, wonderful old Dublin prints, and a background of statuesque plants. Intimate, tranquil Dublin cocktail lounges are often difficult to find—and a lounge that serves a fine afternoon tea is even rarer. The Westbury lounge maintains a quiet European sophistication ideal for a lovely and quiet chat. It's just another reason why this hotel works so well—it fulfills a need. The bedrooms are luxurious, furnished with wonderful antique reproductions—another lovely touch that makes this a superb new hotel.

DINING AT THE WESTBURY: A sense of lightness and elegance pervades the hotel's fine Russell Room. Among the array of starters are seafood Newburg in a pastry shell, Dublin Bay prawns, chicken liver pâté with Cumberland sauce, smoked salmon and—if you really want to splurge— Sevruga caviar. Good soups include prawn with cream and brandy, and beef consommé with truffles. For entrees, the veal dishes here are excellent (perhaps because of the Swiss-trained chef). They include escalope of veal panfried and topped with ham, Gruyère cheese, and sliced mushrooms; sautéed fillets of veal served in lemon juice and ginger sauce; and strips of veal in a white wine cream sauce with mushrooms and onions. Other fine entrees are slices of beef fillet flamed in brandy and served with black peppercorns; freshly boned fillet steak, grilled and served with asparagus wrapped in bacon and topped with mushroom and Madeira sauce; loin of lamb with green peppercorn sauce; rack of lamb; fillet of sea trout with mornay sauce; lobster cooked in mustard and cream and glazed with cheese in shell; lobster with Cognac and cream; fresh salmon and prawns served with vermouth and white wine sauce; scallops in a light tarragon sauce; grilled black sole. The moderate-to-expensive wines are good and special. Lunch, served 7 days a week from 12:45 to 2:30, is moderate. Monday through Saturday, dinner is served from 7 to 10:30; on Sunday, from 7 to 9:30. It ranges from moderate to expensive.

The hotel also boasts the wonderful Sandbar, which is beautifully designed like an old Dublin pub. Here you'll find fresh seafood quiche, fisherman's platter, smoked salmon with brown bread, crabmeat and prawn cocktail, lobster cocktail, grilled steaks, and a duckling casserole with a sauce of red wine, mushrooms, bacon, and onions. There's also a cold buffet of Irish ribs of beef, baked ham, or roast turkey. The food is good and inexpensive. Lunch is from 12:30 to 2:30 and dinner from 6 to 10:45, but this restaurant is closed Sunday.

PARTICULARS: The Westbury (01-791122) is open all year and has a full license. It is expensive, and breakfast is not included, but all major credit cards are accepted. There are 134 rooms, all with bath, phone, and color TV—as well as suites with Jacuzzis. There is a **Best of Irish** shop in The Westbury, which stocks the finest Irish craft and clothing items. There are also underground parking facilities. (U.S. agents: Doyle Hotel Group; Leading Hotels of the World Group; Loews Representation International; Utell International.) *Finding the Westbury*: It's just off Grafton Street and behind St. Stephen's Green—in the most attractive section of Dublin City.

──────

Suggestions for Your Visit   DUBLIN CITY

¶ The important thing to remember about **Dublin** is that it's an exciting old European city with an abundance of memorable places to see and things to do—far too abundant for a short stay. Perhaps that's part of the city's appeal: It leaves you longing for more, thinking you'll have to come back here again. And that puts Dublin on the elite list of the world's most captivating cities. It's fascinating to wander its twisting streets and lanes, getting lost, finding treasures. And it's better to walk than drive, because parking is almost impossible and it's easy to get very lost and exasperated in this bustling city's traffic.

To acquaint yourself with Dublin, you may wish to take one of the inexpensive but well-documented half-day bus tours operated by C.I.E., The Irish Transport Company (787777), from Busaras (bus station),

Amiens Street, or by Dublin City Tours (766887) from 3 Wilton Place, near Baggot Street Bridge.

¶ If a bus tour isn't for you, the Irish Tourist Board publishes a booklet called the *Tourist Trail*. This is a walking guide to all the spots of historic interest on the signposted trail through Dublin. You can pick up the booklet at tourist offices, newsagents, and bookstores. One of the most romantic things to do is to stroll through **St. Stephen's Green**, which is adjacent to the Shelbourne Hotel, a very brief walk from the Westbury, and about a 15-minute walk from the Berkeley Court. This placid, well-kept park—with gazebos, duck ponds, a children's playground, shade trees, quiet gardens, and convenient benches—is quite charming. Donated to the city by Sir Arthur Guinness in 1880 and favored by writer James Joyce, the green was once the heart of Georgian Dublin. The statues of Irish freedom fighters here and there are a continuing reminder of an earlier day, and of the fact that the real Irish cause is—and always has been—peace. It's the sort of place that's pleasant in all types of weather, because it takes on a variety of beguiling moods.

An equally romantic park, although considerably farther away (you might want to take a quick bus or a taxi), is the 2,000-acre **Phoenix Park**. One of Europe's largest, it makes New York's Central Park look like a postage stamp. This absolutely beautiful, ancient tree-scaped terrain encompasses an unusually open zoo (where animals and birds are sensibly given freedom to roam), gardens that match the likes of anything in western Europe or America, a racecourse, a polo ground, and even a cricket pitch. Cattle still graze in some areas of this mammoth park, and late in the evening, you're quite likely to encounter the almost-extinct-in-Ireland deer. Take the time to enjoy one of the park's hillside benches overlooking vast expanses of Irish greenery, which is like none other in the world.

¶ Georgian architecture characterizes **Merrion Square**, said by many Irish historians and writers to contain the finest of this period's architecture in Europe. There are some magnificent buildings here, with stately wine-colored, vine-covered brick façades and fanlighted doorways. Be sure to examine the mammoth doors themselves: Some are plain, some ornate, some are painted in bright colors, while others bear a rich natural-mahogany finish. Their brass hardware is a treasure. Behind these doors once lived Oscar Wilde, William Butler Yeats, and the Irish freedom fighters Daniel O'Connell and Charles Stewart Parnell.

If this has only whetted your appetite, you may wish to stroll down **Fitzwilliam Street**, a few blocks southeast, to linger over the smaller, but very beautiful, **Fitzwilliam Square**. Few of these Georgian townhouses remain private residences. Most have long since been converted into office buildings, but their exteriors provide a vivid reminder of the grace of an age gone forever.

¶ Dublin has many fine museums and libraries, all of which have their points of interest. If you're an art lover, no doubt you will find these among the most appealing:

- **The National Gallery**, on Leinster Lawn in Merrion Square, seems straight from the pages of James Joyce. Opened in 1864, the building houses works of Renaissance masters, along with those of Rubens, Van Dyck, Goya, El Greco, and Murillo. In the Irish section are paintings by John Butler Yeats (W.B. Yeats's father), Walter Osborne, and Sir John Lavery. It's open all year (free admission) from 10 to 6 weekdays and Saturday (open till 9 on Thursday) and from 2 to 5 on Sunday. (There are tours on Sunday at 2:30 and 3:45.) If you're hungry while here, the **National Gallery Restaurant** (also known as Fitzers) offers tasty meat and fish dishes (especially good are the crab pâté and the roast beef). The menu is varied and there's a wine license. Open for lunch and dinner during gallery hours, the restaurant also serves morning and afternoon tea. Prices are inexpensive to moderate; AmEx, Diners, Master, and Visa are accepted.

- **The National Museum**, on Kildare Street, houses all the major ancient art finds, including prehistoric goldwork, the Cross of Cong, the Tara Brooch, the Ardagh Chalice, Viking artifacts from the oldest section of Dublin City, and collections of Irish silver, glass, and Belleek china. It's open all year—Tuesday through Saturday from 10 to 5 and Sunday from 2 to 5. Admission is free.

- The 16th-century **Trinity College** on College Green, with its most enjoyable Parliament Square and the library housing the legendary Book of Kells, is a must. The book, a masterpiece of Celtic art, is believed to date from the 8th century. It depicts the gospels magnificently in text and illuminations. The library is open all year from 10 to 5 weekdays and 10 to 1 Saturday. It's closed Sunday.

- **The Chester Beatty Library**, at 20 Shrewsbury Road in the Ballsbridge section, offers examples of New Testament manuscripts, picture scrolls, Manichaean papyri, Far Eastern jades, rhinoceros horn cups, and Chinese snuff bottles. It's free and open year-round from 10 to 1 and 2:30 to 5:30 Tuesday through Friday and from 2:30 to 5:30 on Saturday.

¶ **Shopping** in Dublin is a must on most Dublin tourists' lists, and there are plenty of special little places to meet your needs. There are 2 major shopping areas (along with a few offshoots) of particular interest to visitors. All are within a stone's throw of one another. Most of the shops in these areas accept AmEx, Master, and Visa; some accept Diners.

The Powerscourt Townhouse Shopping Centre, covering the block from William to Clarendon streets, is an exciting new shopping complex created within the vast 4-story Georgian townhouse of Lord Powerscourt, which was built in 1774. (One American counterpart of this center is Boston's spectacular Quincy Market in the Faneuil Hall area.) Powerscourt's magnificent plasterwork ceiling (which documents the country's transition from the rococo to the neoclassical period) and its grand exterior attest to its status as one of the country's finest examples of Georgian architecture. But the shops within—along with a few very pleasant and reasonable dining places—make this a special treasure. There's a wonderful level containing 9 antiques shops, offering furniture, crystal, jewelry, home furnishings, silver, goldwork, original oils, and maps. Another level is devoted to Dublin's young craftsmen and features woodwork, leatherwork, prints, batik fashions, stoneware, porcelain, and jewelry. Dozens of other boutiqes stock Belleek, Royal Tara china, Donegal tweeds, linens, tweed caps and hats, and gourmet foods (jams, smoked salmon and trout, wine, excellent Irish cheeses). By all means, save several hours for Powerscourt, which is streets ahead of any other shopping center in Ireland. While you shop or dine, musicians play in the open center of Powerscourt's first floor so people on all the tiers of the complex can enjoy them.

Among the restaurants at Powerscourt are **The Periwinkle** (one of Dublin's best new mini-restaurants, with nautical decor against a gleaming white background; fast-but-delicious seafood such as crabmeat sandwiches, shrimp rolls, periwinkles, salads, plus zesty wines—all inexpensive; open 11 to 6 daily, closed Sunday); **Timmerman's Wine Bistro** (in the original vaulted kitchen of Viscount Powerscourt's Dublin home with church pew seating; odd yet cozy restaurant serving hearty homemade soups, excellent seafood salads, pasta dishes, and good wines at relatively inexpensive prices; AmEx and Visa accepted; open from 11 A.M. to 11 P.M.—11:30 P.M. during summer—Sunday, all year, noon to 10; entertainment nightly—folk ballads, jazz, bluegrass); **The Pink Bicycle** (unique self-service place; homemade soups, salads, tacos, hot chicken dishes, and desserts; you can sip wine on balcony terraces overlooking the Powerscourt Centre, while an ever-changing parade of musicians entertains far below; inexpensive; open from 11 to 6 daily, except Sunday).

When you're ready to leave Powerscourt, take the Clarendon Street exit. Cross Clarendon to **Johnston Court** and meander down this small, European-style lane where aspiring young musicians play tin whistles and violins; visit the little antique jewelry stores as you move toward Grafton Street.

When you come to **Grafton Street**, you are in the heart of Dublin's other major shopping area. **Brown Thomas** and **Switzers** are opposite one another here. Few Irishmen, or anyone who knows Ireland, would deny that these are 2 of the country's finest department stores. Switzers

Shopping for crystal at Brown Thomas, Dublin

is usually bustling, while Brown Thomas has a leisurely, boutiquelike atmosphere and carries everything from Irish high fashions, tweeds, and knitwear to china, crystal, linens, lace, crafts, and Irish gourmet foods.

After this, you might like to stop at **Bewley's** for a masterful cup of coffee and a sugary currant bun (see Special Restaurants, chapter 14).

While there are many other shops on Grafton Street, special attention should be paid to **Weirs**. This shop opened in 1869 (you can still see the original door with its frosted-glass lettering) and still offers an excellent selection of china, crystal, jewelry, clocks and watches, pens, leather goods—but above all else, superb hallmarked antique Irish silver and china. Also antique jewelry.

Off Grafton Street are several other narrow, short streets of shopping interest: **Anne Street, Duke Street, Anne's Lane, Duke Lane.** Here you'll find tiny craft and antiques shops, pubs, and little cafes.

At the foot of Grafton Street's slope, you'll see Nassau Street to the right. Follow it along, opposite the gardens of Trinity College, and you'll pass the **Genealogy Bookshop** (which may be of interest if you're into tracing family roots) and later the **Free Hanna Bookshop**, with fine books of Irish interest. Next you'll come to the corner of Nassau and Dawson streets, where you'll see **The House of Ireland**. This large, boutiquelike complex houses a wide variety of high-quality items under one roof. These include crystal (Waterford, Galway, Cavan, Silver Crystal); china and porcelain (Belleek, Lladro, Wedgwood, Aynsley, Noritake, Royal Tara); fashions (Aran knitwear, kilts, sweaters, tweeds, linens, mohair capes, shawls, and rugs); Irish crafts (Celtic jewelry, pewter, shillelaghs, character dolls, family crests). Just up Dawson Street from here is **Fergus O'Farrell**, a small craft shop with Irish pottery, ceramics, and a special emphasis on carved wooden figures of many of Ireland's legendary personalities.

Backtracking to the **St. Stephen's Green** area and the nearby Westbury Hotel (whose own fine shop, **Best of Irish** has already been noted), there's the **Westbury Mall**, attached to the hotel. This conservatory-type shopping area houses 20 elegant shops offering antiques and fine jewelry.

Near the Shelbourne is one of the city's most fashionable new shops, **Cleo's** on Kildare Street. Here Kitty Joyce and Marie Murtagh offer elegant country tweeds and handknits made to their own specifications and designs for both men and women. The shop, which also carries some unusual children's wear, has another branch across from The Park Hotel in Kenmare, County Kerry.

Farther out in the **Ballsbridge** area—especially for those staying at the Berkeley Court on Lansdowne Road (which, as has already been mentioned, has its own fine Berkeley Shops)—there's another special shop in nearby Jurys Hotel called **Shop at Jurys**. The shop prides itself on undercutting everyone. The tweed jackets are less expensive than in most other shops. So are the Blarney sweaters (even cheaper than at the Blarney headquarters), the fisherman knits (and of better quality), the Belleek, in some cases even the Waterford crystal. The fine assortment of Irish jewelry is several Irish pounds lower than in the Dublin City shops. Also, there's a selection of books of Irish interest. This place is a real find. It's open from 8 A.M. to midnight.

Again for those of you staying at the Berkeley Court (patrons of the Shelbourne and the Westbury may wish to seek this out as well), as you walk toward St. Stephen's Green, first following Lansdowne Road then crossing the major Merrion Road and walking along Pembroke Road (with fine restaurants), you'll come to Baggot Street Bridge. On the canal here in Bridge House is one of the world's most delightful bookstores—**Parsons**. This is about a 10-minute walk from the Berkeley Court; it's another 5 minutes to St. Stephen's Green. Run by Miss May O'Flaherty and opened little more than 35 years ago, this place has an aura of old literary Dublin that no other bookshop in the city achieves. Although small and cramped, it houses a wealth of material by Irish writers—as well as by the rest of the world's finest writers. If you love books, this is a place to savor. There's a special timelessness about it. As you browse, you almost expect a gaunt but dapper James Joyce to walk in, hat cocked back on his head, or to glimpse bespectacled young William Butler Yeats hovering over ancient folkloristic volumes in the corner. Parsons has exerted a magnetic pull on Irish writers almost since the day it opened, as Miss O'Flaherty and her associate, Miss Mary King, will tell you. Brendan Behan, Frank O'Connor, and Liam O'Flaherty all used to drop by—and never wanted to leave. The Monaghan writer Patrick Kavanagh visited here daily. Today you're likely to see the current crop of fine Irish writers drifting in—among them Benedict Kiely, Seamus Heaney, Thomas Kinsella, and John Montague. But for all this, there isn't a hint of snobbishness. It's as natural and unassuming as a country bookshop. Yet its charm and grace will strike you the moment your eyes alight on its old brick façade and fine display windows. This place truly is a treasure.

Other than the antiques shops at **Weirs** of Grafton Street and the **Powerscourt Townhouse Shopping Centre**, there are many other fine sources of antiques in Dublin. Some of the best include:

- South Anne Street: **H. & E. Danker**, No. 10, silver, jewelry, paintings, Georgian tea sets. **Dillon Antiques**, No. 27, 18th- and 19th-century Irish and English furniture, glass, china, silver, watercolors, oils. Picture gallery on first floor. Specialists in exporting items to the United States. **Rembrandt Antiques**, No. 24, good porcelain, ceramics, Belleek, small silver items, jewelry, treenware (woodware). Very large stock. **M. Samuels**, No. 12, antique silver and jewelry, old Belleek, porcelain, Victorian jewelry. **J.W. Weldon**, No. 18, Irish and English silver, jewelry (with a branch at 55 Clarendon Street).
- Kildare Street: **McDonnell Antiques**, No. 15, 18th- and 19th-century furniture, crystal, porcelain, objets d'art. Reputed to be Dublin's leading antiques dealer. **Kildare Antiques**, near McDonnell's, fine porcelain and paintings. **Cynthia O'Connor**, No. 35a, Irish paintings and watercolors.
- Molesworth Street: **Jane Williams Antiques**, No. 23, ivory, tortoiseshell, treenware, small items of furniture.
- Nassau Street: **John Morton Ltd.**, No 48/49, opposite Trinity College gardens, antique jewelry and silver.
- Clare Street: **Greene's**, No. 16, old books (new ones, too) dealing with Dublin and Irish provincial folklore.
- Lower Merrion Square: **European Fine Arts**, No. 6, 17th-century Dutch and Flemish Old Masters, European paintings, drawings and prints up to the 19th century.
- South William Street: **Patrick F. Brown**, No. 15, paintings and art. **Saskia Antiques**, No. 43, 17th- and 18-century furniture, paintings, rugs, carpets.
- Lower Pembroke Street: **T.J. Mitchell Antiques**, No. 1a, furniture, antiques restoration, cabinet reproductions.
- Mill Street: **S.B. & J. Orken**, No. 33b, Regency furniture, ceramics, brass.
- Francis Street: In this, one of the oldest parts of Dublin and somewhat removed from the tourist areas (take a taxi), an antiques market is growing up with interesting places offering a surprising number and variety of antiques (from small crystal, porcelain, and brass items to period furniture) at cheaper prices than elsewhere. The **Decora** market is especially interesting, and there's a large antiques warehouse here called **Cooke's**, which deals mainly with retailers. But if you're of the mind, you can stop by and strike a bargain or two.

NOTE: Even with the high cost of shipping furniture items to America, very often it's cheaper to buy items here and have them sent air freight than it is to drop into one of the trendy antiques shops in New York, Chicago, or Beverly Hills and purchase similar items. Irish antiques are still an enormous bargain.

¶ There has been a revolution in Irish dining in recent years, and much of it has taken place in Dublin. Today there are so many superb restaurants that you could spend your entire holiday just visiting them. Of course, it's impossible to review them all here, but those described are among the best.

Since they are all on Dublin's south side, the restaurants are reviewed in alphabetical order. Most of them are relatively close to one another, so just ask for directions. You can walk to many of them within a few minutes. But always reserve first.

A number of Dublin's restaurants are of such superior quality that they are featured in chapter 14, Special Restaurants. These include **Le Coq Hardi, The Kish, The Lord Edward**, and **Bewley's**. In addition to these, don't forget the fine restaurants at the **Shelbourne**, the **Westbury**, and the **Berkeley Court**.

Beefeaters—House of Beef, 99/100 Baggot Street Lower (760784), is a modern, trendy new Irish beef eatery ensconced in the basement of an old Dublin townhouse. It has superb Irish beef at low (by any country's standard) prices—everything from gourmet burgers to steak béarnaise and Chateaubriand. The menu also has a roast prime rib lunch and a dabbling of good seafood entrees. But the emphasis, by at least 90 percent, is on the steaks. And when you can pick up a 20-ounce prime sirloin cooked to perfection and at an inexpensive price yet, that's saying a mouthful—in more ways than one. Beefeaters has a wine license and offers good wines at equally unbelievable prices. The capacity here is only 65, and it's popular (with good reason), so *do* reserve. Monday through Friday lunch is from 12 to 3; Monday through Saturday dinner is from 6 to 11 (closed for lunch Saturday and bank holidays and all day Sunday). All major credit cards accepted.

Broph's, 16 Merrion Road, Ballsbridge (605288), is another of Dublin's hot new restaurants. Run by Kevin Brophy, who has had extensive haute cuisine experience, the restaurant has a casual Art Deco seafood wine bar in front and a more formal, intimate dining room in back. Some of the top-notch appetizers include hot duck liver salad, mussels in Bordelaise sauce, lively seafood chowder, and mushrooms stuffed with snails and served with a succulent lemon verbena sauce. There's a wide selection of memorable entrees. It's difficult to choose from offerings such as sole on the bone with a fine spinach soufflé stuffing, monkfish perfectly laced with peppercorns and flamed in brandy, seafood selections with sea urchin sauce, roast venison with hearty game sauce, chicken breast layered with salmon and beautifully highlighted with creamy prawn sauce, and duckling with an appropriately rich sour-cherry-and-blackcurrant sauce. The roast Wexford lamb, either stuffed or served with honey and thyme, is unusually good. Food is moderately priced, as are the good wines (wine license only). Open for dinner from 7 to 9, but closed Sundays and bank holidays. All major credit cards accepted.

Dobbins Wine Bistro, 15 Stephen's Lane (764670/764679), opened in the early 1970s, is a disarmingly cozy, cafelike restaurant that has become an old chestnut with Dubliners and seasoned tourists as well. There's a variety of meat, fish, and salad dishes here, along with lots of good wines—and all at moderate prices. Dobbins's real appeal is its totally disarming charm. It is tucked away from the rest of the city on a lonely lane (if you've never been there before, you'll have to ask for directions when you make your reservations or you'll never find it except by taxi); you enter through a narrow wine cellar into a long, rustic room with a stone floor, red-and-white-checked tablecloths, and sturdy wooden booths. At one end are a wine bar and a patio (used when weather permits). Newcomers may think they've seen the place be-fore—and they have. It was used as one of the key settings in the film *Educating Rita*. This is the perfect place to linger for an afternoon or evening of intimate conversation. It's open for lunch Monday through Friday from 12:30 to 2:30 (closed Saturday and Sunday lunch). Dinner is served Tuesday through Saturday 6:30 to 11:30 (closed Sunday and Monday dinner as well as bank holidays). All major credit cards are accepted.

Ernie's Restaurant, Mulberry Gardens, Donnybrook (693300), is another of Dublin's recent entries on the romantic cafe society scene. Built around a courtyard that centers on a large mulberry tree, the restaurant is small and intimate. Its walls are covered with striking original Irish landscape paintings, including some by Jack Yeats, brother of W.B. Yeats. Owner Ernie Evans, who hails from restaurateuring in County Kerry, brings to Dublin his flair for the preparation of fine fish dishes. People have been pouring in to sample his fine lobster, salmon, and prawn-stuffed sole dishes. He also does charcoal meat specialties. Ernie's is expensive, as are the good wines (wine license only). It's open for dinner 7 to 12 every day but Sunday. All major credit cards are accepted.

The Grey Door, 23 Upper Pembroke Street (763286/766890), located in the cozy basement of a former Georgian townhouse, feels like someone's home rather than a restaurant. The small, dark-wood tables and chairs, cushioned in a deep masculine brown, are offset by pink tablecloths, fresh flowers, and candles. The focal point, a grand dark-wood fireplace, is lightened by an enormous mirror over the mantelpiece. The emphasis here is on rich Russian and Scandinavian dishes. You can sip Russian champagne while you dine on chicken Kiev, salmon in fresh cream and dill sauce, and unusual but tasty veal and beef dishes. To enhance the intimate mood, a Russian guitarist plays the folk music of his motherland. The meals are moderately priced, with fine wines the same (wine license only). It's open for lunch 12:30 to 2:15, except Saturday and Sunday; dinner is from 7 to 11, except Sunday. All major credit cards are accepted.

Kilmartin's Wine Bistro, 19 Upper Baggot Street (686674), once was a bookie joint. Now it's a small, intimate rendezvous spot with the same name. The menu is brief but good in this surprisingly inexpensive place with wine license. The brandied chicken liver pâté and the oversized steak-and-kidney pie are very good, as are the spicy chili con carne and the cannelloni. It's open daily from noon to midnight (Sunday, 12:30 to 10) and closed on bank holidays. AmEx, Visa, and Diners are accepted.

The Lobster Pot, 9 Ballsbridge Terrace (680025), is a romantic little place located in a converted terraced house. It has a masculine feel to it, with a brick floor, dramatic fireplace, and wooden armchairs clustered around intimate tables. Lobster sautéed in a white wine cream sauce with avocado and cheese is a specialty, as are monkfish thermidor and numerous flambéed dishes. Sliced scallops meunière in garlic, and fresh prawn and lobster bisque are fine starters. The restaurant, with a wine license, is moderately expensive. It's open for lunch Monday through Friday from 12:30 to 3:30 and for dinner Monday through Saturday from 6 to 11. AmEx, Master, Visa, and Diners are accepted.

Locks Restaurant, 1 Windsor Terrace, Portobello (752025), is nestled on the secluded banks of Dublin's Grand Canal, in one of the city's quietest and oldest areas. This small and extremely cozy French provincial restaurant was once a farmhouse. The food is excellent, and it's difficult to choose from among such entrees as Gaelic steak, beautifully prepared game (in season), sweetbreads in brown butter sauce, and monkfish, salmon, and mussel dishes. Deep-fried Camembert wedges, fried mushrooms with aioli, and fresh prawn salads are excellent starters. Meals are moderately priced, with good wines, which are moderate as well (wine license only). It's open for lunch Monday through Friday from 12:30 to 2:30, dinner Monday through Saturday from 7 to 11 (closed Sunday and bank holidays). AmEx, Diners, and Visa are accepted.

Rajdoot Tandoori Restaurant, 26/28 Clarendon Court (772441/772643), is another new arrival on the elegant Dublin restaurant scene. It boasts an Irish rarity—air-conditioning. Located in the posh Westbury Hotel complex, this ambitious room with authentic Indian decor and atmosphere offers many dishes. A specialty is chicken tandoori, marinated in a spiced yogurt and roasted in a tandoor (a charcoal-heated cylindrical clay oven). Kebabs, moghlai, and subtle curry balance a fine and unusual menu. The restaurant runs the gamut in prices from inexpensive (a special 4-course weekday businessman's lunch and a Saturday shopper's lunch) to moderate (a regular full menu luncheon) to expensive (dinner). It's open Monday through Saturday for lunch from 12 to 2:30 and for dinner from 6:30 to 10:30 (closed Sunday and bank holidays). Wine license only. All major credit cards are accepted.

Restaurant Patrick Guilbaud, 46 James Place, Lower Baggot Street (764192), was designed by Arthur Gibney, one of Ireland's bold architects. This intimate restaurant would be a knockout anywhere because of the romantic French elegance of its decor, which includes pink-striped upholstery, an interior garden, and a skylight. You'd have to go far in Dublin to find a place with anything close to this Mediterranean kind of lightness. The menu is strictly French haute cuisine, with some dishes tastier than others. If it's on the menu, try the John Dory, a hearty white fish served with a delicious red wine sauce. Very good as well are the prawns in brandy sauce and the poached sole with leeks. If you favor salmon, it's done here in an unusual light pastry that seals in all the flavor and aroma. The rack of lamb with green peppercorn sauce, the chicken with truffles, and the very different (somehow it works well) veal fillet with onion puree are other good possibilities here. Do try the hot pâté or the hot oysters with spinach as a starter, if they are on the menu. The wine list will take you a day to read, and much of it is expensive, as are the dinners (luncheons are moderate to expensive). However, there are some very good (though few) moderately priced wines. The restaurant is open Monday through Friday for lunch from 12:30 to 2 and for dinner Monday through Saturday from 7 to 10. All major credit cards are accepted.

Shrimps Wine Bar, 1 Anne's Lane (713143), is a tiny little place not unlike a Greenwich Village bistro with a lovely fire and either classic or jazz background music. Painted a cool green and adorned with mirrors, the room seems larger than it is. The menu is rather unusual and changes daily. It can range from pizza to fish pies, from crabs to curries, from chili con carne to seafood salads. It's moderately priced, with wines ranging all the way from inexpensive to expensive (wine license only). It's open from noon to 11 P.M., but closed Sunday and bank holidays. AmEx, Master, and Visa are accepted.

Pub luncheons are another feature of the Irish dining scene. Often you can get large quantities of food at low prices. While a large number of pubs now offer some foods, here are a few of the best:

- **Casper & Guimbini's**, Wicklow Street (775122), on the site of the old Wicklow Hotel, is a spacious pub-restaurant that somehow manages to be bright and glittery despite its dim, Tiffany-shaded lighting. The bar is massive, the chair stools comfortable. And there's air-conditioning, unusual in Ireland. Chicken and fish platters, smoked salmon, submarine sandwiches, salads, shepherd's pie, and bangers-and-mash are among the good, reasonable, and plentiful offerings. Brunch is served on Saturday. There's a resident pianist during lunch and most evenings. It's open daily from noon to midnight and on Sunday from 12:30 to 11. All major credit cards are accepted.
- **The Castle Inn bars**, in the Castle Inn, Lord Edward Street (780663), are posh and comfortable. The food is hearty—hot meat and fish dishes—or you can have a lighter but tasty salad. They are open daily for lunch from 12:30 to 2:30, except Sunday. All major credit cards are accepted.
- **The Granary Bar**, 34/37 East Essex Street (713187), is a marvelous Victorian pub with excellent food: cold buffet, soups, meats, seafoods. It's open for lunch from noon to 2:30, but closed Saturday, Sunday, and bank holidays.
- **The Dubliner Bar** in Jurys Hotel, Ballsbridge (767511), is a woody-masculine, simulated Victorian drinking parlor. Carvery luncheons from joints (roasts) of the day are thick, tender, and bountiful. There are a dozen different salads to choose from, and a vegetarian meal as well. You wouldn't get this for double the price in most Dublin restaurants in the evening. The pub is open daily for lunch from 12:30 to 2, but closed Saturday, Sunday, and bank holidays. All major credit cards are accepted.
- **The Lord Edward**, 23 Christchurch Place (752557), is a woody

Victorian pub-lounge on the second floor of the old 3-story Lord Edward complex. The menu offers salads and delicious hot meat and seafood dishes. It's a popular businessman's haunt, with lunch from 12:30 to 2:30, but closed Saturday, Sunday, and bank holidays. All major credit cards are accepted.

¶ For those who are addicted to the theatre, Dublin couldn't be a finer place. Sean O'Casey, W. B. Yeats, J. M. Synge, Lady Augusta Gregory, Brendan Behan, Samuel Beckett, George Bernard Shaw—and, in recent times, Brian Friel, John B. Keane, and Hugh Leonard—are the Irish theatre, abounding in brilliance. The wealth of drama is truly astonishing for such a small country. Most foreigners traveling to Ireland feel an evening at the theatre is a must. In Dublin, there are a number of choices.

- **The Abbey Theatre**, Lower Abbey Street (744505), is Ireland's world-renowned national theatre. It performs works by Irish playwrights past and present. Fire destroyed the original Abbey in 1951, and the current house opened in 1966. Reserve tickets as soon as you can. Curtain is at 8 sharp. If you are late, you won't be seated until after the first act.
- **The Peacock Theatre**, Lower Abbey Street (744505), is a special smaller theatre beneath the Abbey that's an extension of the national theatre group. It does such special productions as prose and poetry readings, one-man shows, and children's theatre—and also hosts out-of-town theatre companies. Evening performances are at 8.
- **The Gaiety Theatre**, South King Street (771717), is a newly renovated 19th-century theatre offering plays and opera. Curtain at 8. Here you find restored house bars and a restaurant called **Chez Beano** that's becoming quite popular.
- **The Gate Theatre,** Parnell Square (744045), stages modern Irish drama as well as the best from the contemporary international scene. The curtain rises at 8.
- **The Olympia**, Dame Street (778962), stages everything from operettas and variety shows to serious drama in its time-honored house. Check newspapers for schedules and times.
- **The National Concert Hall**, Earlsfort Terrace (711888), is Dublin's newest and first concert hall, with mostly classical programs. (Concerts also are held on a sporadic basis at other venues.)
- **Project Arts Centre**, 39 East Essex Street off Dame Street (713327), does works by contemporary and new playwrights. Curtain is at 8.

The Irish Times is a good source for checking on theatrical events. The cost of tickets is extremely modest compared to those of most American houses. Tickets may be booked through **The Ticket Bureau** in Dublin's Westbury Mall, near St. Stephen's Green (01-794455), for Irish entertainment as well as for London and New York theatres.

Remember that Dublin usually holds its annual **Theatre Festival** during the first 2 weeks in October, or the last week in September and the first week in October. Irish, European, and American theatre people and aficionados attend the openings of Irish and international productions (many of them new). It can be a busy time, so it's advisable to reserve in advance (lodgings as well as tickets).

¶ Now comes the time to speak of Dublin pubs. Here you have a wide choice—sophisticated, memorably pleasant (in a chatty sense), and downright bawdy (booze, booze, booze—smoke, smoke, smoke). The middle ground is probably best here. But remember that Irish pubs, especially in Dublin, are often as capricious as the weather. They take on a seemingly stable quality at one time of day, only to switch into reverse at another—and this can happen quite suddenly. In Dublin, it's important to remember that pubs close daily Monday through Saturday from 2:30 to 3:30 (they say it's just to get people back to work) and on Sunday from 2 to 4 ("holy hour"). Choose your times carefully. Off hours are definitely the best if you want quiet conversation, although you'll want to keep in mind the daytime closing hours. Most pubs serve fairly acceptable wines by the glass, and they serve soft drinks if you don't want alcohol. Some even serve coffee and tea. The following listing includes some of the best and most romantic:

The Brazen Head, 20 Lower Bridge Street, is probably Dublin's oldest pub. As early as the 1600s (during the reign of Charles II), it was a popular haunt. In the late 1700s, it became the meeting place of Irish freedom fighters. Such patriots as Wolfe Tone, Robert Emmet, and Daniel O'Connell crossed its cobble-stoned courtyard to frequent the pub's dim, lantern-lit bar and its ghostly parlors reached by a creaking staircase. In later years, James Joyce, Oliver Gogarty, and Brendan Behan were patrons. (Even if you're looking for this place, you could easily miss the unmarked arch that leads to the courtyard entrance, but it's worth the search.) The bar serves no draft stouts or lagers, and its trappings seem as old as the place itself. Patrons often sing late into the evening, although this is primarily a conversation pub.

The Long Hall, 51 South Great Georges Street, is a long, narrow 200-year-old bar with a cozy snug (which ladies used to frequent so the regular clientele wouldn't see them drinking). Its splendid dark-wood bar trimmed with copper and gold plate, magnificent stained-glass panels, gilded mirrors, old crystal chandeliers, and grand pendulum clock (more than 300 years old) qualify this pub as an historic monument. A must-see conversation pub. For more intimate chats, try the snug.

Doheny & Nesbitt, at 5 Lower Baggot Street near Merrion Row, is thoroughly enjoyable and a marvelous monument to Dublin Victoriana, with spectacularly intricate wood-trimmed bar and ceiling, marble tables, carved frame clocks, and snug.

Ryan's, on Parkgate Street (near Phoenix Park), is esteemed by many Dubliners as the finest of the old pubs. James Joyce, among others, was particularly fond of the place, which boasts a handsome mahogany bar, ornate mirrors, graceful oil lamps, snug, and antique bar trappings. It's definitely worth seeing, but stay away on Saturday and Sunday, because the place is mobbed then.

Davy Byrnes, on Duke Street, is mentioned in James Joyce's *Ulysses*. Bloom reflects on it as a "nice quiet bar. Nice piece of wood in the counter." These aspects are the same today, as are the 19th-century murals, but the back snug, in what Bloom thought of as his "moral pub," has long since been modernized into a lounge, and the bare floors are now carpeted. Today it's one of Dublin's slicker pubs, attended by a well-dressed youthful crowd.

Neary's, on Chatham Street, is a turn-of-the-century pub with an elegant pink-and-gray-marble bar supporting enormous brass-stemmed globe lamps. Its massive mahogany-framed mirrors, paneled ceiling, and cozy settees help make it one of Dublin's pleasantest pubs. It's popular with a prosperous young to middle-aged crowd. There's fine food here, too: smoked salmon and brown bread, oysters in season.

The Horseshoe Bar, in the Shelbourne Hotel, St. Stephen's Green, is a well-established meeting place for trendy Dubliners as well as the international set. Small and intimate, it has a grand curved bar and enormous mirrors to reflect the beautiful people who patronize it. This is a wonderful place for a quiet conversation, except on Friday evening, when Dublin executives pour in to initiate the weekend. Cocktails are excellent here, too.

¶ Dublin has 2 major annual events that may be of interest. But even if they are not, keep them in mind if you are planning to visit Dublin when they're in progress. Make reservations for your lodgings well in advance—and make restaurant bookings early in the day, if not a day or more in advance. The **Dublin Horse Show**, usually held the second week in August, attracts the horsey set from America and the Continent, making it Ireland's best-attended special event. The **Dublin Theatre Festival**, usually scheduled for the first 2 weeks in October, is not quite as well known as Scotland's Edinburgh Festival, but it's immensely popular and attended by a cross section of theatre people from around the world. For exact dates, contact the Irish Tourist Board.

¶ There's enough to do in Dublin to occupy the tourist for a month without even considering sports, but for those with an abiding interest, the possibilities are endless: dozens of golf courses, running in 2,000-acre Phoenix Park, swimming in a vast number of seaside haunts near Dublin, fishing (sea and river), yachting all around Dublin, hunting in neighboring counties, polo in Phoenix Park, tennis in Rathgar, Gaelic football and hurling in Dublin's Croke Park. For specifics, check with the Irish Tourist Board.

¶ For the literary romantics who long to visit the spot where Leopold Bloom first made love to his passionate Molly, you'll need to travel the 9 miles from Dublin's city center on the north side to **Howth** and **Howth Head**. It's better not to drive because of complicated directions, and taxis are expensive, but the very inexpensive No. 31 bus departs from the north side, at O'Connell and Lower Abbey streets. It takes about 40 minutes. The last bus returns from Howth to Dublin City center at 11:30 P.M.

There are other reasons besides James Joyce for going to Howth—such as the wonderful **King Sitric** seafood restaurant (see review in chapter 14). If you go by bus, you might opt for lunch, so you won't have to worry about missing the last return bus to Dublin. Another unusual place here is **The Abbey Tavern** (322006). In this fishing village on the northern arm of Dublin Bay, the large and bustling tavern offers a good Irish ballad sing every night except Sunday. This, combined with a fine seafood restaurant (Old World decor), cozy turf fires, stone walls, flagstone floors, and gaslights, makes for a memorable evening. There's the traditional song pub here, too. Stroll down toward the shore afterward and watch the twinkling lights of the boats at sea. It's spectacular, especially on a starry night. The Abbey is open from 7:30 to 11 (closed Sunday). It has a full license, accepts all major credit cards, and is moderate to expensive.

Also in Howth is the **Howth Lodge Hotel and Restaurant** (390288), which emphasizes good French/Irish cooking at moderate prices. It accepts all credit cards, has a full license, and is open evenings from 7 to 9:30, but Sunday from 12:30 to 2 only. The hotel also has good, inexpensive pub food in its lounge.

If your heart is set on a quiet evening, opt for the King Sitric, as the entertainment aspects of the Abbey Tavern really do take over.

¶ If you are interested in the beautiful seascapes and mountains south of the city, and your plans include traveling through the southeast of Ireland, you may wish to postpone seeing this area, with its pleasant little coastal villages, until you are ready to leave Dublin. To do this, leave Dublin from Ballsbridge on the T44, Merrion Road. After a short distance, you'll skirt the shores of Dublin Bay, across which is dramatic Howth Head. After about 3 miles (from Ballsbridge), you'll come to **Blackrock** village, where there's a new and popular restaurant called **The Park** at 26 Main Street (886177). Owner/chef Colin O'Daly has dreamed up an imaginative and delicious menu consisting of such choices as lamb casserole with fresh cranberries and ginger, squid with gooseberries, and cod baked with coconut and Amaretto. It's open for lunch from 12:30 to 2 and dinner from 7 to 9. Prices are moderate to expensive and there's a wine license.

Leaving Blackrock, bear to the left onto the road signposted for Dun Laoghaire. This is Newtown Avenue. In about a half mile, bear left again onto Seapoint Avenue, signposted for **Dun Laoghaire Pier**. If it's a good day, stop for a stroll on this famous pier with magnificent views of Dublin Bay. The neighboring pier is the terminal point for the ferry that crosses to and from Holyhead in Wales. When leaving this area, you will pass the car ferry entrance and come to traffic signs. Follow the road signposted to Dalkey, and after about 1½ miles, you'll come to a T-junction. To the left is **Sandycove**. Here, on Marine Parade, **Restaurant Mirabeau** has reopened under new management. It's an excellent restaurant but open only for dinner. (See the review in chapter 14.) Another Sandycove restaurant is **Russell's** (808878), on Glaasthule Road. It's a moderately priced French bistro with good and simple meat and fish dishes and a wine license. It's open evenings from 6:30 to 11, but closed Sunday. No credit cards are accepted. Nearby is an 18-century martello tower built as part of a defense system against a Napoleonic invasion. Once the temporary home of James Joyce, it appears as a setting in the opening pages of *Ulysses*. The tower now houses the **James Joyce Museum**, with a fascinating collection of Joyceana. From May 1 to September 30, it's open Monday through Saturday from 10 to 1 and from 2 to 5:15. On Sunday, it's open from 2:30 to 6. (The admission fee is very low.) Next to the tower is the famous (in Dublin circles) **Forty Foot** bathing area, where men frequently swim in the nude. From here, return to the T-junction and continue until you come to another junction, where you take the sign-

posted road for Dalkey. On your approach to Dalkey, you'll come to
another T-junction, where you'll turn left onto Castle Street. At the
end of this street, follow the signposted road to the right for Killiney.
At **Killiney**, you might like to stop and take the **Killiney Hill cliff
walk**, with monumental views in all directions—dazzling Killiney Bay,
the mountains of Wicklow (Big and Little Sugarloaf), Bray Head, Dun
Laoghaire, Joyce's tower, and Dublin. There's a car park, but you can
traverse the hill, following Sorrento and Vico roads, by car. Next,
travel on to Shankhill. Just before you come to the village of **Bray**
(about 13 miles from Dublin), take the road for Enniskerry, which is
another 3 miles. From here, you may wish to travel to Glencree, where
you can pick up the narrow, lonely Military Road through Sally Gap
and the heart of the Wicklow mountains, down to the verdant valley
of Glendalough. This would be 32 miles from Dublin. (For details on
this portion of the journey and other County Wicklow sites, see Suggestions in chapter 10.)

It should be noted that **Dalkey** has a number of interesting and
intimate restaurants. These include **The Guinea Pig** at 17 Railway
Street (good seafood with emphasis on shellfish; wine license; moderate
to expensive; all major credit cards; dinner 7 to 11:30, except Sunday,
Easter week, and August 1 through 15); **Restaurant Baroque** on Main
Street (everything from tasty seafood and game in season to suckling
pig; full license; moderate to expensive; Visa, Master; dinner 7 to 11,
but closed Sunday, Monday, bank holidays); **Nieves Restaurant** at 26
Castle Street (good meat and seafood dishes; wine license; moderate;
AmEx, Diners, Master, Visa; dinner from 6:30 to midnight). In **Killiney**
village, there are 2 good hotel restaurants—**The Island Restaurant** in
the Court Hotel (Victorian seaside hotel with modern wing and a dining
room overlooking Killiney Bay); **Fitzpatrick Castle Hotel Restaurant**
(lots of Victoriana and silver trolleys). Should you want to stay in this
beautiful seaside area, the Court and Fitzpatrick Castle both have rooms
(see chapter 13 for reviews of the hotels and their restaurants).

13 OTHER LODGING POSSIBILITIES

I whispered, 'I am too young.'
And then, 'I am old enough';
Wherefore I threw a penny
To find out if I might love.
'Go and love, go and love, young man,
If the lady be young and fair.'
Ah, penny, brown penny, brown penny,
I am looped in the loops of her hair.
                    —W. B. Yeats
                    "Brown Penny"

Carrigart Hotel   CARRIGART, COUNTY DONEGAL

While a little modern, the Carrigart (074-55114) is a very pleasant lodging in this quaint resort town on the shores of Mulroy and Sheephaven bays at the beginning of the spectacular Atlantic Drive. It is not a place to go if you wish to stay away from children. Families frequently come here to take advantage of the resort's many facilities, which include a heated indoor swimming pool, squash court, tennis, croquet, crazy golf, table tennis, playground, sauna, sunbed, masseur, pony trekking, golf, boat trips. There's also dancing, plus sing-songs. There are 56 relatively inexpensive bedrooms (42 with bath), and breakfast is included. No credit cards are accepted. The food, especially the seafood, is very good. Meat dishes are available as well. Wines are quite acceptable and moderate, as is the food. Dinner is served from 7 to 9. The hotel, which is open April 5 through September, is right in the village of Carrigart.

Ernan Park Hotel   DONEGAL TOWN, COUNTY DONEGAL

This hotel (073-21065), located on the wooded, 9-acre St. Ernans Island, is named after the 7th-century monk Ernan (man of iron). (The island now is connected to the mainland by a causeway.) The estate's house was built in 1824 and is run as a lodging by Mary and James Morris. Many of its bay windows have spectacular views of Donegal Bay. There are marble fireplaces, antiques, and a fine collection of books at this house with 10 bedrooms—all with bath and breakfast included. The dining room with a fireplace serves good, traditional Irish meat and fish dishes, plus equally fine vegetables and desserts. Dinner is at 7. Open all year, Ernan Park is moderately priced for room and food, has a full license, and accepts AmEx, Master, and Visa. Nearby are golfing and fishing, and there is ocean swimming off the estate. (U.S. agent: E & M Associates.)

Ballincar House   ROSSES POINT, COUNTY SLIGO

This lodging (071-5361/2/3) was formerly a private homestead that has been transformed into a 20-bedroom (moderately priced, with breakfast included) establishment. While the bedrooms (all with bath and color TV) are rather too modern, the public rooms maintain their old-fashioned appeal. This is the best hotel in the Sligo Town area (2 miles away), and it's in the heart of Yeats country. While the dining room isn't especially intimate, the food is superb. If lobster mornay is on the menu, don't miss it. Salmon is another good choice, as is the panfried trout. Lamb cutlets are extremely delicate and tasty. The delicious seafood cocktail starters are delicate as well as rich. The wonderful strawberries taste like the wild variety. Meringues and rhubarb desserts are equally fine. The really good Latour wines match the reasonable prices of the food. Lunch is served from 1 to 2:30, dinner from 6:30 to 9. The hotel is open all year and accepts AmEx, Master, and Visa. Facilities include sauna, squash court, and sunbed. This is an excellent base for touring the Sligo area. (U.S. agent: Reservations Systems.) This is a good place to stay if you want to dine at the wonderful Reveries at Rosses Point which is only about two miles away. (See chapter 14 for review.)

Knockmuldowney Country House STRANDHILL, COUNTY SLIGO

This charming Georgian manor house (071-68122) was originally a fine restaurant. But with customer encouragement, owners Charles and Mary Cooper have at last opened its 6 tastefully furnished bedrooms (all with bath) to the public. They're moderately priced, as is the award-winning cuisine, which includes beautifully prepared simple fish dishes as well as those of excellent Irish lamb and pork. An orange soup is a surprisingly special treat, as are the desserts. Knockmuldowney has an enormous wine list and a full license. Dinner is at 8. Breakfast is included. All credit cards are accepted. With Knockarea Mountain just behind the estate and Ballisodare Bay in front, climbing and swimming are just across the road. Surfing, tennis, golfing, and riding are nearby. Knockmuldowney is open March to mid-November and is located four miles west of Sligo Town on the L132. (U.S. agent: Robert Reid.)

Mount Falcon Castle BALLINA, COUNTY MAYO

More mansion than castle, Mount Falcon (096-21172) is a Victorian structure with a sinister-looking entrance hall that belies the charm of the rest of the house. It's very informal, despite period gilt, mirrors, chandeliers, and old china and silver. In addition to the cozy sitting room and a library, there's a pantry with a bar where you make your own drinks (keeping track for billing purposes). The 15 moderately priced bedrooms (with bath and breakfast included) are spacious and have old furniture. Be sure to notice proprietor Constance Aldridge's beautiful paintings, done by her brother-in-law, the well-known English painter John Aldridge. Dining at Mount Falcon is an interesting experience. All the guests sit at a long mahogany table near a roaring fireplace while Mrs. Aldridge carves away at the delicious lamb or beef that is the main course of the one set meal. The lovely vegetables she serves come from the estate's own farm. Good wines are also served. While this is going on, Mrs. Aldridge, a transplanted Englishwoman, chats merrily away about everything under the sun—but especially the old days. (She and her late husband opened Mount Falcon as a lodge in 1932.) Dinner is at 8—and is very moderately priced. There's a full license. AmEx, Diners, Master, and Visa are accepted. Besides ocean swimming from deserted beaches, salmon and trout fishing, horse riding, and golfing are nearby. Rough shooting is possible in winter. This is an ideal locale for exploring the remote areas of County Mayo. Mount Falcon is slightly south of Ballina Town on the N57. It's closed Christmas week, February, and March. (U.S. agent: Robert Reid.)

Enniscoe House, Crossmolina   COUNTY MAYO

Enniscoe House (096-31112) is another antique-filled Georgian country home. Owned by Susan Kellett, a descendant of the original occupants, this high-ceilinged home offers a grand drawing room with antique French furniture and wallpaper dating back to the early 1800s. Here you'll find fascinating oil paintings of Mrs. Kellett's ancestors. There's a large, but cozy, living room with a fine big fireplace. Off this room and under a glass-domed roof is a spiral staircase that rises to the bedroom floor. This is the house where French soldiers paused for refreshments in the late 18th century as they made their way south in what was to become a failed attempt to overthrow the British armies. Enniscoe has 7 moderately priced rooms (3 with large baths and four-poster, canopied beds); breakfast is included. The rooms with baths overlook the grounds and lovely Lough Conn. There's top-notch basic Irish meat and fish dishes here. Food and wine are moderately priced. Dinner at 7. AmEx, Visa, and Master are accepted. (U.S. agent: Robert Reid.) The estate offers good brown trout fishing; boats and ghillies (guides) are available. Nearby are golf courses, riding stables. Enniscoe is open from April to October, and by special arrangement during the winter for woodcock and pheasant parties. From here, there's easy access to remote northern Mayo areas. The house is about 3 miles south of the village of Crossmolina on the R315.

Connemara Gateway Hotel OUGHTERARD, COUNTY GALWAY

Formerly a very modern motel, this lodging (091-82328) was not the sort of place that would suit this book. But no more. The whole complex has been completely stripped and refurbished to resemble a fine old country inn. Charles Sinnott, the cordial owner/manager, feels the rustic new look blends beautifully with the surrounding Connemara countryside. The interior decor emphasizes the rustic as well. All native Irish materials and crafts have been used, including furniture, rugs, pottery, and artwork. Irish farm implements are prominent among the memorabilia. There's a library, along with a heated swimming pool, tennis court, putting green, croquet lawn, and extensive gardens. There are 62 moderately priced bedrooms, all with bath, shower, radio, and tea- and coffeemaking facilities. Breakfast is included. Master, Visa, and Diners are accepted. The restaurant serves good Irish fare, such as a tasty traditional Irish stew, roast duckling, roast stuffed shoulder of pork, fresh salmon steak prepared to your liking, plaice with orange and whiskey butter. A fine starter is the smoked salmon salad or the fresh cream of celery soup. Desserts and wines are good. The moderately priced dinner is served from 7 to 9. In the bar is traditional entertainment. Fishing, golfing, and pony trekking are nearby. The hotel offers its own excellent walking (or running) and driving itinerary brochures of the area, with exact mileages. The Connemara Gateway is located on the N59 Galway-to-Oughterard road, just before you reach Oughterard village. It's closed from November through January.

Sweeney's
Oughterard House OUGHTERARD, COUNTY GALWAY

Overlooking the rippling, salmon-rich waters of the Owenriff River, Sweeney's (091-82207) is a perfectly charming and totally disarming old chestnut of an Irish Georgian country house covered in ivy. The gleaming white, bay-windowed structure is enhanced by manicured lawns, lovely gardens, and ancient beech trees. Tranquility is the keynote at Sweeney's, with its cozy, turf-fired lounges, country gentleman's bar, and 20 snug, expensive bedrooms with bath. Breakfast is not included. The rustic dining room serves poached salmon hollandaise, grilled trout, prawns, crabmeat dishes, steak béarnaise, roast lamb— and all are very good. Wines are good and moderate to expensive, as is the food. Dinner is served from 7:30 to 9. Sweeney's also serves a good bar lunch, including smoked salmon and brown bread, plus homemade fruit cake, scones, blackberry jam, pies, and fresh vegetable soup. It's served from noon to 3. Visa, Master, and Diners are accepted. Nearby are fishing and golfing. This is an excellent location for touring Connemara. The hotel, open all year, is located on the N59 on the western outskirts of Oughterard village. (U.S. agent: Reservations Systems.)

Johnston-Hernon
Kilmurvey House   ARAN ISLANDS, COUNTY GALWAY

Located on Inishmore, the largest of the 3 islands, this imposing graystone manor house (099-61218) looks almost as intimidating as Miss Havisham's in Dickens's *Great Expectations*. But once inside, that impression yields to the presence of Bridget Johnston-Hernon, who has more tales to tell than the sea has waves, as they say here. Guests from almost every country have passed through her iron gateway over the years, and her recollections range from the heartbreaking to the comic— including visitors who brought full evening dress to the islands and those who refused to pay their bill because it sprinkled during their visit. She can tell you about the old days when they burned kelp on the strand while the men drank *poteen* and told ancient tales. Her life has not been easy, but it exemplifies the experience of struggle and survival on these windswept islands in the harsh Atlantic. Unfortunately, much of the old furniture in the manor has been replaced by modern pieces. There are 10 inexpensive bedrooms (breakfast included), none with private bath. Good, basic Irish meals are served at inexpensive prices, but there's no alcohol license (a pub is not far away). It's open May 1 through September 30; no credit cards are accepted. The best ways to get here are: to catch the daily steamer from Galway

City (this takes about 3 hours each way) or to take one of the frequent small vessels from Rossaveal in Connemara, which take an hour each way. Then there are several short Aer Aran flights (more expensive) each day from the outskirts of Galway City.

Ardilaun House   GALWAY CITY, COUNTY GALWAY

Located on Taylors Hill, Ardilaun House (091-21433) once was a stately mansion. Now expanded, it has 73 moderately priced rooms (breakfast included), all with bath. Set amid sheltering trees, shrubs, and gardens in the town's finest residential section, it's as quiet as a country hotel. Especially pleasant are the sitting rooms with grand fireplaces and the cozy bar. The intimate dining room has huge windows that overlook the lawn and gardens; it serves a wide variety of meat and seafood dishes—from escalope of veal in white wine and cream sauce to sole Florentine. The pâté maison is good, the fresh seafood chowder excellent. Entrees include coquilles St. Jacques (scallops sautéed in vermouth butter), crepes aux crevettes (thin pancakes filled with prawns and glazed with cheese), and the house specialty—rack of lamb. All are excellent. Meals are moderate to expensive and good wines are the same. Lunch is served from 1 to 2:30, dinner from 7 to 9. The hotel is open all year and accepts all major credit cards. (U.S. agent: Salt and Pepper Tours.)

Great Southern Hotel   GALWAY CITY, COUNTY GALWAY

One of Galway City's 2 best hotels, the Great Southern (091-64041) is centrally located on Eyre Square, in front of the railway station. Built in the Victorian era, this rambling structure has a modern wing. Of the 125 moderate-to-expensive bedrooms (breakfast included)—all with bath, phone, and television—the old, high-ceilinged ones are by far the best. The grand lobby houses the Railway Bar and Lounge, where the international set often alights. Also here is the Oyster Room offering everything from fine snacks to grilled dishes and good 3-course meals from 7:30 A.M. to 11 P.M. daily, at inexpensive to moderate prices. On the rooftop is the hotel's expensive Claddagh Room restaurant, serving Galway Bay's catch-of-the-day—excellent seafood. But this is not to slight the outstanding meat dishes, especially the Gaelic steak flamed at the table in whiskey, cream, and brandy. Crabmeat salad and poached salmon are unerring choices here, too. Lunch is served from 1 to 2:30 and dinner from 7 to 11. AmEx, Diners, Master, and Visa are accepted. The hotel has a pool, sauna, health complex, sunbed, and fine Irish crafts boutique. (U.S. agents: Great Southern Hotels; Utell International.)

Ballykilty Manor   QUIN, COUNTY CLARE

Until recently, Ballykilty Manor (065-25627) was the longtime homestead of the Blood family—in fact, since the early 1600s. One of the members of this family stole the British crown jewels during the reign of Charles II. Part of the original building is still used, along with the later Georgian portions, which include a fine entrance hall, complete with a marble fireplace and grand staircase, and finely pargeted high ceilings. The antiques here are more Victorian than Georgian. It should be said of this house, which has 11 moderately priced bedrooms (all with bath and breakfast included), that it is comfortable and clean but not posh. Its owners, Tom and Maura Conroy, are most amiable. The moderately priced dinner, served at 7 in the rustic dining room, consists of good, basic Irish cuisine. Ballykilty is open all year, has a full license, and accepts AmEx, Master, and Visa. Fishing and river swimming are available on the grounds; riding, hunting, and golfing are nearby. (U.S. agent: Reservations Systems.) It's about a 5-mile, 15-minute drive from Shannon Airport.

Dunraven Arms   ADARE, COUNTY LIMERICK

This long, creamy-yellow, 2-story hotel (061-86209) is situated in one of Ireland's most charming villages, where thatched cottages, shops, and restaurants abound in pastel shades. Little has changed in Adare, which is 25 miles from Shannon Airport, since the 19th century. The hotel stretches out behind flower beds and verdant lawns on the main street. Its cozy interiors are a catchall for antiques of various periods, and the sitting-room lounge is extremely pleasant and warming. Of varying sizes, the 24 expensive (breakfast not included) rooms all have baths. The comfortable Maigue Restaurant serves excellent food, including such entrees as tender prime ribs of beef, superb tournedos béarnaise, tasty pheasant with truffles, fine panfried scampi flamed in brandy, and wonderful poached salmon hollandaise. Vegetables and fruits are fresh from the hotel's own gardens. Wines are good and moderately priced, as are the meals. Lunch is served from 12:30 to 2:15, dinner from 7:30 to 9:30. The bar has inexpensive and good pub grub at lunchtime. AmEx, Diners, Master, and Visa are accepted. Golf, fishing, hunting, and riding are nearby. Dunraven specializes in fox-hunting holidays and makes all arrangements for guests. The hotel has entertainment during the summer months and also caters functions. It's open all year. (U.S. agent: Reservations Systems.)

Adare Manor, Adare

ADARE, COUNTY LIMERICK

Adare Manor (061-86125) is the epitome of the grand country mansion. Originally built in the 18th century, it was the home of the Dunraven family. The second, and gout-ridden, Earl of Dunraven found the original 2-story, 7-bay structure a little too modest and plain for his blood, so he spent his days envisioning a sumptuous Tudor-Revival-style home and spent his heiress-wife's money achieving his fantasy. They lived in the old house, while the new one grew up around them. When enough of the latter was finished, much of the old house was demolished. Work by local craftsmen and leading architects continued through several family generations until Adare Manor grew into the spectacular 19th-century achievement we now see. It's a 3-story asymmetrical composition of bay and mullioned windows, relieved by a Gothic cloister on one side. The structure is dominated by an Irish-battlement tower with a truncated roof that resembles a pyramid. The entrance hall doors are of carved gray marble. The enormous entry hall is divided down the center by huge Gothic stone arches. A similar arch appears in front of the grand staircase. There's also a carved oak minstrels' gallery on this floor. On the second floor, a vaulted passage leads to the long gallery, which is 130 feet long and 30 feet high. The ceiling is timbered, and there are marvelous carved wood panels throughout the room. The third floor houses the grand bedrooms. The wonderful news here is that the Ashford consortium, which owns and operates Ashford and Dromoland Castles, has acquired Adare Manor and is restoring its yesteryear elegance so it can be opened as one of the country's finest lodging and dining manors. It will also be one of the largest of its type with as many as 60 bedrooms, open all year. (U.S. agent: Ashford Castle Inc.) Adare Manor is located right in the village.

Great Southern Hotel   KILLARNEY, COUNTY KERRY

Close to the railway terminal in Killarney, the Great Southern (064-31262) is a very old hotel. It was opened in 1854 and is still surrounded by 40 acres of gardens and lawns, where guests once played croquet. The rambling structure has recently been refurbished in the grand Victorian manner. Besides its sitting rooms and lounges recalling an elegant past, there are 180 expensive bedrooms, all with bath (breakfast is not included). There are 2 moderately priced restaurants, both emphasizing good Irish and French food. The hotel has a full license and accepts all credit cards. Facilities include an indoor heated pool, sauna, tennis courts, and good boutique. Nearby are 2 championship 18-hole golf courses. From May through September, the hotel presents Siamsa Tire, the National Folk Theatre of Ireland, on four weekly nights. The Great Southern is open mid-March through December. (U.S. agents: Great Southern Hotels; Utell International.)

Parknasilla
Great Southern Hotel   PARKNASILLA, COUNTY KERRY

Once the palace of bishops, the Parknasilla Great Southern (064-45122) is a graceful 19th-century mansion set dramatically on the banks of the Kenmare River, near where it flows into the sea. Here, amid nearly

300 acres of semitropical gardens with palm trees, you may golf (private 9-hole course), play tennis, ride horses, hike, and run. Off its shores, you may fish, sail (or take sailing lessons), boat, and swim. In other words, you could stay for months and never even go inside. But once you do, you'll find a heated saltwater pool, a sauna, table tennis, and snooker. After a rather grand foyer, the 60 expensive bedrooms—all with bath, phone, radio, and TV—are simply decorated but cozy (breakfast not included). Be sure to ask for one in the older section rather than in the modern wing. The spacious, yet intimate, Pygmalion Restaurant—so named because George Bernard Shaw loved Parknasilla and made frequent visits to this mansion (the bar is called the Doolittle)—has a menu that has won cuisine awards. The fresh seafood dishes are the best. The restaurant is open for lunch from 12:30 to 2:30, for dinner from 7 to 9. It's moderate to expensive, with AmEx, Diners, Visa, and Master accepted. Often there is evening entertainment. The Great Southern, perfectly located for exploring the Ring of Kerry, is on the Ring (T66), about 19 miles west of Kenmare, and is open April through October. (U.S. agents: Great Southern Hotels; Utell International.)

Aisling House CASTLEGREGORY, COUNTY KERRY

On the threshold of Dingle's breathtaking Conor Pass and Brandon Head, Aisling House (066-39134) is a modern doctor's house, but it works like a charm—all because of the doctor's wife, Mrs. Healy. This totally disarming woman could enchant the sourest of persons. Extremely knowledgeable about Irish history, especially of the Dingle area, this strikingly graceful woman will converse colorfully at great length. She's also a whiz at things current, such as restaurants and shops of the nearby Brandon area and the Dingle Peninsula. It would take pages to describe this woman, who has made this house—through antiques and good taste—a true find. There are 6 rooms (only 2 with private bath), but you'll miss out if you don't stay here. It's also inexpensive, with a delicious breakfast included. No lunches or dinners are served, but Mrs. Healy can provide a sizable list of nearby good food places. (One simple place that must be mentioned is **Marilyn Spillane's**, way out [a few miles] on a jutting, jagged peninsula off Castlegregory called the

Magharees, which splits Tralee and Brandon bays. Marilyn, a Canadian transplant, serves delicious hearty hamburgers and fresh [picked nearby] mushroom soup.) Aisling House, which is open from May 1 to October 1, accepts no credit cards.

Seaview   THE SPA, TRALEE, COUNTY KERRY

On the northern shore of Tralee Bay, this house (066-36107), part of which was built as early as 1836, has both pleasures and drawbacks. The O'Donnells, owners of the house, have great charm. Relax in one of the sitting room's overstuffed chairs and listen to Mr. O'Donnell speak of the distant past, when an enormously wealthy but ugly Tralee leather merchant beguiled a beautiful Kerry maiden into marrying him and moving into this remote seaside Georgian mansion. When she came out of her trance and realized her folly, she drifted off into al-coholic oblivion and death. Some say her ghost still haunts the house. The furniture is very basic, and the 6 inexpensive bedrooms (with breakfast included) have only hot and cold running water. Bathrooms are adjacent. There is no alcohol license. A real bargain (no credit cards), it's open all year. Boating, sailing, surfing, swimming, fishing, and riding are available locally. A golf course is adjacent. It's 4 miles from Tralee (with good shops, restaurants, Gaelic mime/music/dance/ theatre), on the Fenit Road. Also nearby are the Oyster Tavern (sea-food) and the Tankard Bar (meat and seafood dishes).

Milltown House   DINGLE, COUNTY KERRY

This is a very plain, unpretentious, turn-of-the-century house (066-51372) overlooking Dingle Harbor, on the outskirts of the village of Dingle. Except for its gleaming white stucco exterior, with dramatic bay windows and spacious, high-ceilinged interiors, this lodging has little to offer in the romantic sense. But it's about as close as you'll come to that on the remote, spectacularly romantic Dingle Peninsula. There certainly is nothing wrong with Milltown House. It's immaculately clean and quiet, but modern furniture does nothing to enhance the fine, old features of the building. The 7 bedrooms, all with baths, are sizable and inexpensive, with breakfast included, so it's a real bargain. No other meals are served, but in the very attractive Dingle village are 2 wonderful and intimate seafood restaurants—Doyle's Seafood Bar and The Half Door (see chapter 14). Milltown House is open from April 1 through September 30. No credit cards are accepted.

NOTE: Two other lodgings that are acceptable in this very scenic area are **Alpine House** and the **Hotel Skellig**. Alpine (066-51250) is relatively modern, inexpensive (breakfast included), and has 14 rooms, all with bath. The owners are very friendly and accommodating. Open March through October. Skellig (066-51144) is a moderately priced modern hotel (breakfast included) with 79 rooms, all with bath. While it had once slipped from favor, it is now under new management and is on the rise again. Overlooking Dingle Harbor, it has an outdoor pool and a tennis court. The restaurant is improving as well—serving a mix of Irish/French dishes and basic seafoods. The hotel accepts AmEx, Diners, Master, and Visa, and it is open March 15 through October 31.

Another lodging possibility is the very pleasant, though modern, bed-and-breakfast **Cleevan**, which is about a mile west of Dingle village on the R559. There are only 5 bedrooms, all with bath. Run by the friendly Sheehy family, it is open Easter through September. Only breakfast is served. Credit cards are not accepted, but it's inexpensive.

_____

Arbutus Lodge   CORK CITY, COUNTY CORK

This hotel (021-501237) was built as an elegant hilltop townhouse in 1802. The entrance hall still maintains the aura of that period, with antiques, a grand staircase, and high, pargeted ceilings. But the 20 moderately priced bedrooms, all with bath and breakfast included, are modern and of varying sizes. Each contains a private wine/liquor chest with mixers. The major reason for including this lodging here is the restaurant. It is so splendid that you may wish to stay for several days just to enjoy the food. (A review of the Arbutus dining room appears in chapter 14, Special Restaurants.) There is a window-walled bar (overlooking the sweep of Cork City and the River Lee) that serves an inexpensive-to-moderate bar lunch (fresh seafoods, homemade soups, pâté, smoked salmon) from 12:30 to 2:30. Its patio, used in good weather, gets you even closer to the magnificent view. The Arbutus is open all year, has a full license, and accepts AmEx, Diners, Master, and Visa. It is in the hilly Montenotte section of Cork City.

Lotamore House   CORK CITY, COUNTY CORK

Set on 4 acres of wooded land, Lotamore House (021-822344) is a Georgian manor built in 1791 by a sailor for his young bride. Today it's owned by Brendan and Marion Long and Gerard Keane, who have renovated it, keeping the grand staircase, the exquisite pargeted ceilings, and the white marble fireplace in the sitting room. This is one of the very few old lodgings in Cork City. Although the furniture is modern throughout, it is quite comfortable. There are 20 moderately priced bedrooms, each with private bath, shower, phone, and color TV. Breakfast is included. Tea and snack foods are available, but no lunch and dinner or alcohol license. If guests don't want to travel for dinner, the owners have built a path to the next-door Hunter's Lodge, which serves very good dinners. Lotamore accepts AmEx, Master, and Visa and is open all year. It is in the Tivoli section, on the main road to Waterford and Dublin, just past the Silver Springs Hotel as you leave Cork City. (It's about a 4-minute drive from city center.)

Ballylickey Manor House   BALLYLICKEY, COUNTY CORK

Ballylickey Manor House (027-50071) was an old shooting lodge built by Lord Kenmare, which in recent times, under the ownership of the Graves family, had become one of Ireland's grand country inns. So popular was it that chalets and a poolside French restaurant were added to the estate to accommodate more guests. Then some years ago there was a fire, and the lodge was badly burned. While the chalets, restaurant, and gardens remained open to the public, careful reconstruction of the manor ensued. Now the south and east wings have been beautifully restored, and bedrooms and suites are now available. Chalets remain open. So once again here in Ballylickey Town amid rolling hills, gardens, and secluded wooded landscapes is the perfect romantic retreat. There are 11 bedrooms and suites, including the chalets, all with bath, phone, and breakfast included. The chalets are moderately priced, while those rooms in the manor are expensive. AmEx and Visa accepted. The colorful, intimate bar with fireplace and the restaurant with a wood-fired grill are extremely romantic. There's gourmet French cuisine, with seafood a specialty. As a starter, try the heavenly feuilleté de champignons (pastry filled with mushrooms in a cream and cheese sauce) if it's on the menu. John Dory and brill dishes serve as excellent entrees. The vegetables and local cheeses are superb, as is the moderately priced wine; the house wine is fine. Food is moderate to expensive. Lunch is served from 1 to 2:30, dinner from 7:30 to 9:30. The estate has a full license and is open mid-March through November. Closed Thursdays. Nearby golfing, tennis, mountain walks. Ballylickey is an ideal center for touring southern County Cork. (U.S. agents: David Mitchell; Robert Reid.)

Sea View Hotel   BALLYLICKEY, COUNTY CORK

The Sea View (027-50073) is a gleaming white Victorian estate overlooking Bantry Bay and highlighted by mountains. Built in 1890, it is beautifully situated amid gardens, trees, and verdant lawns. The interior, including a very pleasant sitting room with fireplace, is cozy and very attractive. Period antiques furnish the public rooms and the 12 moderately priced bedrooms (11 with bath). Breakfast is included. No credit cards are accepted. Owner Kathleen O'Sullivan has developed an intimate dining room that specializes in seafoods. Crab lasagna is an excellent starter, as are the deep-fried tidbits. There's an excellent turbot dish served with prawn sauce as an entree; the plaice is very good, though plain. Veal and beef dishes are also tasty. There are excellent vegetables, good moderate-priced wines, and a full license. Lunch, 1:30 to 2:30, is inexpensive. Dinner, 7 to 9:30, is moderate. Two golf courses, fishing, shooting, pony trekking—all are nearby. Ballylickey is an ideal base for touring beautiful West Cork and parts of Kerry. The Sea View is on the main road (T65) in Ballylickey, between Glengarriff and

Bantry. It's open mid-March through October. (U.S. agent: Reservations Systems.)

Rectory House　　　　　　　　DUNDRUM, COUNTY TIPPERARY

Comfort is emphasized at Rectory House (062-71115), an old country home set peacefully among trees on the Tipperary plains. There's a very pleasant sitting room with a log fire, and the 10 tastefully decorated bedrooms (7 have baths) are moderately priced (breakfast included). The dining room, offering good meat and fish dishes at moderate prices, is open for dinner from 6 to 9:30. Rectory House has a full license, is open all year, and accepts Master, Visa, and AmEx. Golf and riding facilities are nearby. It's only a short drive from here to the Rock of Cashel. (U.S. agent: Best Western Hotels.)

Knocklofty House Hotel　　　CLONMEL, COUNTY TIPPERARY

Once the estate of the Earls of Donoughmore, Knocklofty House Hotel (052-38222), is an 18th-century mansion on 100 acres of grounds. All the wonderful rooms are furnished with beautiful antiques from various periods and Oriental carpets. But by far the most interesting room is the enormous library with log-burning fireplace and grand piano (a pianist entertains here every Saturday through the year). It is 2 stories high with a balcony and special oak ladders that roll around the walls of bookshelves. There are 11 moderately priced, well-appointed bedrooms, with bath and breakfast included. The oak-panelled, candlelit dining room overlooks the River Suir and serves good French nouvelle cuisine at moderate prices. Try the fillet steak wrapped in bacon and served with a mushroom béarnaise sauce. Dinner is from 6:30 to 10:30, lunch from 12:30 to 2:30. Afternoon tea is also served. AmEx, Master, and Visa are accepted. Facilities include a snooker room, indoor pool, exercise room, sauna, jacuzzi, riding, golf driving range, and nearby hunting. Knocklofty is open all year and is 4 miles southwest of Clonmel on the R665.

Blenheim House   BLENHEIM HEIGHTS, COUNTY WATERFORD

Among Ireland's most romantic lodgings, Blenheim House (051-74115) was built by a Quaker family in 1763 as an enormous Georgian country residence. Pages could be written about its antiques (early 19th-century walnut French beds with lockers to match, 18th-century bow-ended beds, bar tables, granny and granddad chairs, Scotch chests, and on and on). Despite its size, there are only 6 bedrooms (which makes it very exclusive) in this immaculate house with a grand sitting room. All have baths and are inexpensive (*very* inexpensive when you consider the quality), with breakfast included. The only drawback to Greg and Clare Fitzmaurice's splendid home overlooking gardens and a river is that it doesn't serve lunch or dinner. However, they are quick to suggest a number of area restaurants. Blenheim House is open all year, does not accept credit cards, and is not licensed to serve alcohol. It is a 10-minute drive from Waterford City. Nearby are beaches, horse riding, golf, fishing (sea and river), and historic Waterford City. You can also tour the Waterford crystal factory (closed most of August) or take a dinner cruise run by Galley Cruising Restaurants (see chapter 14, Special Restaurants). From Waterford City take the R688 until you see a signpost for Blenheim Heights, after which you will see the sign for the house.

Waterford Castle   BALLINAKILL, WATERFORD CITY

Waterford Castle (051-78203) is a magnificent 19th-century castle built around an old Norman keep by the Fitzgerald family and is located on a 310-acre island on the River Suir, about 2 miles from Waterford City's center. It is reachable only by car ferry. Recently purchased by Eddie Kearns for approximately 500,000 Irish pounds, the castle and grounds are undergoing renovations (costing a million Irish pounds). The castle, built entirely of stone, has Elizabethan-style wings and a turreted roof. Inside, the great hall sets the tone of the castle. Its walls are of Portland stone relieved by majestic panels of oak and there's a fine stone fireplace. The stately dining room is paneled in oak and a fireplace carved from oak has the Fitzgerald family crest. There are 19 elegant and expensive bedrooms ranging from standard size to deluxe suites, all with bath but breakfast not included. Dining is expensive. Food is served on a specially designed Waterford Castle suite made by Wedgwood. Likewise, beverages are served from crystal created from a special new pattern designed by Waterford Crystal. All major credit cards accepted. The Castle is open all year. Sporting activities are fishing, shooting, horse riding, tennis, running, swimming (heated indoor pool). An indoor health and fitness center and a squash court are available. There are nearby polo and golf facilities. However, Mr. Kearns is in the process of creating a golf course on the island, as well as a helicopter landing pad. (U.S. agent: BTH Holidays.) To reach the castle, take the road that branches off where the city's main Quay and Mall roads meet. It's called Adelphi Terrace. Drive to the pier, and the car ferry journey is 2 minutes.

The Old Rectory
Country House   WICKLOW TOWN, COUNTY WICKLOW

For some attentive owners, this lodging (0404-67048) could be just what its rather austere exterior suggests—a drab old 19th-century rectory. But open the door. It's alive with fresh, happy colors that work in harmony with stately rooms of high, pargeted ceilings and dark marble fireplaces. Likewise, the antique and modern furniture blend beautifully. The house's special romantic charm, maintained by owners Linda and Paul Saunders, would make this a perfect place for a honeymoon. The 5 moderately priced bedrooms blossom with pastels offset by gleaming whites. All have bath, phone, fresh flowers, coffeemaker, and brochures suggesting tours of the Wicklow area. Breakfast is included. The Saunderses have turned their intimate, candlelit dining room into a gourmet paradise, serving such starters as farmhouse parsnip-and-bacon soup, Dublin Bay prawns grilled in garlic butter, fondue, and fresh tomato soup with mint. Among the fine entrees are breast of chicken with orange in pastry, lobster with pineapple-coconut and white rum, sea trout en papillote, and marinated fillet steak topped with pâté. Vegetarian dishes are also available. Wines are good and moderate to expensive. Dinner is served from 7:30 to 9. No credit cards are accepted. There is a choice of full Irish breakfast, Aberdeen breakfast (porridge and kippers), or Swiss breakfast (fresh fruit and muesli). (The Swiss breakfast may be served in bed.) Tennis, golf, horseback riding, cycling, swimming—all are nearby. The Old Rectory is on the main N11 Dublin Road, on the edge of town. It's open April through October. (U.S. agent: Robert Reid.)

Tulfarris House   BLESSINGTON, COUNTY WICKLOW

Tulfarris House (045-64574) is a restored grand Georgian manor overlooking Poulaphouca Lake in the front but sheltered by the Wicklow mountains to the rear. It has a leisurely yet elegant sitting room with chandelier and white-marble fireplace and vast window overlooking the gardens. There are 20 tasteful bedrooms, including some suites, all of which have baths and phone, and are moderate to expensive with breakfast included. Tulfarris has a dining room with full license that serves moderate to expensive French cuisine and a less expensive courtyard bistro. Lunch is from 12:30 to 2:30, dinner is from 7:30 to 9:30. It's open all year, and all credit cards are accepted. The estate incorporates its own 9-hole golf course at lake shore and offers trout and course fishing, croquet, a putting green, and pleasant woodland walks. The house is less than 5 minutes from riding stables and for the racing enthusiast, it's about a 20-mile drive to the Curragh, Naas, and Punchestown race courses. It's also promoted as a good locale for small business conferences and is an excellent center for touring the beautiful Wicklow hills. (U.S. agent: Reservation Systems Inc.) Tulfarris is 25 miles south of Dublin City and 6 miles south of Blessington, just off the N81 and is marked.

Kilkea Castle   CASTLEDERMOT, COUNTY KILDARE

Almost 800 years old, Kilkea Castle (0503-45156) was built in the late 12th century. This bleak, turreted Norman structure, sitting bolt upright on the plains of Kildare, has an endlessly fascinating history. Home of the Fitzgeralds, the Earls of Kildare, its greatest attraction is that it's haunted and has been for centuries—since Garrett Og Fitzgerald ("Wizard Earl") practiced black magic. A secret room here was used for the purpose. Apparitions and battle sounds are said to occur still. There are 53 high-ceilinged bedrooms (unfortunately, they are plainly furnished) with baths and phones. Rooms are moderately priced, but breakfast is not included. While the meals are basic hearty Irish fare (duckling, roast loin of pork, sirloin steak, grilled salmon steak) and moderately priced, the great hall in which they are served is too flashy and needs to be refurbished to recapture a quality and sense of the past. There is a house dinner dance on Friday and Saturday nights. Lunch is served from 12:30 to 2:30, dinner from 6 to 10. The bars (full license) are rustic enough, and there's good pub grub, especially seafood. Facilities include a sauna, gym, and outdoor heated pool. Riding and tennis are nearby. The hotel frequently caters functions. AmEx, Diners, Master, and Visa are accepted. Kilkea Castle, 3 miles northwest of Castledermot on the road to Athy and 40 miles southwest of Dublin, is open April 1 through October 31. (U.S. agent: Best Western Hotels.)

Ariel House   DUBLIN CITY

Dating from 1850, Ariel House (01-685512) is a red-brick Victorian townhouse built for a wealthy marquis. It is so popular that owner Michael O'Brien has added an entire wing. Now there are 16 moderately priced rooms, all with bath, color TV, and phone. Breakfast is included. Be sure to specify if you want one of the Victorian rooms. Take the time to enjoy the Victorian antiques in the entrance hall and sitting room. O'Brien himself is a major reason for staying in this spotless house in the central Ballsbridge area, a 15-minute walk from St. Stephen's Green. Not only is he congenial, but he knows Dublin and its history and is more than eager to put you at ease and help you plan your itinerary. His restaurant, overlooking gardens and lawns, is a marvel, with excellent, beautifully prepared meals, both meat and seafood, at inexpensive prices. Ariel House is open all year. Its restaurant, with wine license, is open for dinner from 6 to 10:30 (closed Sunday). Nonresidents must make reservations. Ariel House is at 52 Lansdowne Road, near Jurys Hotel and the Berkeley Court Hotel.

Fitzpatrick Castle Hotel   KILLINEY, COUNTY DUBLIN

Built in 1791, Fitzpatrick Castle (01-851533) now has more of a Victorian aura. Its spacious, high-ceilinged lobby is filled with period antiques and dark oil paintings and warmed with a fine white marble fireplace. Although it has a leisurely, old-fashioned ambience, this 9-acre estate next to the peaceful 250-acre woodland preserve of Killiney Hill is run as efficiently as a Dublin City establishment. There are 3 cozy cocktail bars, including one in the dungeon, and 94 bedrooms and suites, all with bath, phone, TV, and radio. Furnished with antiques and reproductions, including four-poster beds, the rooms are expensive (breakfast not included), with AmEx, Diners, Master, and Visa accepted. The Truffles Restaurant, with antiques and silver trolleys, offers excellent carvery roast beef, lobster, steak, and rack of lamb—served by candlelight at night. Lunch, from 12:30 to 2:30, is inexpensive to moderate; dinner, from 7 to 10:30, is moderate. The restaurant is closed Sunday. The less expensive Jester's Restaurant, for grills, is open daily from 12:30 to 11 (it closes at 10 Sunday). Facilities include an indoor heated pool, sauna, squash and tennis courts, solarium, and men's and women's hair stylists. A courtesy coach to Dublin is available. Nearby are golfing, horseback riding, fishing, and ocean swimming. Fitzpatrick Castle is open all year. (U.S. agents: American Wolfe International; BTH Holidays.) It's on the main Dublin-to-Killiney road, 11 miles from Dublin.

The Court Hotel   KILLINEY, COUNTY DUBLIN

Considered to be a fine example of a Victorian villa, the Court Hotel (01-851622) was built in the late 1800s. This rambling, pale-green stucco structure with white trim and numerous extensions has become a noted seaside resort just 10 miles from Dublin City. Now there are 32 bedrooms, all with bath and moderately priced (breakfast is not included). Try to obtain one of the more spacious rooms in the high-ceilinged portion of the original villa overlooking Killiney Bay. You'll note the Victorian influence in the ornately pargeted high ceilings of the public rooms and the period ship's gear. Unfortunately, the furniture isn't antique, but the lounge bar, with grand windows facing the grounds and bay, is most pleasant. The Island Restaurant, also facing the bay, offers a wide selection of good seafood and gourmet meat dishes, as well as more adventurous game and international cuisine. Lunch is served from 12:30 to 2:15, dinner from 7 to 10. Prices are moderate. There's less expensive fare in the Library Grill, where you can browse through old books while you eat. A must is the hotel's antiques shop, with excellent buys on small items. AmEx, Master, and Visa are accepted. Ocean swimming (with private walkway) is available at the hotel; nearby are waterskiing, riding, tennis, and squash facilities. Open all year, the Court Hotel is located adjacent to the railway station on Station Road at Killiney Bay and seafront. (U.S. agent: Robert Reid.)

Hilton Park   CLONES, COUNTY MONAGHAN

A magnificent Georgian estate with its own private lake, the Hilton Park (047-56007) has been the home of the Madden family for 8 generations. Now Lucy and John Madden have opened it for all to enjoy. All the rooms are furnished with fine period antiques. There are 6 bedrooms, 2 with bath. Some have antique four-poster beds and sweeping views. The dining room serves superbly prepared traditional Irish cuisine, including fresh, locally grown vegetables. Vegetarians are welcome, but prior notice is required for special foods. Specialties include Lucy's fresh breads and pastries, as well as her homemade, award-winning, herb-flavored Irish cream cheese. Dinner is at 8. Cozy Hilton Park is moderately priced, with a wine license, and accepts AmEx. It has its own golf course, and fishing, swimming, and boating are available on the private lake. Open from April to September, Hilton Park is on the N54, southwest of Clones. (U.S. agent: Robert Reid.) While staying here, try to visit the newly opened Marble Arch Caves.

¶ Two palatial old manors are being readied to open as Irish country lodgings. **Mount Juliet** in Thomastown, County Kilkenny, is a sweeping 3-story, 18th-century homestead built by the first Earl of Carrick across the River Nore from his family's Ballylinch Castle. Architectural features here include the long hall, the ballroom, and unusual plaster-work ceilings—one detailing a full hunting scene and another of a man shooting. **Luttrelstown Castle** in Clonsilla, County Dublin, is a stunning structure most likely dating to the 14th century that has dramatic Gothic battlements and turrets and a Tudor-Revival banqueting hall added in the 19th century. The latter was later refurbished in early 18th-century design. A library and ballroom are noted rooms here as well. Luttrelstown was originally the home of the Luttrel family, one of whom was murdered in Dublin and another sentenced to clean the streets of Augsburg in Germany for pickpocketing. The castle is said to be haunted by the family.

Until recently, **Jurys Hotel** in the fashionable Ballsbridge section of Dublin (01-605000) was a big, modern hotel with nothing to distinguish it from other big, modern hotels of Europe. This has now changed with the renovation of its lobby and public rooms—which includes the addition of a spectacularly beautiful three-story atrium/skylight entryway housing a variety of unusual flora and the refurbishment of the hotel's Dubliner Bar with an array of Victoriana. It's still a big hotel, and its 290 moderate to expensive bedrooms have been tastefully redesigned.

14 SPECIAL RESTAURANTS

She's the white flower of the blackberry,
she's the sweet flower of the raspberry,
she's the best herb in excellence
for the sight of the eyes.
  —Irish traditional folk song, before 1789

Reveries   ROSSES POINT, COUNTY SLIGO

Named after a little-known Yeats poem, Reveries (071-77371) is a charming new entry on the Irish restaurant scene with a cool yet elegant Mediterranean design. Tables are set with pale blue linen, plus china and crystal, and the superb cuisine and wines are worthy of such treatment. Good starters are the homemade soups and the deep-fried Irish cheeses served with fresh cranberry sauce. But it's the entrees that are particularly imaginative and memorable: venison with juniper-berry sauce, pigeon in port, veal in fresh dill and mustard sauce, panfried freshwater trout with vermouth and almonds. While there are fine desserts, most people prefer to sample the cheese board, which may have as many as 10 Irish varieties. The romantic dining room, overlooking Sligo Bay with Knocknarea Mountain in the distance, is operated by Damien Brennan, brother of Francis Brennan, who owns one of Ireland's finest hotels—The Park in Kenmare, County Kerry. Both brothers have great flair with cuisine. Reveries is moderately priced, with wine license only, and accepts all credit cards. It's open for dinner only from 7 to 10, but closed Sunday. Reservations are strongly suggested.

Doon   MOYARD, COUNTY GALWAY

Doon (091-85115) is a charming little luncheon-only seafood place. Even though it's signposted, when you arrive you'll think you've made a mistake. After driving between vast rows of fuchsia, you come to a white, flower-skirted cottage that looks like someone's private abode. It is. Fraser and Moira Stephenson live here, and they'll usher you into their small, polished-wood-floor dining room filled with intimate flower-bedecked tables and rustic leather and wood chairs. The room overlooks the grounds. After Fraser takes your order, Moira most likely will chat with you from her adjacent kitchen as she prepares your meal.

And a lovely midday meal it is. It's headed by homemade breads and soups, such as fresh prawn bisque, cream of mussel soup, or vegetable soup (a delicious blend of carrots, lettuce, cauliflower, and onions from the Stephensons' garden). The entrees might include prawn salad, poached brill with herb sauce, cold lobster and crab plates. All are perfectly prepared. The desserts include delicious homemade berry tarts, and there's a very good Irish cheese board. The wine list is small but good and very reasonable, as is the inexpensive-to-moderate food. There is a wine license only. No credit cards are accepted. Doon is open from 12:15 to 3, but closed Wednesday and from November through March. Reservations are advised. It's located on the Clifden-to-Westport road, N59, in Moynard.

Drimcong House   MOYCULLEN, COUNTY GALWAY

One of Ireland's hottest new restaurants, Drimcong House (091-85115), is touted by many knowledgeable cuisine enthusiasts to be among the country's best. This is easily understood when you note that Gerry and

Drimcong House Restaurant, County Galway

Marie Galvin, who once ran one of County Cork's most popular restaurants (the Vintage in Kinsale), are the bright sparks of Drimcong. This truly delightful and intimate dining room (seating no more than 50) is located in a 300-year-old country manor. Here you will find a variety of simple yet superb dishes prepared with a French touch. The menu frequently changes, but a sampling of the delicious starters could include Camembert cheese and oyster tart, stir-fried vegetables and almonds in sesame oil, avocado and fish served with fresh mayonnaise. Entrees might include a beautifully prepared chicken breast with a succulent Madeira sauce, a seafood/shellfish pancake flavored with wild sorrel, or a delicious Irish pork dish. Desserts offered are hot baked pear in crème de cassis, homemade ice creams, and a variety of perfectly ripened Irish cheeses (some unusual). Drimcong is very moderately priced and has a fine wine list at reasonable prices. AmEx, Diners, Master, and Visa are accepted. Sadly, Drimcong is open only at night, from 7 to 10, and closed Sunday and Monday. Also closed Christmas through February. Word of the exceptional quality is spreading fast, so reservations are definitely recommended. The restaurant is 8 miles north of Galway City on the Moycullen-to-Oughterard road. The entry drive is signposted.

Moran's   KILCOLGAN, COUNTY GALWAY

Moran's (091-86113)—or Moran's Oyster Cottage, as it is often called— is the best in the country for the delicacies served (in season) with delicious homemade brown bread and a creamy glass or pint of Guinness. But so much more is available at this white, thatched pub/restaurant with antique trappings. Among the great (and inexpensive) taste sensations—which may range from a snack to a full meal—are fresh salmon, smoked salmon, prawns, crab claws, crabmeat sandwiches, crabmeat plates, summer salads, and seafood cocktails. And there are wonderful, wonderful soups, such as salmon and prawn chowder and lobster bisque. This 200-year-old establishment is a marvelous little gem of a place where you can drop by at almost any hour and be served in the quaint romantic atmosphere. Watch carefully for the small signpost in Kilcolgan, because the restaurant is off the main road and very easy to miss. Moran's is open daily from 10:30 to 10:30, and on Sunday from 4 to 10:30. It has a full license but accepts no credit cards.

MacCloskey's   BUNRATTY, COUNTY CLARE

Without question, MacCloskey's (061-74082) is the finest little restaurant in the Shannon Airport area. Relatively new, it is so good that it already has an international clientele. Gerry and Marie MacCloskey have lovingly restored the cellars and basement of this 18th-century manor. With gleaming whitewashed walls, pastel tablecloths, and candles, it takes on a rustic, country-French atmosphere that's the epitome of romance.

Indeed, this would be a charming place to come even if you didn't eat. But when you do, you'll find out how much more it has to offer. Gerry is truly an adventurous entrepreneur. Originally he ran the lovely Courtyard Restaurant in remote Schull, County Kerry, where he built an exemplary reputation as a chef. He takes the finest of Irish meat and fish dishes and simply transforms them into a nouvelle Irish-French cuisine that remains incredibly memorable long after the meal. For instance, the black sole on the bone produces a hauntingly delicate taste sensation and is touted by many to be the best-prepared version of the dish in the country. But you'll be equally hard pressed to find a better Gaelic steak. The steak au poivre is perfection, and the simple veal and salmon dishes are equally winning. In addition, Gerry is a wine connoisseur and has some wonderful and reasonably priced vintages (wine license only). His meals are moderately priced and well worth it. AmEx, Diners, Master, and Visa are accepted. Dinner only, from 7 to 10, but reserve early—preferably a day or more beforehand. It's closed Sunday and Monday, plus December 24 through January 31. The restaurant is behind Bunratty Castle, on the main Limerick-to-Shannon road.

The Mustard Seed   ADARE, COUNTY LIMERICK

A lovely little (seats only 26) romantic restaurant, the Mustard Seed (061-86451) is located in one of the most charming towns in Ireland. It's across the road from the old Dunraven Arms coaching inn, in an early 19th-century village house with the original kitchen intact. And what comes from this kitchen is a surprisingly inventive array of Irish nouvelle cuisine. A sprinkling of the zesty appetizers includes crab puffs with Tipperary blue cheese sauce, veal and pistachio nut terrine with orange and ginger sauce, confit of duck with blackcurrant vinegar and hazelnut oil dressing, smoked ox tongue salad with homemade chutney. Equally fine entrees are panfried salmon in a light lime sauce, marinated rack of lamb, escalope of veal with fresh mushroom and sherry sauce, roast pork tenderloin with wild rice and orange sauce, and a unique sweet-and-sour rabbit with chocolate and pine nuts. Vegetables are fresh and beautifully prepared. Desserts, including homemade ice cream, are especially tempting. Food and wines are moderate to expensive (wine license only). Master and Visa are accepted. It's open for dinner from 7 to 10:30, and closed Sunday and Monday, plus January through April and October through December. (It's only closed Monday between May and October.) Adare is on the N21, Limerick/Killarney road.

Gaby's KILLARNEY, COUNTY KERRY

This bright, Mediterranean-style cafe (064-32519), with its special romantic charm, rates a 10 on a 10-point scale by any standards. It's one of Ireland's best seafood restaurants. The wonderful fresh shellfish platter is so enormous that it has to be served on an elevated platform so your dining partner (or partners) will also have room to eat. Magnificent oysters, prawns, shrimp, lobster, and crab adorn the platter. Equally wonderful entrees are the smoked salmon platter, lobster salad, cold or hot whole lobsters from the restaurant's own tank, lobster in crème Cognac, oyster platters, and black sole in cream sauce. Although the entrees are enormous, you may still be interested in the starters, among which the lobster bisque and the smoked mackerel pâté are excellent. Prices are moderate. Nor do you have to spend a fortune on a fine complement to these deserving meals: The less-expensive wines are very trustworthy. Gaby's has a wine license only and accepts AmEx, Diners, Master, and Visa. It's open for lunch from 12:30 to 2:30, but closed Sunday and Monday. It's open for dinner from 6 to 10, but closed Sunday (also closed from December 1 through January 13). Reservations are not accepted, so arrive early or you could have a long wait at this very popular spot. But don't miss it. It's at 17 High Street in Killarney Town.

Doyle's Seafood Bar DINGLE, COUNTY KERRY

It seems that people from all over the world have made their way to Doyle's (066-51174), the town's best-known restaurant. Americans remember it with such fondness that they make a strong point of directing their friends here. Doyle's is very rustic and intimate, with flagstone floors, rock walls, pine tables, and *sugán* (traditional rope and rough wood) chairs. It only seats 30, and there are *no* reservations, so go early or you will have to stand in line for ages. (If you do, however, there is a pleasant bar for waiting.)

You'll hear the ecstatic gasps from diners as they start each of John and Stella Doyle's delicious dishes. If you truly love seafoods, you will have a difficult time selecting from the frequently changed blackboard menu. Smoked mackerel pâté, tuna pâté with tomato puree, crab claws, and a crabmeat and brown sauce soup are delicious starters. Lobster is an entree specialty. Boiled in seawater and served with drawn butter, it is incredibly succulent. Other special dishes are salmon with sorrel sauce, crab claw cassoulet, and brown trout in mushroom sauce. Wines are good and very reasonable. There's a full license. Food prices are moderate. AmEx, Diners, Master, and Visa are accepted. Lunch is served from 12:30 to 2:15, dinner from 6 to 9 (closed Sunday and from mid-November to mid-March). Doyle's is at the bottom of John Street in Dingle Town.

The Doyles have recently acquired the house next door to their restaurant and have turned it into a charming rustic lodging with eight bedrooms with Victorian furniture and private baths—all moderately priced. Guests staying here may make reservations in the restaurant.

The Half Door   DINGLE, COUNTY KERRY

Some say that the Half Door (066-51600), next door to Doyle's, is its equal in serving fine seafood. This rustic, intimate place has rock walls and polished pine floors and ceiling. It seats 38 and *does* take reservations, so you're assured of not having to wait in line. The staff is extremely friendly and attentive. Everyone seems to love the crab quiche as an appetizer, although the seafood soups are all fresh and wonderfully tasty as well. Good entrees range from trout in oatmeal, mussels in garlic butter, poached salmon or sea trout to panfried scallops (with wine, cheese, and garlic) and memorable shellfish au gratin (lobster, prawns, crabs mixed with eggs, white wine, and cream). Lobsters are excellent—again prepared simply. Desserts are special, as are the reasonable wines (a large variety) selected by owner John Slye at French vineyards. Moderately priced, the restaurant is open for lunch from 12:30 to 2 and for dinner from 6 to 9. (It's closed Tuesday and from December through mid-March). The Half Door has a full license and accepts all major credit cards. It's located at the bottom of John Street in Dingle Town.

Arbutus Lodge   CORK CITY, COUNTY CORK

Aficionados insist that the restaurant at the Arbutus Lodge Hotel (021-501237) is the finest French restaurant outside of France. Whether or not it's that fabulous, it certainly serves among the best French cuisine in Ireland. This very sedate (yet intimate), darkened Victorian dining room tends to make patrons swoon over its extensive offerings, which include sautéed lobster with fresh fennel, sea bass with Pernod sauce, roast mallard, ris de veau in a succulent lemon/cream/shallot sauce, medallions of venison with fried aubergine (eggplant), wine-poached turbot. If you like beef, the fillet of beef with Beaujolais sauce à la

Arbutus Lodge Restaurant, County Cork

moelle is outstanding. And these are just a few of the dishes available. (The accompanying vegetables are also excellent.) The wine list also goes on forever. It ranges from moderate to extremely expensive, but moderately priced selections are fine. All major credit cards are accepted. Dinner, served from 7 to 9:30, is expensive. Lunch, from 1 to 2, is more moderately priced. The restaurant is closed Sunday. Reservations are required. If you're lucky, you may get the bay-window table overlooking Cork City. The Arbutus, located in the Montenotte section of Cork City, is open all year. It also has rooms if you'd like to stay here and be close to the dining room (see chapter 13 for a lodgings review).

Lovett's   CORK CITY, COUNTY CORK

A small restaurant in a grand Georgian period townhouse, Lovett's (021-294909) boasts bright red walls, floral draperies, rich old oil portraits, and small vases of flowers. The specialty in this friendly place is seafood, and each dish receives a wonderful special touch. Particularly good are the offerings *en papillote* (baked in a sealed, buttered paper). The John Dory prepared this way with herbs is memorable; likewise the salmon. Even plaice, an ordinary fish, takes on a new dimension when wrapped in lettuce and served with a lemon *beurre blanc* sauce. The shellfish dishes, especially lobster and crabmeat, are worthy of citations. Even a simple crabmeat salad is superlative with the addition of freshly made mayonnaise. If you like scallop dishes, they're especially good here, too. Lovett's also offers meat dishes, which are said to be very good. Owner Dermot Lovett's wines range from inexpensive to expensive, with house wines being agreeable. The food is moderate to expensive. The restaurant accepts all major credit cards and has a full license. It's open all year for lunch Monday through Friday, 12:30 to 2, and for dinner Monday through Saturday, 7:30 to 10 (closed Sunday, Saturday lunch, and bank holidays). Reservations are advised. Lovett's is on Churchyard Lane in the Cork City suburb of Douglas.

Blairs Cove DURRAS, COUNTY CORK

Blairs Cove (027-61127) is housed in a 250-year-old stable. Yes, a stable. And that probably makes it the most unusual restaurant in Ireland. It's a superb one to boot. The stable and its adjoining courtyard are part of a Georgian country estate that includes the splendid Blairs Cove House. The restaurant has been converted into the epitome of Irish rusticity, with old stone walls and floors, an extraordinary high-beamed and chandeliered ceiling, and a gigantic oak-burning fireplace used for cooking. Attended with ease and utmost care by young chef-restaurateur Philippe de Mey, it is worth a visit at all costs. You'll make your selections from a blackboard menu in the cozy fireside lounge, where you can sip an aperitif. Then you'll dine at charming candlelit tables set with vases of cut flowers, while a quietly played grand piano provides background music. Splendid entrees include sautéed veal with fresh raspberry sauce, medallions of lamb with fresh herbs, monkfish flambé, and oak-broiled turbot and sole. A smorgasbord of delightful appetizers is attractively displayed on a table in the center of the room. Here you can sample fresh trout, freshly picked mushrooms in a delicate sauce, tomato mousse, pork pâté, gamebird pâté, and shellfish. Just remember to save room for the soup course and the entrees. Delicious desserts include cheesecake, crème caramel, and fresh fruits. Wines are excellent and moderately priced, as are the meals (wine license only). AmEx, Diners, Masters, and Visa are accepted. Reservations are advised. Lunch is from 1 to 2, dinner from 7:30 to 9:30. Blairs Cove is closed Sunday night and all day Monday (also January 1 through February 28, and Monday through Thursday during March and October 16 through December). The pianist plays daily during the summer months, when guests may dine on the equally romantic courtyard veranda overlooking a fountain and rose gardens. Blairs Cove is a mile south of Durras village on the L56. If you're arriving from the north, keep going straight when you come to the village and *don't* take the road that branches off to the left.

NOTE: The Blairs Cove owners also operate some splendid self-catering (rental) houses facing the courtyard and in the nearby area. (See the review in chapter 15, Special Holidays.)

The Blue Haven   KINSALE, COUNTY CORK

While in truth it is a hotel (it has 10 inexpensive bedrooms, 7 with bath), the Blue Haven (021-72209) is far better known for its gourmet pub and restaurants in this truly beautiful coastal village. So good is the food here that when Bloomingdale's in New York planned a huge Irish promotion a few years ago, owners Brian and Anne Cronin were wisely chosen to do the presentation of Irish cuisine. In this woody, rustic, and quite intimate atmosphere, you'll have difficulty selecting from the array of offerings, especially the seafood. Starters include a wonderful seafood pancake as well as a smoked mackerel and salmon pâté. If you like soup, try the shellfish chowder. Then you can graduate to such delicious entrees as fillet of brill with shrimps and capers, shellfish casserole, sole stuffed with mussels and shrimp, and poached salmon hollandaise. The sautéed beef with mead sauce is robust, as are the chicken breasts in Irish whiskey/mushroom/cream sauce and steak au poivre with brandy sauce. For dessert, try the coupe Blue Haven— a mixture of assorted homemade ice creams, fresh fruits, grated chocolate, and whipped cream. The oak-paneled Haven Bar and Buttery serves food all day, while the more formal (though still relaxed) Sovereign Room serves dinner every day from 7 to 11:30. There's a full license, with good and moderately priced wines. Inexpensive to moderate lunch, moderately priced dinners. AmEx, Diners, Master, and Visa are accepted. The Blue Haven, on Pearse Street in Kinsale Town, is closed during January and February.

Aherne's Seafood Bar   YOUGHAL, COUNTY CORK

Decorated with a sprightly nautical motif, Aherne's (024-92424) is a marvelously refreshing pub/restaurant. Located in a quaint, equally charming seaside town, Aherne's has won food awards and very favorable mentions in international food guides. In the bar, the Fitzgibbon family serves an array of tasty foods: rock oysters, Rossmore king oysters, fresh salmon mayonnaise, dressed crab, fresh prawn cocktail, Youghal Bay sprats grilled in lemon juice and butter. Smoked salmon with brown bread is another fine choice, as are the zesty seafood pies. The pub also offers a vegetarian salad, sandwiches, and shepherd's pie. But it's the seafoods that you should relish. In the equally memorable restaurant, you'll find superb fresh trout, salmon, and black sole from the nearby Blackwater River estuary, as well as simply and beautifully prepared lobster and crab dishes, prawn platters, and scallop casseroles. The bar food is inexpensive and available all day. The restaurant prices for lunch (12:30 to 2:15) are inexpensive; for dinner (6:30 to 10), moderate. Aherne's has a full license and serves good (especially white) wines at moderate prices. It accepts AmEx, Diners, Master, and Visa. Aherne's is open all year but closed Monday (except in August). It's at 163 North Main Street in Youghal village.

Chez Hans   CASHEL, COUNTY TIPPERARY

Originally a small Gothic stone chapel, Chez Hans (062-61177) has been converted into a rather spooky-looking restaurant with blue-painted walls, dim nave lighting, spotlighted tapestries, and gleaming silver. In this unusual setting, adventurous owner Hans-Peter Matthiä presents French cusine that's both intriguing and rewarding. Zesty ham mousse with fresh tarragon leaves, quenelles (dumplings) of turbot, rock oysters, avocado-based seafood salad with prawns and smoked salmon, and courgette (zucchini) soup do equally thrilling justice to the appetizer list. Among the exceptionally fine main courses are veal in tarragon cream sauce or with Gruyère cheese, steamed prawns in sorrel sauce, sea bass in Pernod *beurre blanc*, and tender cuts of roast lamb in rich wine-laced juices. Desserts are good, especially the sorbets. There are equally good cheeses and moderately priced wines. The restaurant is expensive, and no credit cards are accepted. It's open for dinner only from 7 to 10 (closed Sunday and Monday and Christmas to March). Reservations are required. Chez Hans is at the base of the Rock of Cashel, in Cashel Town.

Galley Cruising Restaurants   NEW ROSS, COUNTY WEXFORD

A new dimension in romantic dining accompanies the Galley Cruising Restaurants (051-21723). You decide whether you want lunch (noon), afternoon tea (3 P.M.), or dinner (6 or 7 P.M.). Then you climb aboard and cruise for a few hours up the Nore or the Barrow river. Some feel that the tranquility of the journey, combined with the magnificent pastoral scenery, is worth the price alone. Happily, owner/host Dick Fletcher provides so much more. The very moderately priced lunch (inexpensive, in fact) consists of an enormous buffet of freshly prepared soups, hot and cold meat dishes (such as chicken and turkey), a variety of salads, and rich desserts. The inexpensive afternoon tea includes a large selection of freshly baked cakes, buns, and scones. Dinner is 6 impressive courses long, and it is moderately priced. All cooking is done by Fletcher's competent staff. There's a full license, and the moderately priced wines are good. No credit cards are accepted. Reservations are essential, and they will be held until 10 minutes before departure. Cruises operate daily from Easter through October but are closed for dinner on Sunday and most Mondays. (Weather is not a factor.) Some extended sailings combine both lunch and afternoon tea at a somewhat higher fee. There are also some cruises that depart from Waterford City.

Doyle's Schoolhouse
Restaurant   CASTLEDERMOT, COUNTY KILDARE

Doyle's (0503-44282) is just what the name says it is—a restaurant in an abandoned schoolhouse. The building, from the Victorian era, maintains the original windows and floor and enhances the flavor with original watercolors. Owner/chef John Doyle prides himself on a menu of unusual and varied dishes. Some of the entrees include rabbit casserole using fresh grapefruit juice and cream, poached salmon served with hollandaise flavored with fresh strawberry juice, sea bass *en papillote*, roast guinea fowl, lamb's brains in garlic butter, baked pike, curried beef pancakes. Pâtés are the favored starters here. The wines are excellent and moderately priced, as is the food. Four inexpensive, antiques-furnished cottage bedrooms with baths are now available for those wishing to stay overnight. Doyle's is on the main Dublin-to-Waterford road, 50 miles from Dublin City. Doyle's is open all year. From April through September, dinner is served from 6:30 to 10:30, and it is open for Sunday lunch from 12:30 to 2. From October through March, dinner is from 7:30 to 10, but there is no Sunday lunch and it is closed on Mondays.

Le Coq Hardi, Dublin

Le Coq Hardi

DUBLIN CITY

Not only is Le Coq Hardi (01-689070) an outstanding restaurant and one of Ireland's finest; it must be among the world's best. Chef/patron John Howard and his charming wife, Catherine, continue to garner citations from all quarters (Michelin, Egon Ronay, Good Food, Woodford Bourne Wine Awards). A few years ago, the Howards moved into this marvelous Georgian townhouse and decorated it in the regal manner. When you arrive, you're escorted to a basement sitting-room bar with masculine deep-brown tones, white marble fireplace, richly appointed loveseats, a magnificent black-leather chaise, and handsome oil lamps. Vases of long-stemmed mums grace the tables. Aperitifs are served while you nibble on nonfilling (rightly so) crisp celery and freshly picked cherries (on the stem) as you ponder the menu.

What a menu. Scallop, lobster, prawn, mussel, turbot, sole, and angler dishes were the seafood selections on one memorable evening. Meat and fowl included rack of lamb, Gaelic steak, sweetbreads, calf's liver, ribs of beef, fillets, and chicken. Roast goose is a specialty. Everything is prepared in the grand French manner and served in the elegant first-floor dining room featuring rosewood and mirrors. The lobster salad appetizer is served in the shell, the rack of young lamb entree is served in its own rich juice laced with fine wine. John Howard whisks up the hollandaise sauce for the Argenteuil asparagus after you've ordered it, just as he does for all the sauces. (You can hear the whisk if you are seated at the table near the kitchen.) The wine list is enormous: excellent wines, moderate to very expensive.

Meals are absolute perfection here, and the subdued sighs and murmurs of other diners confirm that assessment.

A word on desserts. They're excellent, but the cheeses are even better—so good that Le Coq Hardi has won dairy awards, and that's rare in Ireland. Do try the Irish Mileens, a tangy, smooth cow cheese that tastes like one of the great French goat cheeses.

If you have but one life to live in Ireland—or one night in which to go money-mad—and you appreciate superlative food in elegant, yet intimate, surroundings, go to Le Coq Hardi. Not only will you not regret it, you'll never forget it.

Lunch is served from 12:30 to 3, dinner from 7 to 11. All major credit cards are accepted. It's closed Sunday and bank holidays. Le Coq Hardi is located in Dublin's "restaurant row" at 35 Pembroke Road, not far from Jurys Hotel and the Berkeley Court, or about a 10-minute walk from St. Stephen's Green. Reservations are necessary.

The Lord Edward   DUBLIN CITY

An historic house in the most ancient quarter of old Dublin, the Lord Edward (01-752557) exudes a woody Victorian charm. And it's the real thing—so much so that you'll feel you're going back in time before you even enter the building, which spans 3 generations. This is a rather unusual place that includes an expensive and fashionable, though rustic, upper gourmet level, a businesspeople's elite middle-level lounge, and a real down-to-earth Dubliner bar on the lower level. Don't be put off by the first-floor bar, where the best of the Dublin grassroots *bowsies* reside.

The upper level has a very pleasant romantic quality about it, especially if you obtain a bay-window table that overlooks old Dublin. Here you'll find a vast array of fish and shellfish dishes prepared in a variety of ways from simple to fancy French. You'll have to choose what suits you best, because they're all good. And so are the wines. The restaurant has a full license, is expensive, and accepts all major credit cards. It's open for lunch Monday through Friday from 12:30 to 2:30 and for dinner Monday through Saturday from 6 to 10:45 (closed Sunday and bank holidays). Reservations are recommended.

The second level here—the Lord Edward Bar—is open for lunch only Monday through Friday from 12:30 to 2:30. You'll find a wide range of salads and seafood salads and a hot dish of the day for a very inexpensive price—and it's good. All major credit cards are accepted.

Bewley's   DUBLIN CITY

You won't find the likes of Bewley's (01-776761) anywhere else in Ireland—or in the rest of the world, for that matter. It's unique. Actually, Bewley's is a series of Dublin cafes, and although all are fine, the 78/79 Grafton Street location is the most interesting and probably the closest to your lodgings. It is *not* an intimate restaurant—unless you relax and turn it into that by enjoying its quaint atmosphere. Established in 1840 as a classic tearoom/coffeehouse, Bewley's has changed very little. Mahogany paneling, stained-glass motifs, enormous dining rooms with shared tables, displays of tea chests and baked goods—and, above all, the wonderful aroma of coffee—make Bewley's memorable. A cross section of Dublin life sits and sips its coffee and tea here each day. Some rush, some pause—to chat or often eavesdrop, to read the papers or browse casually through poetry anthologies. Others just watch the passing parade—as James Joyce once did. And what marvelous baked goods are served here: fresh cream cakes, sugary currant buns, scones, eclairs, rock buns. They're enough to drive you to distraction if you are trying to diet—because you can't resist them with that wonderful coffee and tea (the best in Dublin).

If you wish, you may have more than pastries at Bewley's. Sandwiches and hearty full meals are available, including breakfasts. The fried-plaice-and-chips platter is delicious. Bewley's is open throughout the year from 8:15 to 6. AmEx and Diners are accepted in the new downstairs restaurant, but the upstairs restaurant is far more interesting. Bewley's also has a wonderful shop for buying exquisite teas and coffees,

Bewley's, Dublin

along with chests and pots. Plus there's a pastry and bread shop. The flat, oblong, whole-grain loaf is like none other in the world. Take home a loaf with a pound of Irish butter, lightly toast the bread, serve it with this marvelous butter—and you're in heaven.

The Kish

Located in Jurys Hotel, the Kish (01-605000) is a very modern, yet quite elegant, seafood restaurant. Overlooking the hotel's unusual skylit Pavilion Bar and gardens, this terraced room was named after a lighthouse in Dublin Bay. Here you will find truly delicious dishes with an emphasis on the fancier French concoctions—but simpler versions also are available. Strongly recommended are the sea trout with a lighter-than-usual béarnaise sauce, poached salmon, and lobster Newburg. All of the lobster dishes here are quite special. The shellfish salads and the seafood soups make good starter choices. The Kish is expensive. The wines, which are moderate to expensive, are perfect complements for the fish. It's open for dinner from 6:30 to 10:45 all year, except Sundays. Reservations are suggested. All major credit cards are accepted. The hotel is in Ballsbridge, just a few minutes' drive (or a 15-minute walk) from St. Stephen's Green.

King Sitric   HOWTH, COUNTY DUBLIN

One of the country's early trend-setting (for fine cuisine) restaurants, King Sitric (01-325235) opened in the early 1970s and still maintains its reputation. This charmingly sleepy place, located in the coastal village of Howth (9 miles from Dublin City center on the L86), was once the harbor master's house. Predinner drinks (wine license only) are served in the cozy lounge, where you can watch the lonely flickering lights of distant boats under the star-washed sky. In the intimate, rambling candlelit dining room, the seafoods are almost all first rate. Delicious though simple sole amandine takes on a new taste sensation, the lobster in drawn butter is beautifully done (as are the more complicated lobster dishes), the braised brill *en cocotte* is basic but beautiful. There are poultry and wild game (in season) entrees here, but they tend to be extremely robust. Not that there's anything wrong with that, but it's a shame to miss the infinitely more delicate and memorable tastes of owner Aidan MacManus's seafood delights. If you're wise, you'll also opt for the seafood appetizers. The white wines rule the roost here, but they tend toward the expensive side. All major credit cards are accepted. Lunch, from 12:30 to 2:30, is moderately priced; dinner, from 6:30 to 11, is expensive. Reservations are required. King Sitric is open all year but closed Sunday and bank holidays (also Monday in the wintertime).

White's on the Green   DUBLIN CITY, COUNTY DUBLIN

Open only a few years, this magnificent restaurant (01-751975) just across from romantic Stephen's Green has risen to the pinnacle of the Irish gourmet scene. After getting off to a slow start, it now draws an international clientele, with people often phoning from afar to ensure reservations. White's, which seats 60, has a dazzling white and green decor filled with vibrant fresh flowers. Diners order their meals in a sumptuous, yet cozy, basement cocktail lounge before being taken upstairs to dine. But what's mood without food. And the food prepared by chef Michael Clifford, formerly of Claridge's in London, the Lancaster in Paris, Kersitol in Amsterdam, and the Arbutus in Cork, is superb. Starters might include smoked spiced beef served with a leaf of lovage and clusters of fresh black currents, a salad of roasted young quail and fresh mangos, asparagus sprinkled with boiled and chopped quails' eggs, nettle soup or gazpacho. Entrees may be such dishes as succulent noisettes of lamb, poached brill with tomatoes, onions, and a touch of garlic, grilled sea bass with soya butter and leeks, or wonderful salmon prepared in a variety of ways. There's also one curiosity—lamb stew; something you wouldn't expect in a gourmet restaurant. But it is exquisitely prepared with potatoes perfectly cooked. Desserts (try the caramelized grapes) and country farmhouse cheeses are wonderful. There's an extensive list of wines, many expensive; but the lower-priced house wines are very good. Service is superior but not intimidating. Owners Peter and Alicia White have achieved a lighthearted atmosphere where everybody, including the diners, seems blissfully happy. The restaurant is moderate to expensive and accepts all major credit cards. It's open for lunch from 12:30 to 2:30 and for dinner from 7 to 10:30—but make reservations. Closed Sundays.

15
SPECIAL
HOLIDAYS

I have fallen in love, and I cannot hide it, with her spreading
hair, with her calm mind, with her narrow eyebrows, her blue-grey
eyes, her even teeth, her soft face.

I have given also, though I do not admit it, the love of my soul
to her smooth throat, to her melodious voice, to her sweet-tasting
lips, to her snowy bosom, to her pointed breasts.

—Irish, author unknown
probably 15th or 16th century

Rent an Irish Cottage

The perfect way to be completely alone together is to rent an Irish self-catering cottage. There are many such complexes throughout the country, and they are usually available only for a week or longer. One example is the **Donegal Thatched Cottage Complex** on **Cruit Island** (connected to the mainland by a bridge), near Kincasslagh, County Donegal. Spending time here is a wonderful experience. If you really want to know what it's like to live away from the world in frontier style, this is it. But everything is done with finesse. The painstaking taste level of these country houses enriches them with an infectious rural appeal that is very rare. The cottages are gleamingly spotless, with high-beamed ceilings, cozy lofts, open hearths, flagstone floors, *sugán* (traditional rope-and-wood) chairs, and fine oil paintings. There are fully equipped kitchens (including beautiful china, dishwashers, and washing machines) if you wish to cook. The local Coop grocery is only a few miles away in Kincasslagh. There is also a fine nearby seafood restaurant called The Viking. For your fireplace, there's a handy communal turf pile, but the cottages also have oil-fired central heating and electric blankets. There are miles of beautiful, virtually vacant beaches here, and the fishing is superb. Owners Conor and Mary Ward have established a wonderful holiday complex that offers a special picture of Irish country life—presented with taste, dignity, and an attraction that is not only appealing, it's compelling. Despite all this, it's inexpensive (but no credit cards are accepted). You must make reservations well in advance, especially for peak season. Make arrangements through the Sligo exchange—071-77197—or through Conor and Mary Ward, Donegal Thatched Cottages, Rosses Point, County Sligo.

NOTE: There are many other possibilities for renting Irish cottages in locales throughout the country. In fact, there is now an Irish Self-Catering Holidays Association, comprised of more than 40 such cottage complex groups. All are registered and approved by the Irish Tourist Board, which means high standards must be maintained. Remember that rentals are usually a minimum of a week, sometimes longer. If such a vacation interests you, contact the Irish Tourist Board for its full-color *Irish Cottages & Holiday Homes Quality Self-Catering* brochure.

Rent an Irish Country House, Apartment, or Lodge

While not entirely different from renting an Irish cottage (all are self-catering), the **Blairs Cove House** complex in **Durras**, County Cork, is unique to Ireland—and truly wonderful. So unusual, attractive, and varied are these units that an entire book could be produced with photographs of the interiors and exteriors. And, as if this weren't enough, one of the country's best and most attractive restaurants—Blairs Cove (see chapter 14, Special Restaurants)—is right at its doorstep.

Blairs Cove House and its stable (now the restaurant) are 250 years old, and they rest high above the shores of Dunmanus Bay, a mile from Durras village in the ruggedly beautiful yet lush western portion of County Cork. Fortunately, 3 of these complexes (and "complex" is much too harsh a term) are in the courtyard overlooking the rose gardens and a fountain. There's an upper-story apartment plus two 2-story abodes (one of these in the old smokery). All are dreamlike, in that their interiors beautifully incorporate styles ranging from Georgian to modern—perfect for sophisticated travelers. They even have old fireplaces. And while you can zip down the mile into Durras or the 10 miles into much-larger Bantry Town for food and supplies, you can far more easily dine next door by candlelight. Two neighboring lodge-type bungalows with terraces facing the sea are exceptional, but they're strictly modern. All are enchanting and are outfitted with modern conveniences. You may rent by the week or the weekend, and rates are relatively inexpensive. Reserve well in advance (027-61014).

Rent an Irish Castle

If you really want to be lavish—or to impress someone with your true romantic nature—you may wish to rent a castle. It is very expensive (and no credit cards are accepted), but you're treated like royalty—with maids, butlers, and chefs. All dining (and in some cases even the alcohol) is included in the price. A fine example is **Lismore Castle** (058-54424) in **Lismore**, County Waterford. Dramatically positioned overlooking the Blackwater River, the castle was built during the 12th century and has been beautifully preserved and regally appointed. It has a magnificent enclosed garden with walls built in the 17th century. For years, Lismore (originally constructed on the orders of King John) has been owned by the various Dukes of Devonshire. The brother of one of them married the famous dancer Adele Astaire, whose brother Fred became a little more famous and often visited Lismore when Adele lived here. Fred's youthful pictures still adorn the walls. You'll be well looked after here by the Paul Burtons, who manage the castle for the current duke. You may invite guests for afternoon tea, cocktails, or dinner at a slightly higher fee. Or you may sit in candlelit splendor just enjoying each other's company. Laundry service is free. Golfing and river fishing are available on the estate. If you're a hunter or a rider, facilities are nearby. Lismore also has a billiards room. The estate is located in Lismore Town. Another highly touted rent-a-castle is **Mallow Castle** (022-21469) in **Mallow**, County Cork. For further information, write Michael McGinn, 319 Maryland Avenue NE, Washington, DC 20002 (or call 202-547-7849).

Rent a River Boat or Coastal Cruiser

Another marvelous way to spend quiet romantic moments surrounded by enchanting scenery is to rent a river boat. There are 3 main water routes for river-boat cruising in Ireland. The **River Shannon** is the longest waterway, with the largest inland area in Ireland or Britain. It forms at Derrylahan in County Cavan and flows 210 miles southward, through Limerick, to the Atlantic. It is navigable for 140 miles, with 6 locks, and is nontidal for 128 miles. The **River Erne**, second-longest in the country, is navigable for 50 miles from Belturbet in County Cavan up through Northern Ireland to Belleek in County Fermanagh. The **Grand Canal**, which links Dublin with the River Barrow and the River Shannon, has 80 navigable miles with 24 locks.

You may choose from 11 companies that rent a total of 560 luxury cruisers. All have been stringently inspected and approved by the Irish Tourist Board. These self-drive boats have 2 to 8 berths, plus refrigerators, gas ranges, utensils, and toilets. Many have central heating, hot water, and showers—especially the larger vessels. Be sure to request the latter, since the usual minimum rental period is a week (although there are some weekend rentals). Charts, binoculars, and safety equipment are included. Dinghies are provided except on canal cruises, in which case they may be rented. Radios and TVs may also be rented. Groceries may be ordered in advance.

The operator of the boat must be over 21, and the controls must be understood by 2 people, but no license is required. Before you depart, you'll receive an hour's free training (or more if needed).

It is strongly advised that you not drink while operating the boat. The waterways are not jam-packed, but there are other boats, and serious accidents can occur—just as on roadways. Of course, you can always drop anchor or, better still, dock at one of the various towns along your route.

Costs are moderate to expensive, depending on the size of the boat. And, of course, you have to pay for your fuel, which usually is the lower-priced diesel. Most firms require a deposit of one-third of the total fee, with the remainder payable upon embarkation in either cash or traveler's checks. (Credit cards are not usually accepted.) There's also a damage deposit that may range from 50 to 150 Irish pounds (depending on boat size). It's refundable within a week after the cruise if you have incurred no damage. (Greater damages are covered by insurance.) There is also a deposit for any extras (such as a TV). Cancellation insurance is advisable.

You may reserve through the firms listed below. The smaller vessels are emphasized here, since most couples seeking to get away from it all don't travel in large parties or take along their children. However, the larger vessels do tend to have more facilities (namely showers), so you may wish to opt for a larger boat than you need—which could push the cost into the expensive category.

RIVER SHANNON

- **Carrick Craft**, P.O. Box 14, Reading RG36TA, England. Phone (Reading) 0734-22975. 100 craft, some with 2 berths.
- **Emerald Star Line Limited**, St. James Gate, Dublin 8. Phone 01-720244. 153 craft, none with 2 berths, some with 4.
- **Flagline** (1972) Limited, Shancurragh, Athlone, County Westmeath. Phone 0902-72892. 35 craft, some with 2 berths but not with shower.
- **SGS (Marine) Limited**, Ballykeeran, Athlone, County Westmeath. Phone 0902-85163. 80 craft, some with 3 berths, none with 2.
- **Athlone Cruisers Limited**, Shancurragh, Athlone, County Westmeath. Phone 0902-72892. 29 craft, some with 2 berths, but not with shower.
- **Silverline Cruisers**, Banagher, County Offaly. Phone 0902-51112. 21 craft, some with 4 berths and shower, none with 2.
- **Shannon Castle Line**, Dolphin Works, Ringsend, Dublin 4. Phone 01-600964. 25 craft, some with 2 berths but without shower.
- **Atlantis Marine Limited**, Bob Parks Marine Centre, Killaloe, County Clare. Phone 061-76281. 10 craft, some with 4 berths and shower, none with 2.
- **Derg Line Cruisers**, Killaloe, County Clare. Phone 061-76364. 22 craft, some with 4 berths and showers, none with 2.

RIVER ERNE

- **Book-a-Boat Limited**, Belturbet, County Cavan. Phone 049-22147. 10 craft, some with 4 berths and shower, none with 2.

GRAND CANAL
- **Celtic Canal Cruisers Limited**, Tullamore, County Offaly. Phone 0506-21861. 9 craft, some with 2 berths and shower.

Another possibility is a coastal cruise. This is considerably more expensive, and unless you're truly experienced at navigation, a qualified skipper must accompany you. Also, most of these boats are equipped to carry 6 to 9 people. Some have engines and sails, some just sails. If you're interested, the east coast is far calmer than the west. Here's a listing of firms:
- **Dun Laoghaire Sailing School**, 115 Lower George's Street, Dun Laoghaire, County Dublin. Phone 01-806654. Bermuda sloop, 4-berth capacity; short-duration coastal cruising.
- **Irish Atlantic Yacht Charters**, Ballylickey, County Cork. Phone 027-50352. 3 craft ranging from 5- to 9-berth capacity, one with shower and autopilot; long cruising range.
- **Andrew Stott Yacht Charters**, Rossbrin Cove, Schull, County Cork. Phone 028-37165. 2 craft with 5 to 7 berths, one with showers; long cruising range.
- **Oysterhaven Yacht Charter** (through Denis Kiely, Monrovia, Highland West, College Road, Cork City). Phone 021-45374. Skippered craft for long- and short-term sailings.

16
SPORTING HOLIDAYS

Sailing

Ireland is the perfect place to vacation if you love to sail. And that goes for the amateur as well as the experienced sailor. Among the beautiful sailing areas are the sheltered Dublin Bay, Skerries, Malahide, Bray, Arklow, and Wexford on the east coast; the Shannon lakes inland; Waterford, Youghal, Ballycotton, Crosshaven, Cobh, Castletownbere, Kinsale, and Baltimore on the south coast; Dingle Bay and Tralee Bay on the southwest coast; Galway Bay and Clew Bay on the west coast; Lough Gill in County Sligo; Rosses Point, Mullaghmore, and Killybegs on the northwest coast. The east coast usually is calmer, the south and southwest coasts are also sheltered, but the west and northwest coasts face the often-stormy Atlantic and offer plenty of adventure for the experienced.

There are 2 sailing associations in Ireland with full-time secretaries who will answer any of your questions. They are the *Irish Yachting Association*, Haddington Terrace, Dun Laoghaire, County Dublin (01-800239), and the *Irish Association for Sail Training*, I.F.M.I., Confederation House, Kildare Street, Dublin 2 (01-779801). Below is a listing of sailing schools and centers throughout Ireland—for both the experienced and the amateur:

- **Baltimore Sailing School**, The Pier, Baltimore, County Cork (028-20141). Dinghy and cruising courses. Easter through September.
- **Dun Laoghaire Sailing School**, 115 Lower George's Street, Dun Laoghaire, County Dublin (01-806654). Dinghy courses. April through September; off season by arrangement.

- **Fingall Sailing School**, Upper Strand Road, Broadmeadow Estuary, Malahide, County Dublin (01-451979). Dinghy courses. Mid-April through August.
- **Galway Sailing Centre**, 8 Father Griffin Road, Galway City (091-63522, or 091-22564 on weekends). Dinghy courses, also boat rental (rowboats, outboards). Mid-May through September.
- **Glenans Irish Sailing Centre**, 85 Merrion Square, Dublin 2 (01-76775). Dinghy and seamanship courses at bases in Bere Island, Bantry Bay, County Cork; Baltimore, County Cork; Collanmore Island, Westport, County Mayo, Summertime.
- **International Sailing Centre**, 5 East Beach, Cobh, County Cork (021-811237). Ketch and dinghy courses. March to October.
- **Baltyboys Sailing School**, Blessington, County Wicklow (045-67121). Dinghy courses for beginners on scenic Poulaphouca Lake. March to October; winter by arrangement.
- **Teddy Knights Sailing Centre**, Dromineer, Nenagh, County Tipperary (067-24295). Sailing canal barge courses on the River Shannon. March through October. Live-aboard weekend courses.
- **Riversdale Sailing Centre**, Riversdale Farmhouse, Ballinamore, County Leitrim (078-44122). Dinghy courses on Lake Garadice. May through September.
- **Little Killary Adventure Centre**, Salruck, Renvyle, County Galway (095-43411). Gaff-rigged cutter instruction during cruise to local islands of Inishbofin, Clare, Inishturk, Achill, and possibly farther afield. May, June, and July; other dates April through September when there is a group of 5.
- **Voluntary Organizations (Coiste An Asgard)**, c/o Irish Shipping Limited, Merrion Hall, Strand Road, Dublin 4 (01-695522). Irish sail-training vessel *Asgard II* operates instructional cruises around the Irish coast and to British and northern European ports. March to October. Reservations should be made in December, as berths are allocated in February.
- **Skillet Sailing School**, The Pier, Kinsale, County Cork (021-72151). Dinghy and keelboat instruction. Late June to early September.

Other Water Sports

CANOEING: Canoeing—both canoe touring and rough-water canoeing—is developing at a tremendous rate in Ireland. The principal touring rivers are the Liffey, Barrow, Nore, Boyne, Slaney, Lee, Shannon, Suir, and Blackwater. Popular sea-canoeing areas are Kilkee, County Clare; Portnoo and Rossnowlagh, County Donegal; Achill Island, County Mayo; Glenbeigh, County Kerry; Tramore, County Waterford; Saltee Islands, County Wexford; Lahinch, County Clare; Aran Islands, County Galway; Mullaghmore, County Sligo. Canoes are available for rent at many of these places, or from Irish Canoe Hire, 1 Ash-Hurst, Military Road, Killiney, County Dublin (01-807517). Special courses are offered by the Tiglin Adventure Centre, Ashford, County Wicklow (0404-40169), and by Connemara Adventure Holidays, Atlantic Coast Hotel, Market Street, Clifden, County Galway (095-21050). There's a sea-canoeing course during the summer months at Little Killary Adventure Centre, Salruck, Renvyle, County Galway (095-43411).

ROWING: For more than a century, rowing has been a competitive sport in Ireland. Now there are more than 50 clubs, with more than 3,000 members. Visitors may compete in Irish regattas if they wish, but non-competitive rowing and touring activities are also available. For information, contact T. Morahan, 35 Rugby Road, Belfast 7, Northern Ireland. The main centers of coastal rowing are in the area between Dublin and Wicklow and in West Cork. Further information may be obtained from Lorna Siggins, Irish Amateur Rowing Union, 34 Palmerston Road, Dublin 6.

SAILBOARDING: Sailboarding (or windsurfing) is possible on coastal waters as well as lakes and rivers. Contacts are Eddie English, Irish Boardsailing Association, 5 East Beach, Cobh, County Cork (021-811237), and Gary Matthews, Irish Windsurfing Class Association, 1 Havelock Square, Donnybrook, Dublin 4 (01-684703). Courses are available at Skerries Boardsailing School, 7 Convent Lane, Skerries, County Dublin (01-491734); Condell Sailport Boardsailing Centre, Killaloe, County Clare (061-45396); Scubadive Limited, Coliemore Harbour, Dalkey, County Dublin (01-850357)—straight rental as well; Fingall Sailing School, Upper Strand Road, Broadmeadow Estuary, Malahide, County Dublin (01-451979); International Sailing Centre, 5 East Beach, Cobh, County

Cork (021-811237); Castletownbere International Windsurfing School, Castletownbere, County Cork (027-70235); Baltimore Sailing School, The Pier, Baltimore, County Cork (028-20141); Oysterhaven Board-sailing Centre, Oysterhaven, County Cork (021-73738); Little Killary Adventure Centre, Salruck, Renvyle, County Galway (095-43411); Figary Boardsailing School, Roneragh House Hotel, Fahan, County Donegal (077-60265); Glenans Irish Sailing Centre, 85 Merrion Square, Dublin 2 (01-76775); Galway Sailing Centre, 8 Father Griffin Road, Galway City (091-63522, or 091-22564 on weekends). Most of these schools operate from Easter through October, and most provide necessary apparel.

WATERSKIING: One of Ireland's fastest-growing sports for both men and women is waterskiing. Information is available from Sean Kennedy, Irish Water-Ski Association, 7 Upper Beaumont Drive, Ballintemple, County Cork (021-292411). Waterskiing clubs affiliated with the association that offer facilities to nonclub members are Shannonside Water-Ski Club, O'Brien's Bridge, County Clare (061-317166—Andreina Egan); Cork Power Boat and Water-Ski Club, Farren Wood, Farren, County Cork (021-292411—Sean Kennedy); Golden Falls Water-Ski Club, Ballymore Eustace, County Kildare (045-64332); Parknasilla Great Southern Hotel, Parknasilla, County Kerry (064-45122). Most operate May through September.

SURFING: Atlantic waves often pound the beaches with waves comparable to those in California, so surfing is very popular in Ireland. Visitors who intend to surf are advised to bring their own boards. But equipment is available for rental at The Sand House Hotel, Rossnowlagh, County Donegal; Lifeguard Hut, Lahinch Strand, County Clare; Lifeguard Hut, Tramore, County Waterford; Lifeguard Hut, Strandhill, County Sligo; Lifeguard Hut, Bundoran, County Donegal. Further information may be obtained from Roci Allan, Irish Surfing Association, Tigh-na-Mara, Rossnowlagh, County Donegal (072-51261).

DEEP-SEA DIVING: Situated as it is in the path of the Gulf Stream, Ireland is almost unsurpassed for deep-sea diving and underwater swimming. Inclusive diving holidays for *experienced* divers with valid certificates are available at Clew Bay Diving Centre, Bay View Hotel, Clare Island, Westport, County Mayo (098-26307); McFaddens Hotel, Gortahork, County Donegal (074-35267); Valentia Diving Centre, Des and Pat

Lavelle, Valentia Island, County Kerry (0667-6124); MacNamara's Diving Service, Coast Road, Fanore, Ballyvaughan, County Clare; Scubadive Limited, Coliemore Harbour, Dalkey, County Dublin (01-850357); Ostán Synge, Geesala, County Mayo (01-974309). Most operate April through September or October.

SWIMMING: With more than 3,500 miles of coastal Gulf Stream waters and many of the world's finest beaches, Ireland is ideal for the swimmer. A word of warning, though—do watch for and heed the signs indicating waters in which swimming is dangerous or prohibited.

Fishing

GAME ANGLING: A variety of still-water and river locales offer game angling. Salmon, sea trout, rainbow and brown trout are species that are prevalent. Generally all legal rod and line methods are allowed, but some waters have fly-only regulations. There are opportunities to catch salmon from early January through September, but the spring run brings 10- to 20-pound catches from the majority of coastal rivers and their still waters and headwaters. The shorter coastal streams and acid lakes of the south and west coasts provide a bounty of sea trout. Depending on the area, the season runs from as early as May to late October. One inexpensive license is required for both salmon and sea trout fishing—by the week or the season. Some salmon fishing is free or available for a low fee. But nearly all sea trout fisheries are under private or club control, and a day permit (inexpensive to moderate) is required. The largest brown trout are found in the rich limestone waters of the central Irish plains from April through June. Rainbows are found in more than 20 lakes and ponds from April through September. No license is required for brown trout or rainbows, but a permit from the Regional Fisheries Board (low fee) is required. Some river fishing is privately controlled and requires a low-cost permit. Boats and ghillies (guides), as well as equipment, can be found in all major fishing areas. Some hotels cater to fishermen and rent equipment and boats for free or for a nominal fee. For further information, contact Central Fisheries Board, The Weir Lodge, Earl's Island, Galway, County Galway, or Balnagowan House, Mobhi Boreen, Glasnevin, Dublin 9 (01-379206).

SEA ANGLING: Sea angling is a year-round sport in Ireland. For shore fishing, the principal species are bass, whiting, pollock, codling, coalfish, mullet, flounder, plaice, ray, conger, gurnard, and wrasse. Inshore fishing is done within bays and inlets close to shore and from small powerboats. Pollock, cod, bass, monkfish, ray, coalfish, tope, wrasse, skate, and dogfish are the principal species here. In deep-sea fishing, which is usually done from small motor fishing vessels 30 to 40 feet long, there is a choice of ground or bottom fishing for pollock, coalfish, dogfish, ray, skate, shark, or wreck. For lists of deep-sea angling centers, boats, and facilities that have been approved by the Irish Tourist Board, write for its booklet *Sea Angling in Ireland* (Irish Tourist Board Literature Dept., P.O. Box 1083, Dublin 8).

COARSE ANGLING: Coarse angling is centered on the midlands area. Coarse fisheries and fresh waters offer pike, perch, bream, rudd, tench, and dace. No license or permit is required, except at some private fisheries. Principal waterways are the Shannon, Erne, Owenmore and Owenbeg rivers and neighboring lakes; the Monaghan/Meath lakes and some small connecting rivers; the Upper Boyne; the Royal and Grand canals; the Barrow River and Canal; the Munster Blackwater River. Boats and boatmen are available at many points for moderate rates, but tackle usually must be purchased. Prepacked bait may be purchased, but it's best to preorder from Irish Angling Services, Ardlougher, County Cavan (049-26258). You are not allowed to bring your own bait into the country if it's packed in soil or vegetable material.

Horseback Riding

Ireland offers an enormous choice of riding vacations and facilities catering to every type of rider—amateur to experienced. Most stables have ponies or horses available for trekking and riding. The following are selected in areas with the most attractions and finest lodgings.
- **Bel-Air Riding School**, Ashford, County Wicklow—near Rathnew (0404-40385). All year.
- **Broom Lodge Stables**, Nun's Cross, Ashford, County Wicklow—near Rathnew (0404-40404). All year.

Horseback riding, Horetown House, Foulksmills, County Wexford

- **Daveve Farm Equestrian Centre**, Glanmore, Ashford, County Wicklow—near Rathnew (0404-40143). All year.
- **Lisbeg Farm**, Gortogher, Cloghan's P.O., Ballina, County Mayo (096-21970). March 1 through October.
- **Ardnavaha Riding Centre**, Ardnavaha House Hotel, Ballinascarthy, County Cork (023-49135). April 1 through September. Demi-pension in fine grade-A hotel with 36-modern-bedroom wing connected to grand Georgian homestead with fireplace sitting rooms and intimate restaurant. Two hours a day of riding included in moderate fee.
- **Coolcorron Equestrian Centre**, Belgooly, County Cork—near Kinsale (021-71353). All year.
- **Grangemore Riding Centre**, Ardfinnan Road, Cahir, County Tipperary—near Cashel (052-41426). All year.
- **Carrigart Hotel Stables**, Carrigart Hotel, Carrigart, County Don-

egal (074-55114). April 1 through 15 and May 15 through October.

- **Kilkea Dressage Centre**, Kilkea Lodge, Castledermot, County Kildare (0503-45112). All year.
- **Donacomper Riding School**, Donacomper, Celbridge, County Kildare—near Maynooth (01-288221). All year.
- **Errislannan Manor Connemara Pony Stud**, Errislannan Manor, Clifden, County Galway (095-21134). Easter through September. Full board plus riding and lessons at very moderate price.
- **Waterside Riding Centre**, Waterside, Dingle, County Kerry (066-51476). March 1 through October 15; by arrangement rest of year.
- **The Old Rectory Stables**, The Old Rectory, County Sligo (071-73221). April 1 through September.
- **Hillcrest House Riding Centre**, Hillcrest House, Park, Galbally, County Tipperary (062-57915). All year.
- **Dromquinna Riding Stables**, Dromquinna, Greenane, County Kerry—near Kenmare (064-41043). April 1 through October.
- **Bridestream Riding Centre**, Bridestream House, Kilcock, County Kildare—near Maynooth (01-287261). All year.
- **Rye Valley Riding Centre Limited**, Leixlip, County Kildare (01-244157). All year.
- **The Lodge Riding Centre**, Drimcong, Moycullen, County Galway (091-85361). All year.
- **Burkes Riding School**, Ballycar, Newmarket-on-Fergus, County Clare (061-71113). All year.
- **Smithstown Riding Centre**, Main Ennis Road, Newmarket-on-Fergus, County Clare (061-61494). All year.
- **Oughterard Riding School**, Conrower Pony Stud, Oughterard, County Galway (091-82120). April 1 through September.
- **Eileen Murphy's Horse Riding & Driving Centre**, Russagh, Skibbereen, County Cork (028-21589). All year.
- **Sligo Equitation Co. Ltd.**, Carrowmore, Sligo, County Sligo (071-62758). All year.

There are also several all-inclusive (meals and accommodations) trail-riding holidays, generally available from May through October, depending on the area:

- **Drumcliffe Beach and Mountain Trail**, County Sligo. Eileen Blighe, The Old Rectory Stables, Drumcliff, County Sligo (071-63221).

- **The Sligo Trail**, County Sligo. Noreen McGarry, Sligo Equitation Co. Ltd., Carrowmore, Sligo, County Sligo (071-62758).
- **Connemara Trail and Coast Trail**, County Galway. William Leahy, Aille Cross Equitation Centre, Aille Cross, Loughrea, County Galway (091-41216).
- **Dingle Peninsula Trail**, County Kerry. William J. O'Connor, William J. O'Connor Riding Stables, El Rancho Farmhouse, Ballyard, Tralee, County Kerry (066-21840).
- **Killarney Reeks Trail**, County Kerry. Donal O'Sullivan, Killarney Riding School, Ballydowney, Killarney, County Kerry (064-31686).
- **Lough Derg Trail**, Counties Clare, Galway, and Tipperary. Rosetta Paxman, Ballycormac Riding Stables, Ballycormac, Aglish, County Tipperary—near Roscrea (067-21129).
- **Melody's Riding Stables & Pony Trekking Centre**, Ballymacarbry, County Waterford—near Clonmel (052-36147).

Golf

Many, many hotels in Ireland have their own private golf courses. As a matter of fact, a hotel in Downings, County Donegal, calls itself the Rosapenna Golf Hotel, even though it's situated right on a bay and also offers sailboarding, waterskiing, canoeing, and swimming. Most golfers regard Ireland as a paradise. And most hotels throw in the golf free of charge. Chapters 1 through 12 indicate which lodgings have golf courses. Bear in mind also that some hotels without courses have arrangements with local clubs whereby guests may golf for free at certain hours.

There are more than 200 golf courses in Ireland. If you want specifics about any of them or any other golfing information, write J. P. Murray, Golf Promotion Excecutive, Bord Failte—Irish Tourist Board, Dublin 2. You might also request the brochure on the all-inclusive (airfare, lodgings, meals) golf tours of Ireland at very reasonable rates.

The Hunt

In Ireland, the hunt usually means fox hunting, although there are some stag hunts and harriers. Tourists may not hunt deer. The fox-hunting season runs from early November to the end of March, with cub hunting from September to November. Hunting clubs are eager to welcome guests for a cap fee (subscription), but they *must* be experienced. The fee (which is assessed *per meet*), plus the rental of a horse for the day, makes this an expensive sport. There are 85 organized clubs. Those who prefer double banks head for the south; stone walls are in the west; ditches and streams are in the east; single banks are in the southeast. Some all-inclusive hunt tours are available. For details, contact one of the Irish Tourist Board offices listed at the end of this book.

Hunting also means snipe, wild ducks, grouse, partridge, pheasant cocks, and rabbits. But it does not mean pheasant hens, geese, or quail. And, of course, no hunting is permitted in nature preserves. Gamebird hunting is usually done from September to January. Rabbits and foxes may be hunted all year. To bring a hunting weapon into the country, you must obtain permission from the Irish Ministry of Justice, Upper Merrion Street, Dublin 2.

Other Sports

TENNIS: Many hotels have their own private tennis courts, which are usually free to their guests. Chapters 1 through 12 indicate which lodgings have tennis facilities. Also, some tennis clubs, including Dublin's famous Fitzwilliam, allow visitors club privileges for a fee. For further information, check with C. J. Brennen, Irish Lawn Tennis Association, 15 Cill Eanna, Rahenny, Dublin 5 (01-338916). This association, in connection with the Wright Tennis Center, offers all-inclusive (airfare, lodgings, meals, motorcoach tours through the country, along with a week of intensive tennis instruction with a champion player) summer tours at very reasonable rates. The New York City contact for this is I. L. T. A./Wright Tennis Center, 128 East 71st Street, New York, NY 10021 (212-249-3869, or toll-free 1-800-231-8896).

HANG GLIDING: Hang gliding is a rapidly developing sport in Ireland. Prevailing southwesterly breezes sweep in from the Atlantic to the mountainous regions, and they are perfect for the sport. Dangerous airflows found in countries with higher, more jagged mountains are absent here among Ireland's hillish, more rounded mountains. Visiting flyers must contact the Irish Hang-Gliding Centre to be briefed on general air traffic lanes, airport control zones, and other restricted areas. The address is Wits End, Drumbawn, Newtown, County Wicklow (01-819445), and the contact is Peter Willis. Arrangements for rentals and/ or lessons can be made through him. For information and regulations on motorized hang gliders, contact Irish Micro Light Association, c/o Tom Hudson, 60 Hillcourt Road, Glenageary, County Dublin (01-852856). Every pilot must have adequate insurance; a visitor may obtain low-cost insurance with a monthly membership in the Irish Hang-Gliding Association, 41 Newlands, Wexford, County Wexford (053-41276). The contact is Declan Doyle. The main hang-gliding sites of Ireland are Knockalla, County Donegal; Great Sugarloaf Mountain, County Wicklow; Lacken Bowl, County Wicklow; Mount Leinster, County Carlow; Musheramore, County Cork; Mweelin, County Cork; Portmagee, County Kerry; Dingle Peninsula, County Kerry; Arra Mountains, County Tipperary; Devil's Bit, County Tipperary; Maamturk Mountains, County Galway; Minaun Heights, Achill Island, County Mayo; Ox Mountains, County Mayo; Slieve Anieran, County Leitrim; Benbulben, Truskmore, County Sligo.

RUNNING: Each year, running seems to become more popular in Ireland, with running clubs springing up all over the country. You can run almost anywhere in the country. Just be very careful of the traffic on some of the extremely narrow roads. If you want to start your holiday with a marathon, you might want to consider the Cork City Marathon in early April (for information, call 021-23251) or the Dublin City Marathon in late October, usually the day after the New York City Marathon (call Cathal O'Doherty, 01-764647, or write Radio 2, Dublin City Marathon, P.O. Box 1287, Dublin 2). There are often special all-inclusive tour packages for the Dublin Marathon. If a marathon isn't for you, you might like to keep your eyes peeled for some of the shorter, less-publicized races. There's even a 10K on Inishmore in the Aran Islands, County Galway. But above all, if you're a serious runner, enjoy the scenery—and forget about your stopwatch.

17

TOURING IRELAND'S FINEST ESTATES AND GARDENS

Many people travel to Ireland just to see the grand array of historic houses, castles, and gardens. They're open to the public for very modest fees. In most instances, the estates described here are not available as lodgings. Some of the places listed, however, have already been mentioned under itinerary suggestions. If you're mainly interested in these sites, this list should prove particularly helpful.

- **Abbey Leix House and Gardens**, Abbeyleix, County Laois. 18th-century manor house of Viscount de Vesci; fine and varied woodland gardens. Open daily, Easter through September, 2 to 6:30.
- **Annes Grove Gardens**, Castletownroche, County Cork. Extensive multiple gardens, secret paths, cliff beside river. Near 18th-century manor. Open Easter through September, Monday through Friday 10 to 5, Sunday 1 to 6. Closed Saturday.
- **Bantry House**, Bantry, County Cork. Stunning 1750 country mansion with period antiques, paintings, objets d'art; fine grounds and gardens. Tearoom, crafts. Open daily all year, 9 to 6 and until 8 most spring and summer evenings.
- **Birr Castle**, Birr, County Offaly. 17th-century home of Earl and Countess of Rosse (interior open by special advance arrangements; phone 0509-20056). Magnificent, extensive gardens laid out around a lake and along the banks of 2 rivers. Open daily all year, 9:30 to 1 and 2 to 6.
- **Castle Gardens**, Timoleague, Bandon, County Cork. Compact gardens that have been maintained for 160 years; ruins of 13th-century Barrymore Castle. Open daily, June through August, noon to 6.

- **Castle Leslie**, Glaslough, County Monaghan. Originally a medieval stronghold; rebuilt in 1870 by Sir John Leslie, renowned collector and painter. Open daily, mid-June to mid-August, 2 to 6.
- **Castle Matrix**, Rathkeale, County Limerick. Built in 1440 by 7th Earl of Desmond; in 1580 served as the venue for the meeting of Edmund Spenser and Sir Walter Raleigh; some authentic furnishings remain. Open mid-May to mid-September, Saturday, Sunday, Monday, and Tuesday, 1 to 7.
- **Castletown House**, Celbridge, County Kildare. Magnificent Palladian-style mansion built in 1722 for William Conolly, Speaker of the Irish House of Commons; one of the most superbly furnished estates in the country; a must-see. Open January to March, Sunday only, 2 to 5. April through September, open Wednesday, Saturday, Sunday 2 to 6. Closed October through December. Teas.
- **Clonalis House**, Castlerea, County Roscommon. 19th-century mansion of the O'Conors of Connacht; well furnished with Thomas Sheraton furniture. Open May and June, Saturday and Sunday, 2 to 5:30; July to early September, open daily, 11 to 1 and 2 to 5:30. Afternoon teas.
- **Creagh Gardens**, Skibbereen, County Cork. Good collection of shrubs, flowering trees; many exotic varieties on grounds of estate built in 1820. Open daily, Easter through September, 10 to 6.
- **Curraghmore House and Gardens**, Portlaw, County Waterford. Azaleas, bluebells, rhododendrons are most impressive at this 1754 mansion. Open April through September, every Thursday and bank holiday, 2 to 5. (Mansion open only by prior arrangement; phone 051-87102.)
- **Damer House**, Roscrea, County Tipperary. 18th-century homestead with finely carved pine staircase, period Irish furniture. Open mid-May through October, weekdays 10 to 5, Saturday and Sunday 2 to 5.
- **Dargle Glen Gardens**, Enniskerry, County Wicklow. Romantic glen of gardens, including trees, flowers, and flowering shrubs and trees. Open Sunday, May through September, 2 to 6.
- **Derren Gardens**, Lauragh, near Kenmare, County Kerry. Woodland gardens by the sea, planted more than a century ago by Lord Lansdowne. Open April through September, Tuesday, Thursday, and Sunday, 2 to 6.
- **Dunkathel House**, Glanmire, County Cork. Late-18th-century manor with fine collection of antiques and paintings. Open May

through September, Wednesday, Thursday, Saturday, and Sunday, 2 to 6.

- **Fernhill Gardens**, Sandyford, County Dublin. Fabulous array of every type of gardening on 40 acres. Open March through October, Tuesday through Saturday and bank holidays, 11 to 5; Sunday, 2 to 5.
- **Fota House**, Fota Island, County Cork. Splendid example of Regency architecture of the 1820s; period antiques and wall-papers, superb landscape paintings. Open mid-April through mid-September, Monday through Saturday 11 to 6, Sunday 2 to 6. Rest of year, Sunday and public holidays, 2 to 6. A wildlife park is open daily, all year, 10 to 5; Sunday, 11 to 5:15. Sunday teas.
- **Garinish Island** (Ilnacullin), County Cork. Elaborate early 20th-century garden with classic Italian pavilions. Open March through October, Monday through Saturday, 10 to 5:30; Sunday, 1 to 6.
- **Glin Castle and Gate Shop**, Glin, County Limerick. Georgian-Gothic; held by the Knights of Glin since the 13th century; fine period furniture, paintings. Open mid-May through June, 10 to 2 and 2 to 4. Craft shop open April through October, 10 to 5 daily. Lunches and dinners.
- **Howth Castle and Gardens**, Howth, County Dublin. More than 2,000 varieties of plants, trees, flowers, at this garden begun in 1875. Open year round, 8 A.M. through sunset.
- **Japanese Gardens**, Tully, County Kildare. Earliest Japanese gardens in Europe, dating to early 1900s; truly lovely. Open Easter through October, Monday through Friday, 10:30 to 5:30; Sunday, 2 to 5:30.
- **Johnstown Castle**, Wexford Town, County Wexford. Strong Gothic Revival mansion, but you can see only the outside. The finely crafted 19th-century gardens are the appeal here. Open all year, 9 to 5:30; Sunday, 2 to 5.
- **Killruddery House and Gardens**, Bray, County Wicklow. 1820s manor with ponds, canals, gentle gardens. House and gardens open 3 months of the year only—May, June, and September, daily from 1 to 5 (Phone 01-863405.)
- **Kylemore Abbey**, Moyard, County Galway. Magnificent Bene-dictine nunnery and boarding school established from an 1864 abbey. Wonderful mirror-lake waterway. Open daily, May through October, 10 to 6. Tearoom.
- **Lismore Castle and Gardens**, Lismore, County Waterford. Castle

of the Duke of Devonshire from 1748; lovely floral gardens and yew walk. Edmund Spenser wrote part of his *Faerie Queene* here. An earlier 1642 castle played an important part in an Irish siege. Gardens open mid-May through mid-September, 1:45 to 4:45, closed Saturday. (This castle is available for rental as a vacation lodging; see chapter 15.)

- **Lissadell House**, Rosses Point, County Sligo. 19th-century Georgian manor of Countess Markievicz, one of the leaders of the 1916 Rising, and her sister Eva Gore-Booth. W. B. Yeats, who wrote of this house and these beautiful women in his poetry, frequently slept in the bedroom above the porch. House open daily, May through September, 2 to 5:15, except Sunday.
- **Malahide Castle**, Malahide, County Dublin. 12th-century castle; one of Ireland's oldest and most historic, with excellent collection of period furniture, oil portraits. Open all year, Monday through Friday, 10 to 12:45 and 2 to 5. Restaurant.
- **Mount Usher Gardens**, Ashford, County Wicklow. 4,000 different varieties of trees, shrubs, and plants set out on the banks of the River Vantry. Open daily, April through September, 10:30 to 6; Sunday, 2 to 6.
- **Muckross House**, Killarney, County Kerry. 19th-century manor house and gardens on shore of Muckross Lake, second-largest of Killarney's 3 lakes. It serves as the Museum of Kerry Folklife and presents an excellent picture of life in bygone days. Open daily, all year, 10 to 7; summer hours usually extended. Refreshments, craft shop.
- **National Botanic Gardens**, Dublin. 50 acres of shrubs, plants, trees; established in 1795 with curvilinear range of glass houses. Open year round, Monday through Saturday, 9 to 6; Sundays, 11 to 6. In winter, Monday through Saturday, 10 to 4:30, and Sunday, 11 to 4:30.
- **Powerscourt Estate, Gardens, and Waterfall**, Enniskerry, County Wicklow. An 18th-century mansion was gutted by fire in 1974, but fine Italian and Japanese gardens remain, along with a lovely waterfall. Gardens open daily, Easter through October, 10 to 5:30. Waterfall open all year, 10:30 to 7, but closed at dusk in winter. One of Ireland's most dramatic garden sights. Restaurant, souvenirs, boutique.
- **Riverstown House**, Glanmire, County Cork. Built in 1602 and renovated in 1745; chief interest is intricate wall and ceiling plas-

terwork by famed Francini brothers. Open May through September, Thursday through Sunday, 2 to 6.
- **Rothe House**, Kilkenny, County Kilkenny. 1594 Elizabethan merchant's house with interesting trappings. Open all year, Monday through Saturday, 10:30 to 12:30 and 3 to 5; Sunday, 1 to 5.
- **Russborough**, Blessington, County Wicklow. One of Ireland's finest; built 1740–50; home of Sir Alfred and Lady Beit; superb antique furniture, silver, Italian bronzes; originals by Vermeer, Goya, Velazquez, Gainsborough, Rubens, Murillo. Open Easter through October, Wednesday, Saturday, Sunday, 2:30 to 5:30. Another must-see.
- **Slane Castle**, Slane, County Meath. Dates from 1785 with one of the finest Gothic Revival reception rooms in Europe and superb period furniture. Open Sunday 2 to 6. Restaurant.
- **Thoor Ballylee**, Gort, County Galway. 16th-century tower house used by poet W. B. Yeats as a summer home in the 1920s; has rare first editions of his work and items used by him. Open daily, May through September, 10 to 6. Teas.
- **Tullynally Castle and Gardens**, Castlepollard, County Westmeath. Fine 17th-century estate of the Earls of Longford; 30 acres of woodland walks and walled gardens. Castle open daily, mid-July to mid-August, 2:30 to 6. Gardens open June to September 2:30 to 6.
- **The Water Garden**, Ladywell, Thomastown, County Kilkenny. Almost 2 acres of trees, shrubs, aquatic plants; strongly favored by nature lovers for its grace. Open daily, May through September, 10 to 6.

Recently, the Historic Irish Tourist Houses & Gardens Association has opened for the first time these three houses for the public to view at modest fees:
- **Blarney House**, Blarney, County Cork. Restored baronial homestead, circa 17th century, with fine gardens on the grounds. Adjacent to Blarney Castle and five miles from Cork City. Open June through mid-September, Monday through Saturday, noon to 6; closed Sunday.
- **Carrigglas Manor**, Longford, County Longford. Tudor/Gothic revival house, one of the earliest Victorian houses in Ireland. Has much of the original furniture; also excellent period costume collection. Stables and courtyard. Open mid-June through mid-September, Thursday, Saturday, Sunday, 2:30 to 6.

- **Strokestown Park House**, Strokestown, County Roscommon. Palladian mansion complete with ballroom which was later converted into a grand library. One of the last 18th-century mansions to survive in this county; even has a vaulted stable. All the work of famous architect Richard Cassels. Open June through August, Tuesday through Sunday, noon to 5; closed Monday.

18
A GOURMET
COOKING VACATION

A first in the Irish Republic is gourmet Myrtle Allen's cooking school, held near her perfectly wondrous Ballymaloe House lodging in Shanagarry, County Cork. The course lasts a week, and the price (approximately $1,500) covers everything (accommodations, meals, and excursions) except your cost of reaching Ballymaloe. You'll reside at Ballymaloe House and each day travel the short distance to the Regency home of Darina Allen, Mrs. Allen's daughter-in-law, who, along with her brother Rory, will instruct you in the vast, modern Irish kitchen. You'll study the preparation of French cuisine as well as Irish traditional fare, often using Myrtle Allen's own well-tried recipes as source material. The ingredients you'll be using are freshly picked vegetables, fruits, and herbs from the estate's own garden. Fish come from nearby Ballycotton Bay, meat is raised in the family's pastures just down the road at Cloyne, and farmhouse cheeses come from all over the province of Munster. And yes, indeed, you do get to eat what's prepared.

According to the Allens, a typical day at the school starts at Ballymaloe House, with a grand and hearty Irish breakfast of homemade breads and jams, fresh farm eggs, and local bacon and sausages—the whole hog. Then off you go for 3 hours of demonstration and preparation. This forms the basis for your lunch in the school's dining room, where a suitable wine is chosen to complement the meal.

After lunch, you'll be taken on a short excursion, perhaps to visit one of Cork's beautiful country houses and gardens or perhaps to watch pottery being handmade at Shanagarry. After dinner at Ballymaloe, Myrtle Allen's husband might offer a discourse on the fascinating history of Ballymaloe House, or you might rush off to a singing pub to hoist a few pints.

On other days, there's an expedition to buy fish on Ballycotton Pier, then back to school to prepare it. There's usually a trip to the famous Arbutus Lodge in Cork City to experience its award-winning Victorian dining room. Owner/chef Declan Ryan prepares a special sampling of the finest of the menu's dishes. On Sunday morning, you may watch Myrtle Allen making the breads for brunch and planning the Sunday evening buffet. The latter contains up to 30 different dishes, ranging from fresh tongue and sea urchins to potted crabs and poached Blackwater salmon.

There are 6 such cooking courses from May through September. If you're interested, book early. A $400 deposit is payable when you make your reservation. The balance is due 4 weeks before the course begins. If you have to cancel, all fees will be returned, except for $100, if you write at least 2 weeks before commencement of the course.

For further information or reservations, write to The Ballymaloe Cookery School, Shanagarry, Midleton, County Cork, or phone 021-652531. (If you're calling from the United States, dial 011-353-21-652531.)

19 CHRISTMASTIME IN IRELAND

Many Irish hoteliers offer special programs for the Christmas holiday season, which are rapidly becoming very popular with both Americans and Europeans. Among them are a number of lodgings featured in this book. They include The Shelbourne Hotel, Dublin; The Mount Herbert, Dublin; Fitzpatrick Castle Hotel, Killiney, County Dublin; The Park Hotel, Kenmare, County Kerry; The Parknasilla Great Southern Hotel, Parknasilla, County Kerry; The Abbeyglen Hotel, Clifden, County Galway; Renvyle House, Renvyle, County Galway; and Ashford Castle, County Mayo.

A delightful example is that of the elegant Park Hotel, Kenmare. The program begins with a December 24 check-in and a candlelit dinner from 7 to 9. At 10, there are traditional Christmas carols in the foyer, followed by midnight church services. After church, mince pies and tea are served. On Christmas Day, breakfast is served either in your room or in the restaurant, from 8 to 10. At 1, there's a buffet luncheon, and at 2:45 a feature film. During this time, game competitions are held for those interested. Afternoon tea is served at 4:30. Santa arrives at 5, and the children's tea is at 6. At 7:30, there's a cocktail reception, followed by a gala dinner-dance at 8. Dress is formal. On December 26, there's brunch in the restaurant from 9 to 2, while concurrently there's a treasure hunt. The final rounds of the table-tennis competition begin at 3. Afternoon tea is at 4:30 and candlelit dinner at 8, followed by dancing and the presentation of prizes.

The same hotel also offers a New Year's package, which includes a cocktail reception, gala dinner, and formal dance on December 31. Then, on January 1, brunch is served from 9 to 2, followed by a treasure hunt, short scenic drives in the area, indoor games, lounge music, party songs, and dinner from 7 to 9. Checkout follows breakfast on January 2. Considering everything that's included, these holiday offerings seem very moderately priced. The same hotel has a mystery weekend program in November when guests solve a murder case.

Another example of a Christmas package that's becoming very popular is that for Ashford Castle. It's a 3-night program that includes 3 nights' accommodations with full Irish breakfasts, a welcoming cocktail party, a formal Christmas dinner with fine French wines, entertainment, golf, and tennis. There's also a children's package that includes the three nights' accommodations with full breakfasts, a welcoming "coketail" party, Christmas dinner, party favors, and a visit from Santa. Ashford's drawing rooms and lounges are decorated with giant Christmas trees; garlands drape the carved balustrades. Choirs and musicians make frequent appearances in the public rooms. All of this is at a very favorable price considering it's Ashford Castle.

For more information on individual lodgings, the Irish Tourist Board has published a *Christmas and New Year Holiday Breaks* brochure.

20 UNIQUE FEATURES OF IRELAND'S COUNTIES

And then they returned again, dancing and singing, to the country
of the gods.

—James Stephens
The Crock of Gold

Nearly every one of Ireland's 26 counties has something that is unique.
Some counties are famed for their scenery, some are famed for their
handcrafts, and some are famed just for their names. Below are highlights of 13 of the best known.

Donegal

Many of Donegal's road signs are in Gaelic only. People here are
very proud of this heritage, and there are a number of *Gaeltachts*,
communities where only Gaelic is spoken. *Don't* let this put you off
going there. The local people understand and speak English very well,
and they're most cordial to visitors. In some cases, you can interpret
the road signs, in others it's impossible. Don't hesitate to ask. The
county is also famous for its fine handwoven tweeds, and its handknit
sweaters rival the Aran fisherman knits. Also, just across the border
from Donegal, in County Fermanagh, Northern Ireland, is the tiny

village of Belleek, world-famous for its cream-colored china. The factory and shop are open Monday through Saturday from 9 to 5 (closed the first 2 weeks in August). Factory tours run from 10:15 to noon and from 2:15 to 4 at 20-minute intervals. You can purchase china here at about half the price you'd pay in the United States.

Sligo

This county has the reputation of being the most praised for its scenic beauty by a major writer—William Butler Yeats. Poet Yeats did for Sligo what James Joyce did in prose for Dublin. For Yeats fans, the Yeats Summer School is held each year in Sligo Town. (For details, see chapter 2.)

Mayo

This county is the home of the famous Foxford Woollen Mills, in Foxford Town. These mills produce some of the world's finest blankets, throws, and scarves in richly colored wool. While not as well known as Donegal tweed, Foxford tweed is lovely. The factory and shop are open all year, Monday through Friday, from 9 to 5:15, and Saturday, May through September, from 10 to 6. Tours of the factory are given weekdays, April through September. The shop accepts credit cards and handles mail orders.

Galway

Galway is known the world over for its Connemara ponies. You'll notice them right away, because they're like miniatures. Connemara marble is another well-known local product. Quarried here, it is used to make everything from jewelry and small gift items to furniture, and it is considered to be one of the world's finest marbles. Its green colors are as varied as the hues of the Irish landscape. While you can purchase Connemara marble items in other Irish counties, you won't find as much variety as in the many craft shops in the Connemara area. One of the best such shops is at the Connemara Marble Industries factory, at Moycullen. It's open from 9 to 6, Monday through Saturday, throughout the year.

Limerick

Since the days of Georgian Ireland, Limerick lace has been revered. It is made under the supervision of the Good Shepherd Convent on Clare Street in Limerick City. The work is done completely in thread on fine Brussels net, and the products range from handkerchiefs to veils, blouses, and christening gowns. They're all available in the shop here. It's open throughout the year, Monday through Friday, from 9:30 to 5 (closed for lunch from 1 to 2).

Kerry

This county is perhaps the most scenic, with the Dingle Peninsula, Ring of Kerry, Moll's Gap, the charming village of Killarney and its nearby lakes, and the Gap of Dunloe. Outside of County Galway, Kerry has the finest array of craft shops, many of which have been covered in the suggested Kerry itineraries in chapter 6. In the lovely little village of Kenmare, Kenmare lace is made and sold at the Convent of the Poor Clares. The shop is open Monday through Friday from 10 to noon, 2 to 4, and 7 to 9.

Cork

This is the only county where you'll find Murphy's stout. It's made here and competes with the much-more-famous Guinness stout. Murphy's is a softer, more delicate brew, and doesn't travel well. Many here even prefer it to Guinness. In Dripsey is the Dripsey Woollen Mills, famous for its Dripsey tweed. (See Suggestions in chapter 7 for details.)

Tipperary

Other than having a song written about it—"It's a Long Way to Tipperary"—this county is best known for the dramatic ancient ruins on the Rock of Cashel.

Waterford

This county is known the world over for its Waterford crystal. You can visit the factory outside Waterford Town if you wish. It's open throughout the year, Monday through Saturday, from 10 to 2:30, but closed most of August. These are factory touring hours. Waterford Crystal is not on sale at the factory, and therefore there are no special rates on crystal firsts or seconds.

Wexford

Besides being one of Ireland's sunniest counties, Wexford hosts one of the country's most famous festivals—the Wexford Opera Festival. It usually runs for about 10 days at the end of October. Here well-known opera stars perform lesser-known operas. For details, call 053-22144, or write to the Wexford Opera Festival in Wexford Town. Don't wait until the last minute to try to obtain tickets for these well-attended black-tie events. Also in the county, 5 miles south of New Ross, is the 410-acre John F. Kennedy Park, which overlooks the Kennedy ancestral homestead. There are fine gardens and forest walks here, along with a picnic area and a cafe. The park is open daily throughout the year from 10 to early evening.

Wicklow

This county boasts Arklow Pottery in Arklow. It manufactures Noritake and other brands of earthenware in all price ranges. Much of it is exported to the United States, but you can buy it at the factory shop at somewhat lower prices. It's open June through August, from 9:30 to 5:30. Other months, it's open Monday through Saturday, 9:30 to 1 and 2 to 5. Credit cards are accepted. In Avoca is the famous Avoca Handweavers operation. Most of its tweed items are destined for shipment to stores around Ireland and abroad, but you can buy remainders here. It's best, however, to go to the Avoca Handweavers Shop in Kilmacanogue, Bray, County Wicklow. It's open all year, Monday through Friday, from 9:30 to 5:30, and Saturday and Sunday from 10 to 5:30. It accepts credit cards and handles mail orders.

Kildare

This is the horsiest of all the counties in Ireland. It's the home of the National Stud at Tully, which has produced many famous racehorses. East of Kildare Town is the Curragh, where the Irish Derby is held each June.

Dublin

Dublin is famed for many things, and one of them is Guinness stout. You can visit the brewery on James Street throughout the year (Monday through Friday, 10 to 3) and sip a sample. Likewise, if you're in a tippling mood, you may visit the Irish Whiskey Corner, with its museum, on Bow Street. For a very minor fee, you can sample 5 different kinds of Irish whiskeys. You must arrange this in advance by calling 01-725566.

All Counties

Irish country farmhouse cheeses are a recent delicious development. Previously there were only a few basic cheeses that were mass produced by major companies. Thankfully that has changed and wisely so, since Ireland is considered one of the world's finest dairy capitals. Now individual farmers and small companies produce cheeses that are unique to each county, and they truly rival the best French cheeses. They range from blues to goats, to goudas and cheddars, to camemberts and bries and herb-flavored creams. There's even one made from sheep's milk. You may sample these in place of a dessert at many of the country estates covered in this book.

21

IRISH TRAVEL INFORMATION

Traveling to Ireland

Three airlines offer the majority of flights to the Irish Republic from the United States—Aer Lingus, Pan Am, and Delta. (Note: Prices listed are subject to change.)

AER LINGUS offers the most flights and uses 747s. It also carries 70 percent of all American travelers to Ireland, which must say something about the quality of its service.

In the old days, people always said that when you travel to a foreign country, go via the airline of that country. In Ireland's case, this is certainly valid. Aer Lingus carries the country's flavor wherever it goes. Its staff is still all Irish—and it's good. The headphones provide access to a wonderful cross section of the country's entertainment. The menus offer such Irish specialties as smoked salmon, smoked trout, and country pâté. Entrees may include poached salmon, roast pheasant, braised noisette of lamb, fillet steak, as well as veal, pork, and sole dishes. There's also a hearty platter of cold roast meats and salad. All of this is surprisingly good, especially when you consider that it's airline food. The accompanying wines and champagne are also superb.

Special Apex fares (reserve at least 3 weeks in advance and stay at least 7 days) from New York range from around $450 to $600 round trip—depending on the time of year. Regular economy fare is about $1,000 round trip. The fare for the extremely comfortable, and most worthwhile, executive class is about $1,700 round trip. The first-class fare one way is around $1,600. (All of these fares are slightly more if you go to Dublin rather than Shannon.) Aer Lingus has Apex fares to Ireland at very favorable rates from more than 60 cities throughout the United States. These are offered in cooperation with TWA, Pan Am, and Eastern.

Toll-free (all states except New York)	800-223-6537
Toll-free (New York State)	800-631-7917
New York City	212-557-1110

PAN AM operates A-300 jumbo-jet service from New York to Shannon (only) on a daily basis at similar prices. Through the Pan Am network, 23 American cities are linked to the single-carrier service to Shannon.

Toll-free (all states except New York)	800-221-1111
New York State	212-687-2600

DELTA operates 3 nonstop L-1011 flights from Atlanta to Shannon (only) weekly. Special round-trip fares range from approximately $475 to $575.

Toll-free (all states)	800-221-1212
Atlanta	404-765-5000

Access to and from Britain and Continental Europe

BY AIR: There are many flights between Ireland and all the major cities in Britain and mainland Europe. Aer Lingus and the major European airlines offer special excursion fares and a wide range of "all-in" vacation packages, which include self-drive cars. There are some flights with first-class sections.

BY SEA: Ireland is linked to Britain and France by a number of ferry routes. There are a number of sailings weekly to several destinations in Britain; some even operate on a daily basis. There are 1 to 5 sailings per week to the different destinations in France. They offer first-class as well as tourist accommodations. If you are coming from or going to France, it is strongly suggested that you select first class, since the journey takes between 14 and 22 hours, depending on your destination.

B & I Lines and **Sealink** operate joint service between Dublin and Holyhead (northern Wales); Dublin and Liverpool; Rosslare (County Wexford) and Fishguard (central Wales); Larne (Northern Ireland) and Stranraer (Scotland).

Brittany Ferries/Townsend Thoresen operates ferry service between Cobh (County Cork) and Swansea (central Wales).

Irish Continental Lines operates French services between Rosslare (County Wexford) and Cherbourg; Rosslare and LeHavre; Cobh to LeHavre.

Brittany Ferries/Townsend Thoresen operates ferries between Cobh (County Cork) and Roscoff (France).

Check with the Irish Tourist Board (addresses and phone numbers appear later in this chapter) for further sailing information.

Car Rentals and Self-Drive Tours

There are several ways to rent cars in Ireland. First, there's the straight rental from one of the Irish car-hire firms (listed below with their American 800-line numbers).

Several very attractive fly/drive packages offered by Aer Lingus include both the plane fare and an unlimited-mileage car, which you pick up at the airport in Ireland.

Taking this a step further, you may arrange for an even more economical package that includes plane fare, the car, and vouchers to cover stays at a range of the country's hotels. The Aer Lingus "Discover Ireland" promotion is just such a package. And, even more important, it includes many of the marvelous lodgings featured in this book. (Contact the airline for its detailed brochure on this program.)

Also, several tour operators with American bases specialize in self-drive packages that include stays in country manor houses and first-class hotels at special prices. These do not include air fares, however.

Abercrombie & Kent is a top-class travel firm. All of its grand Irish lodgings are included in this book. This company has 9-, 10-, 11-, and 13-day self-drive itineraries linked up with reservations (all made by the firm in advance) at the various lodgings. (Chauffeur-driven limousines also are available.) Information: 1000 Oak Brook Road (head-quarters), Oak Brook, Illinois 60521-2240—phone 312-887-7766 or 800-323-7308 (nationwide); 211 East 51st Street, New York, NY 10022—phone 212-753-8110.

Lynott Tours, Inc. has included among its self-drive/lodgings pack-ages many of the fine hotels featured in this book. Vouchers are provided for each night of your stay. The first night is reserved for you at a hotel near Shannon or Dublin airport. Afterward, you make your own res-ervations from Lynott's listings—or Lynott will make them for you for a fee. Information: 350 Fifth Avenue, New York, NY 10118—phone 212-760-0101 or 800-221-2474 (nationwide) or 800-537-7575 (New York State).

Auto Ireland, Fleming Gaelic Tours includes a large number of places featured in this book in the more than 400 hotel selections available in its special-price, self-drive promotions. (Chauffeur-driven cars also are available.) Optional prebooking is available for a minimum 1-week package via Telex when your final payment is received. One additional lodging may be prebooked for a small fee. Information: 15 Crescent Street, Waltham, Massachusetts 02154—phone 617-899-7733 or 800-343-0395 (nationwide) or 800-852-1000 (Massachusetts).

Worldwide Marketing Associates has included some of the special lodgings featured in this book in its special self-drive/lodgings combi-nation packages. They make reservations for your first night and provide open vouchers for the rest of your stay. If you prefer, they will prebook your entire visit at a low, nonrefundable per couple fee. Address and phone numbers: 7136 West Grand Avenue, Chicago, Illinois 60635; phone 312-889-6015 or 800-621-3405 (nationwide).

Some other firms that specialize in connoisseur tours are: Connois-seurs Tours, Box 13363, Savannah, Georgia 31416 (912-352-8747); Design-A-Tour, 3582 Guava Way, Oceanside, California 92054 (619-967-1330); Owenoak International, Box 472, New Canaan, Connecticut 06840-0472 (203-972-3777); Travel Concepts, 373 Commonwealth Ave., Suite 601, Boston, Massachusetts 02115-1815 (617-266-8450); Travel Times, 17 N. State Street, Chicago, Illinois 60602 (312-726-7197, 800-621-4725).

Another possibility is to take advantage of the package deals offered by some car-hire firms themselves. These include your car and lodgings vouchers. But be sure the lodgings offered are those you're interested in before you become involved.

Car-hire 800-line phone numbers in America are:

Avis Rent-a-Car	331-1212
Boland's InterRent	421-6868
California	262-1520
Budget Rent-a-Car	527-0700
Dan Dooley Rent-a-Car	331-9301
Flynn Brothers Rent-a-Car	343-0395
Massachusetts	852-1000
Hertz Rent-a-Car	654-3131
Johnson & Perrott Ltd.	223-6764
New York	522-5568
Kenning Car Hire Ltd.	521-0643
Murray's Europcar/National Car Rentals	328-4300
Tipperary Car Hire/Kenwel Group	468-0468
New York	942-1932

Vital Points About Car Rentals

¶ In Ireland, as in England, you must drive on the left side of the road. This may take a little getting used to; but if you concentrate on thinking left, this usually works beautifully. Some people find it wise to minimize city driving (especially in Dublin and Cork) by heading directly to their lodging, parking the car, and walking or using city transportation. Some who begin their journey at Dublin wait to pick up their cars until they're ready to head for the hills, as it were. It is also possible to take delivery of a rental car at your Dublin lodging, and the delivery driver then can give expert advice on the best way to leave the city.

¶ As in the United States, you must produce a valid driver's license. If you do not have one of the major credit cards, be prepared to leave a sizable security deposit before you're allowed to rent. You must have a credit card when you pick up your car, whether you paid in advance or not. Some firms will accept personal checks if arrangements are made well in advance. Many car-hire firms will not rent cars to drivers under 24 and over 70, even if they're properly licensed and carry credit cards. Be sure to check age restrictions at the time of reservation.

¶ Reserve your car well in advance—especially if you're planning a vacation in July, August, or early September.

¶ Do not, repeat **do not**, expect that the car you reserve will have automatic transmission unless you have requested it. Unless you state specifically that you must have automatic, you'll end up with standard transmission, and it could prove virtually impossible for you to make a switch once you arrive in Ireland—especially in the peak summer season. Don't let this ruin your vacation.

¶ Rates for car rentals vary according to the rental firms—and, of course, the type of car you choose. You can get a basic (nonautomatic) small car for a low-season weekly rate of around $170 with unlimited mileage. This figure would increase to around $210 to $280 moving into the high season. A basic automatic would run around $260 in low season to about $460 during the peak months. (These figures do not include the 10 percent VAT—Value Added Tax—or insurance.) A chauffeur-driven car for 2 would run upward of $300 per day without tips. Check for the most up-to-date prices, because they do change.

¶ Rental rates are inclusive of third-party and passenger liability coverage, as well as fire and theft claims. The customer is responsible for a portion of the fee for accidental loss or damage to the car. But this may be waived if you agree to pay an additional amount for a collision damage waiver.

¶ Gas (petrol in Ireland and England) is expensive—around $3 per imperial gallon, which is a larger gallon than the American one.

¶ It's always a good idea to fill your gas tank the night before a long journey if you're planning to start early in the morning. Otherwise, you may have to search for a station that's open. And don't count on running into one a little farther down the road. You may (certainly in the urban areas), but then again, you may not—as in the case of the Wicklow mountains or parts of Donegal (to name just a few places), where you may drive for what seems like hours without seeing houses or people, let alone petrol stations.

¶ Another important word about gas stations: Few have public toilets. Your best bet is a pub or a hotel. Public toilets often are labeled in Gaelic, which can be confusing: **Fir** is for men and **Mna** for women.

• Some road-sign terminology:
  A black spot indicates an upcoming dangerous twist or curve.
  A cul-de-sac is a dead end.
  A dual carriageway is a divided highway.
  "No overtaking" means no passing of other vehicles.
  A P with a red line through it means "no parking."
  An arrow with a red line through it means "no entry."

- Some important car terms:
  The bonnet is the hood.
  The boot is the trunk.
  The dynamo is the generator.

¶ A word of caution: Irish laws are strict, and the combination of drinking and driving in the unfamiliar left-hand pattern on strange roads can be doubly hazardous. It's best to drink very little or let another person drive. If you're interested in going to a pub at night, it's wise to park your car at your lodging and walk.

AN IMPORTANT NOTE ABOUT ROAD SIGNS: The Irish Republic is in the process of relettering its road signs. "T" (Trunk) and "L" (Link) routes are being changed to "N" (National) and "R" (Regional) respectively. However, the route numbers will remain the same. For instance, a T-5 will become an N-5 and an L-25 will become and R-25. A suggestion to avoid confusion is to simply go by the road number.

Alternate Transportation

If you don't want to rent a car or hire a limousine, the lodgings listed below are accessible by alternate means of transportation. Included here are only the "super standard" trains and the good express bus coaches. Substandard service—i.e., rural bus services—are not mentioned. The "super standard" trains have a first-class section for a slightly higher fee. They also have smoking and nonsmoking sections. The express buses have seats similar to executive-class airline seats. Remember that when hotels make special arrangements to meet you, as is noted below, they charge a fee that you might want to establish in advance.

LODGINGS DESCRIBED IN CHAPTERS 1 THROUGH 12: Drumlease Glebe House (RR or bus to Sligo Town and taxi 12 miles); Temple House (RR to Ballymote, where guests can be met by staff); Abbeyglen Castle (guests can be met at Galway RR or Shannon; summertime bus service to Clifden); Zetland Hotel (guests can be met at Galway RR or Shannon); Renvyle House (guests can be met at Shannon, Galway RR, or bus at Tully Cross); Dromoland (short taxi from Shannon); Park Hotel (taxi 20 miles from Killarney RR, or owner can arrange for limousine from Shannon); Longueville House (RR to Mallow and short taxi); Assolas

House (RR to Mallow and taxi, or staff will meet); Ballymaloe (staff will meet at Cork airport, or RR); Marlfield House (staff will meet at Gorey RR); Tinakilly House (short taxi from Wicklow RR); Hunter's Hotel (short taxi from Wicklow RR); Shelbourne, Berkeley Court, and Westbury (short taxi from airport, RR, or bus).

LODGINGS DESCRIBED IN CHAPTER 13: Knockmuldowney House (RR to Sligo Town and short taxi); Ballincar House (RR or bus to Sligo, short taxi); Mount Falcon Castle (RR or bus to Ballina, short taxi); Connemara Gateway (summertime bus from Galway RR, or bus); Sweeney's Oughterard House (bus from Galway, or guests can be met by staff at Shannon or Galway RR); Johnston-Hernon Kilmurvey House (RR or bus to Galway, then plane or boat to Kilmurvey, then jarvey or minibus); Ardilaun House (RR or bus to Galway, short taxi); Great Southern, Galway (RR or bus to Galway, walk, or brief taxi); Ballykilty Manor (short taxi from Shannon); Dunraven Arms (guests can be met by staff at Limerick or Shannon); Parknasilla Great Southern (guests can be met by staff at Shannon or Cork airport or Killarney RR); Seaview, The Spa (short taxi from Tralee); Arbutus Lodge (RR or bus to Cork, short taxi); Lotamore House (RR or bus to Cork, short taxi); Sea View Hotel and Ballylickey Manor House (bus from Cork to Bantry, short taxi); Blenheim House (RR to Waterford, short taxi); Old Rectory Country House (brief walk or taxi from Wicklow RR); Kilkea Castle (bus from Dublin); Ariel House (taxi from Dublin Airport, RR, or bus); Fitzpatrick Castle and The Court Hotel (RR to Killiney and taxi, or staff will meet at Dublin Airport).

Irish Tourist Board   OFFICES IN NORTH AMERICA AND ABROAD

The Irish Tourist Board (Bord Failte) is considered by nearly all other tourist organizations to be the finest such organization in the world. It is held in such high esteem by other countries that they consult it for advice in dealing with their own tourism matters. It can provide you with information on all areas of the Irish Republic and all aspects of Irish life—and it does so with great pride and pleasure. So don't hesitate to call, write, or stop in if you have any questions not answered in this book. There are also Tourist Board offices all over the Irish Republic that will do the same (see following section).

- **New York City:** 757 Third Avenue, 10017. 212-418-0800.
- **Chicago:** 230 North Michigan Avenue, 60601. 312-726-9356.
- **San Francisco:** 625 Market Street, 94105. 415-957-0985.
- **Toronto:** 10 King Street E., M5C 1C3. 416-364-1301.
- **Belfast,** Northern Ireland: 53 Castle Street, BT1 1GH. 084-227888.
- **Derry,** Northern Ireland: Foyle Street. 0504-369501.
- **London:** 150 New Bond Street, W1Y 0AQ. 01-4933201.
- **Paris:** 9 Boulevard de la Madeleine, 75001. 1-4261-84-26.
- **Milan:** Via Galleria Passarella 2, 20122. 02-700080/783565.
- **Frankfurt:** Untermainanlage 7, 6000/Main 1. 69-236492.
- **Amsterdam:** Leidsestraat 32, 1017PB. 020-22-31-01.
- **Copenhagen:** Den Irske Stats Turistkontor, Store Strandstraede 19, 1255 K. 01-158045.
- **Stockholm:** Irlandska Statens Turistbyra, P.O. Box 45092, 10430. 08-307960.
- **Sydney:** MLC Centre, 38th Level, Martin Place, 2000. 02-232-7177.
- **Auckland:** Dingwall Building, 2nd floor, 87 Queen Street, P.O. Box 279. 09-793708.

Irish Tourist Board (Bord Failte)   OFFICES IN IRELAND

- **Cork:** Tourist House, Grand Parade, 021-273251
- **Dublin City:** 14 Upper O'Connell Street, 01-747733
- **Dublin Airport:** 01-376387/8 or 375533
- **Dun Laoghaire:** St. Michael's Wharf, 01-806984/5/6
- **Galway:** Aras Failte, Eyre Square, 091-63081
- **Killarney:** Town Hall, 064-31633
- **Letterkenny:** Derry Road, 074-21160
- **Limerick City:** Michael Street, 061-317522
- **Shannon Airport:** 061-61664
- **Skibbereen:** 14/15 Main Street, 028-21766
- **Sligo:** Temple Street, 071-61201
- **Tralee:** 32 The Mall, 066-21288
- **Waterford:** 41 The Quay, 051-75788
- **Westport:** The Mall, 098-25711
- **Wexford:** Crescent Quay, 053-23111

Lodgings

The majority of the establishments in this book have private baths, which usually means a toilet, sink, tub, and shower. A few even have bidets. Some have a tub but no shower. Other places have some rooms with private bath and some without. This often means that the bath and toilet are across the hall and are yours alone (not shared). In some instances, sharing might be necessary. If there's any question, be sure to inquire in advance. Don't be shy about asking for what you want. Increasingly, the number of rooms without private baths diminishes in these elegant, upscale places—so don't be fearful. Many even provide color TV and phones; some even are direct dial. Among the facilities, you may find saunas, pools, and an occasional exercise room.

Restaurants

Dining hours in Ireland are somewhat more restricted than in the United States. Breakfast is rarely served after 10 and in some cases not after 9. In some places, you can get coffee or tea, rolls, or a cold cereal between breakfast and lunch, but that's about all. Usually you can get breakfast as early as 7 or 7:30—or, in some cases, even earlier upon request. Breakfast is rarely served in the bedroom in the Georgian homes, but it is—for a fee—in many of the larger hotels.

Most places serve lunch from noon or 12:30 to 2, 2:30, or 2:45—rarely later. If you've missed the boat, many pubs throughout the country serve delicious pub grub at all hours. This means anything from homemade soups and pâtés to hamburgers, Irish stews, and shepherd's pies to fresh seafood salads. Not all pubs serve food of equal quality. Some are *not* desirable. Walk in and look around. If you don't like what you see, leave. Usually a pub that's serious about its food business will have a menu posted outside, or certainly inside.

Another possibility for daytime food is the Irish craft shops. Some of them have adjoining tearooms that serve tea, coffee, scones, and other delicious baked goods. Many have sandwiches and perhaps hot dishes.

Dinner usually runs from 6:30 or 7 to around 9, sometimes to 10.

Nearly all of the fine places described in this book—whether hotels, Georgian estates, or restaurants—require dinner reservations. Even if you're a hotel or estate guest, it's a good idea to book early in the day, or upon arrival. If you forget, the proprietors usually will make every effort to accommodate you, but sometimes this is difficult. If you're a nonresident, reservations are essential.

Pubs

Pubs are open daily from 10:30 A.M. to 11:30 P.M. throughout the year. Sunday hours are from 12:30 to 11:30 P.M. throughout the year. Wine may be served in restaurants up to midnight. Hours for hotel bars are the same as those for pubs. However, as a visitor, you enjoy a special status. If you're a resident of a lodging that has a bar, you may legally be served alcoholic beverages at any hour—although few places will accommodate you all night long, and with good reason.

Licensing

All hotels have a full license to serve all alcoholic beverages—and that also applies to the restaurants and bars on the premises. In the cases of the Georgian estates and the separate restaurants included in this book, some have a full license, others only a wine license, and a very few no license at all. (A reference to this appears in each individual lodging and restaurant review.) It's important to note that a wine license allows for the sale of wine only (including sherry, other aperitif wines, and port) and does not allow for the sale of beer, stout, lager, or brandy. All pubs have full licenses, but this does not mean that all pubs stock wine. Many do, and the list is growing every year as wine becomes increasingly popular. However, don't expect to find a wide array of superlative wines in a pub. It is better to ask what kind of white or red wine they have before committing yourself, because some of it (especially in the more rural areas) can be pretty poor quality. On the other hand, many of the country's restaurants have become very sophisticated about wines, and an ever-growing number have a finer selection than many of the top American restaurants.

Credit Cards

Most hotels accept the major credit cards: American Express, MasterCard, Visa, and Diners Club (referred to in this book as AmEx, Master, Visa, Diners). Castles (Ashford and Dromoland) and some of the elegant Georgian lodgings also take them. (This has been specified in the individual descriptions in this book. Restaurants that accept cards are also noted.) Almost all major stores and many smaller ones (including craft shops) throughout the country accept at least one major credit card. Rarely—for obvious reasons—are personal checks accepted. Of course, traveler's checks are welcome everywhere.

Tipping

Be sure to check your dining bills to see if a 10- to 15-percent service charge has been included. If so, no additional sum is required unless you feel the service rendered and the quality of the meal were so extraordinary that you'd like to leave a little more. Never tip for drinks at a bar, but you may wish to tip a waiter or waitress for drinks served at a table near the bar. Taxi drivers usually are tipped 10 percent of the total meter amount, while porters should receive from 50 pence up to 1 or 2 pounds, depending on the number and/or weight of the bags.

Taxis

As in the United States, taxis are expensive. They do seem to be more so in Ireland—but then gasoline is far more expensive, and the drivers have to live. A ride from Dublin Airport into the city (6 miles) can run about $15, maybe more. In many areas of the country, there are "gypsy" cab drivers with no meters. If you look prosperous, you may be charged Park Avenue prices. It's best to establish the fee before you enter the vehicle.

Climate and Clothing

Ireland lies within the Gulf Stream and therefore has a springlike climate most of the year. This does not mean that it's eternally balmy, however. It can be cold and rainy or warm and rainy. It can be cold and cloudy or warm and cloudy. It can also be dazzling, under halcyon skies. You can be prepared for all these conditions by packing mediumweight clothing and a little rainwear. Forget all the heavy tweeds and bulky sweaters. You'll rarely need them. What you have to be concerned about—especially during the peak season—is the heat. Everyone, and every travel guide, insists that the average temperature during the peak season ranges from 60 to 66 degrees Fahrenheit. While this may be true at times, there have been several recent years in Dublin when that figure has risen well above 80. There are very few hotels or restaurants capable of coping with this, since few have air-conditioning. So if you drift in wearing heavy tweeds, you will wilt immediately. Stick to the medium weights, but be sure to slip in some lightweight wool sweaters (you may want to purchase some beautiful ones in Ireland) for extra layers if it turns cold.

Regardless of the weather, be prepared with an easy system of dressing up for one of the fine city or country evening-out experiences. Many people think of Ireland as completely rural and jeans-oriented. Not so—at least, not anymore. Men should pack a tie, dress shirt, and sport coat or blazer; women should pull together a dressy evening outfit.

Don't forget swimwear, running shorts and shoes, golfing and tennis apparel, if you're so disposed. Since many Irish lodgings do not provide washcloths (or facecloths, as they're called in Ireland), you may want to pack a few of these.

Time

Ireland is 5 hours ahead of U.S. East Coast time—except during part of March, when there is a 6-hour difference in favor of Ireland due to different time changes.

Passports

To visit Ireland, Americans need only an up-to-date passport. No visa is necessary. Don't fail to have your passport, however, when you land in Ireland. Very close checks are made at American airports before you are allowed to board, but occasionally there is a slipup.

Electrical Current

The standard Irish current is 220V; the standard U.S. current is 110V. Be prepared. Even if there's a conversion button on the appliance, you will need plug adapters if you want to use your favorite hairdryer. Such adapters, designed to fit the array of Irish outlets, are available in many U.S. drug and hardware stores. Most major hotels will be able to supply you with an adapter, but few of the Georgian lodgings would be able to do so. Most hotels and Georgian lodgings have wall units for electric razors that convert to 110V and accept the standard American razor plug.

Shopping

When you see something you're dying to purchase—don't wait. Buy it. The likelihood of your finding it cheaper somewhere else is remote, since Ireland is not discount-oriented like America. Then, too, you're much likelier not to see the same item again in another locale.

Pay attention to customs allowances. When you return to the U.S., you must declare all goods over $400 Irish prices. Included in the allowances are 200 cigarettes and 1 liter of alcoholic beverages or 2 standard bottles of wine.

Gifts not exceeding $25 retail may be sent to friends and relatives in the U.S. duty free—if the same person does not receive more than $25 in gift value in a day. But you *must* write the words "unsolicited gift" on the package and label it "under $25." You must also indicate the contents. *Do not* ship alcoholic beverages or tobacco.

Irish shops are normally open from 9:30 A.M. to 5:30 P.M., Monday through Saturday. In some towns, there is an early closing day once a week at 1 P.M. This is usually Wednesday, but it may be a different day in some areas. Visitors who have the stores mail purchases back to America do not have to pay VAT (Value Added Tax), which can be substantial. Visitors who carry the goods with them must pay the VAT, but refunds are possible. To request a refund, ask the store to give you an invoice and an envelope preaddressed to: VAT Refund Division, Foreign Exchange Company of Ireland Ltd., P.O. Box 1485, O'Connell Street, Dublin 1. When you leave the country, you'll need to have an Irish customs officer stamp the invoice. Send in the stamped invoice, together with your name and address, and the Foreign Exchange will issue you a refund check. Or, if you have time, go to the special window at the airport for a cash refund.

INDEX